Carlo Emilio Gadda and the Modern Macaronic

Crosscurrents

Crosscurrents: Comparative Studies in European Literature and Philosophy
Edited by S. E. Gontarski

Improvisations on Michel Butor: Transformation of Writing, by Michel Butor; edited, annotated, and with an introduction by Lois Oppenheim; translated by Elinor S. Miller (1996).

The French New Autobiographies: Duras, Sarraute, Robbe-Grillet Rewriting History, Story, Gender, by Raylene L. Ramsay (1996).

The Ghosts of Modernity, by Jean-Michel Rabaté (1996).

Carlo Emilio Gadda and the Modern Macaronic, by Albert Sbragia (1996).

Carlo Emilio Gadda and
the Modern Macaronic

ALBERT SBRAGIA

University Press of Florida
Gainesville/Tallahassee/Tampa/Boca Raton
Pensacola/Orlando/Miami/Jacksonville

Copyright 1996 by the Board of Regents of the State of Florida
Printed in the United States of America on acid-free paper
All rights reserved

01 00 99 98 97 96   6 5 4 3 2 1

Library of Congress Cataloging-in-Publication Data
Sbragia, Albert.
Carlo Emilio Gadda and the modern macaronic / Albert Sbragia.
  p. cm.
Includes bibliographical references and index.
ISBN 0-8130-1463-8 (cloth: alk. paper)
1. Gadda, Carlo Emilio, 1893-1973—Criticism and interpretation.
2. Macaronic literature—History and criticism. I. Title. II. Series:
Crosscurrents (Gainesville, Fla.).
PQ4817.A33Z873 1997
853'.912—DC20   96-14691

Publication of this book was made possible in part by a grant from
the University of Washington.

The University Press of Florida is the scholarly publishing agency for the State
University System of Florida, comprised of Florida A & M University, Florida
Atlantic University, Florida International University, Florida State University,
University of Central Florida, University of Florida, University of North Florida,
University of South Florida, and University of West Florida.

University Press of Florida
15 Northwest 15th Street
Gainesville, FL 32611

To Dawn Amber

Contents

Foreword, by S. E. Gontarski   ix

Acknowledgments   xi

Abbreviations   xiii

Introduction: The Modern Macaronic   1

ONE: The Poetics of Polarity   28

TWO: In Search of a Necessary Style   72

THREE: Grotesque Tragedy: *La cognizione del dolore*   106

FOUR: Macaronic Pastiche: *Quer pasticciaccio brutto de via Merulana*   129

FIVE: Satura tota nostra est: *Eros e Priapo*   159

Notes   183

Selected Bibliography   197

Index   209

Foreword

The Crosscurrents series is designed to foreground comparative studies in European art and thought, particularly the intersections of literature and philosophy, aesthetics and culture. Without abandoning traditional comparative methodology, the series is receptive to the latest currents in critical, comparative, and performative theory, especially that generated by the renewed intellectual energy in post-Marxist Europe. It will as well take full cognizance of the cultural and political realignments of what for the better part of the twentieth century have been two separated and isolated Europes. While Western Europe is now moving aggressively toward unification in the European Community, with the breakup of the twentieth century's last colonial empire, the former Soviet Union, Eastern Europe is subdividing into nationalistic and religious enclaves with the collapse of the Communist hegemony. The intellectual, cultural, and literary significance of such profound restructuring—how history will finally rewrite itself—is difficult to anticipate. Having had a fertile period of modernism snuffed out in an ideological coup not long after the 1917 revolution, the nations of the former Soviet Union have, for instance, been denied (or spared) the age of Freud, most modernist experiments, and postmodern fragmentation. While Western Europe continues reaching beyond modernism, Eastern Europe may be struggling to reclaim it. Whether a new art can emerge in the absence—or from the absence—of such forces as shaped modernism is one of the intriguing questions of post–Cold War aesthetics, philosophy, and critical theory.

This current volume in the Crosscurrents series brings to the fore one of the neglected masters of Italian modernism. In his study, *Carlo Emilio Gadda and the Modern Macaronic*, Albert Sbragia brings to the English-speaking world the first full historical and thematic appreciation of one of Italy's greatest twentieth-century writers. His focus is twofold. First is to see Gadda as part of the linguistic experimentalism of the macaronic, a polyglossia or plurilingualism that Sbragia defines broadly as "literary works of a composite linguistic nature," from the Renaissance to the present day. Sbragia's historical sweep is impressive: "A European genealogy of the modern macaronic traces its premodern roots to the original Renaissance macaronic and Rabelaisian comic, its amalgam of comic parody and melancholic subjective totality to the Romantic theorists, its crisis of mimetic realism to Flaubert (who becomes the veritable father of sorts in the encyclopedic parody of received ideas and bourgeois inanity of *Bouvard et Pécuchet*)."

Gadda, however, is very much a modernist author, and so Sbragia's second front is to situate Gadda within the tradition of monumental European modernism. For Sbragia the novel *is* "the genre of modernity," and Gadda ranks with those masters of "modern macaronic" narrative James Joyce and Louis-Ferdinand Céline while remaining within the genealogy of the historical macaronic: "It is by recognizing this broader European genealogy that the occasional and intuitive comparisons of Gadda to other macaronic modernists such as Louis-Ferdinand Céline or James Joyce can gain in substance and justification."

"Gadda's linguistic experimentalism," according to Sbragia, then, "hinges on his complete exploitation of [a] rich linguistic variance (phonological, morphological, lexical, syntactic) of literary Italian and its constitutive archaicism." But, according to philologist Gianfranco Contini—who championed Gadda's work and wrote the introduction to the 1963 edition of *La cognizione del dolore*, published as *Acquainted with Grief* in 1969, with a modern twist—Gadda's was a "macaronic art exercised on Freudian material."

Only two of Gadda's works are readily available in English: the aforementioned *Acquainted with Grief*, which won the prestigious Formentor Prix International de Littérature in 1963 (although it was written between 1938 and 1941); and the Roman detective novel, *That Awful Mess on Via Merulana*, published in Italy in 1957 as *Quer pasticciaccio brutto de via Merulana* and translated into English in 1965. One hopes that books such as the *Modern Macaronic* will do much to remedy such neglect.

The series henceforth will continue to critique the developing, often conflicting currents of European thought through the prism of literature, philosophy, and theory.

S. E. Gontarski

Acknowledgments

I thank Gian Paolo Biasin for having introduced me to Gadda during my years as a graduate student at the University of California at Berkeley and for his gracious advice and enthusiastic support in the years since. I would also like to thank Nicolas Perella, Francine Masiello, Douglas Collins, Cynthia Steele, Anthony Tamburri, Alan Gowing, Robert Dombroski, and Gregory Lucente for their advice, comments, and assistance. The University of California provided a traveling research grant, and the University of Washington has provided continuing research support for my work. For her herculean editing and proofreading, her keen sense of appropriateness, and her loving concern, my deepest gratitude goes to my wife Dawn Perkins Sbragia.

English translations of passages from *La cognizione del dolore* and *Quer pasticciaccio brutto de via Merulana* are from William Weaver's *Acquainted with Grief* (AWG) and *That Awful Mess on Via Merulana* (TAM) and are so indicated. Occasionally I have changed a word or phrase for a more literal translation. All other translations of Gadda's works and correspondence and of Italian critics whose work is cited in Italian in the bibliography are my own.

Abbreviations of Gadda's Works and Correspondence

A	*L'Adalgisa (disegni milanesi)*. In *Opere*, vol. 1, 1988.
AAF	*A un amico fraterno. Lettere a Bonaventura Tecchi*. 1984.
AG	*Accoppiamenti giudiziosi*. In *Opere*, vol. 2, 1989.
AS	*Altri scritti*. In *Opere*, vol. 5, part 1, 1993.
C	*La cognizione del dolore*. In *Opere*, vol. 1, 1988.
C$_2$	*La cognizione del dolore*. Turin: Einaudi, 1987.
CU	*Il castello di Udine*. In *Opere*, vol. 1, 1988.
EP	*Eros e Priapo (Da furore a cenere)*. In *Opere*, vol. 4, 1992.
GA	*Gli Anni*. In *Opere*, vol. 3, 1991.
GGP	*Giornale di guerra e di prigionia*. In *Opere*, vol. 4, 1992.
IDM	Interview with Dacia Maraini. In Maraini 1973.
IF	*L'ingegnere fantasia. Lettere a Ugo Betti*. 1984.
LAM	*Lettere agli amici milanesi*. 1983.
LAS	*Lettere alla sorella (1920–1924)*. 1987.
LGC	*Lettere a Gianfranco Contini a cura del destinatario*. 1988.
LGS	*Lettere a una gentile signora*. 1983.
LPGC	Letters to Piero Gadda Conti. In Gadda Conti 1974.
LS	Letters to *Solaria*. In Manacorda, ed., 1979.
LSG	"Tre lettere di C.E. Gadda a Silvio Guarnieri." 1983.
M	*La meccanica*. In *Opere*, vol. 2, 1988.
MF	*La Madonna dei Filosofi*. In *Opere*, vol. 1, 1988.
MI	*Le meraviglie d'Italia*. In *Opere*, vol. 3, 1991.
MM	*Meditazione milanese*. In *Opere*, vol. 5, part 1, 1993.
MS	*I miti del somaro*. In *Opere*, vol. 5, part 1, 1993.
P	*Quer pasticciaccio brutto de via Merulana*. In *Opere*, vol. 2, 1989.
PL	*Quer pasticciaccio brutto de via Merulana (redazione di "Letteratura," 1946–47)*. In *Opere*, vol. 2, 1989.
PLF	*Il primo libro delle favole*. In *Opere*, vol. 4, 1992.
PO	*Il palazzo degli ori*. In *Opere*, vol. 5, part 1, 1993.

RaI   *Racconti incompiuti.* In *Opere,* vol. 2, 1989.
RD   *Racconti dispersi.* In *Opere,* vol. 2, 1989.
RI   *Racconto italiano di ignoto del novecento.* In *Opere,* vol. 5,
      part 1, 1993.
SA   *Schede autobiografiche.* In *Opere,* vol. 4, 1992.
SD   *Scritti dispersi.* In *Opere,* vol. 3, 1991.
TLI   "Tre lettere inedite a Giuseppe De Robertis," 1983.
TR   *Traduzioni.* In *Opere,* vol. 5, part 1, 1993.
VC   *Verso la Certosa.* In *Opere,* vol. 3, 1991.
VM   *I viaggi la morte.* In *Opere,* vol. 3, 1991.
VS   *La verità sospetta.* Milan: Bompiani, 1977.

The Modern Macaronic

Sed prius altorium vestrum chiamare bisognat, o macaronaeam Musae quae funditis artem.

TEOFILO FOLENGO, *Baldus* 1:5–6

Connais-tu les livres de Gadda, et son dernier: *Quer pasticciaccio brutto de via Merulana?* Je t'en parlais dans ma dernière lettre. La fureur de Sade est inégalable; mais la fureur de Gadda est digne qu'on la dise une véritable fureur. Le récit: c'est Flaubert l'auteur auquel il fait plutôt penser: tout Flaubert, y compris, bien entendu, *Bouvard et Pécuchet.* Le langage: Gadda sans doute est plus près de Rabelais que de Joyce, mais il n'oublie pas qu'il y a eu dernièrement sur terre Joyce, tout en suivant naturellement la tradition italienne.

GIUSEPPE UNGARETTI TO JEAN PAULHAN

The first half of the twentieth century was witness to the rebirth of the ancient tradition of the macaronic. The verbal and archetypal gigantism of Teofilo Folengo and François Rabelais relived in transmuted form in the polyphonic plurilingualism and physicality of authors such as James Joyce, Louis-Ferdinand Céline, and Carlo Emilio Gadda. Their works are emblematic of a strain of modernism that grapples with the crisis of nineteenth-century mimetic realism by exasperating its precepts. They seek innovation and adequate metaphors for the complexity or horror of modernity by evoking its premodern representational origins. Having worked for many years in Italy and abroad as an electrotechnical engineer, Carlo Emilio Gadda (1893–1973) remained for most of his career a difficult and obscure author. Much of his work consisted of narrative "fragments" or *poèmes en prose* (Contini 1989, 19) written in the 1920s, 1930s, and 1940s, published in elite literary journals such as the Florentine *Solaria* and *Letteratura* and appreciated by a small coterie of critics and literati. In 1957 the publication in volume of his stunning Roman detective novel, *Quer pasticciaccio brutto de via Merulana* (*That Awful Mess on Via Merulana*), propelled the reclusive Milanese author to instant national fame. "I've become a sort of Lollobrigido, of Sophio Loren," he wrote to friend Domenico Marchetti (LAM 60–61). Six years later, in 1963, the seventy-year-old Gadda became a European cause célèbre when *La cognizione del dolore* [*Acquainted with Grief*] was also published in volume and was awarded the Formentor Prix International de Littérature, attracting essays by major European authors and men of culture such as Michel Butor and Hans Enzenberger.[1] Both works had originally been written years earlier, *Cognizione* in 1938–41 and *Pasticciaccio* in 1946, and their republication led to the ransacking of Gadda's numerous unfinished manuscripts and correspondence, which have been published in the succeeding years. As was the case some four decades previously with one of Italy's first great modernists, Italo Svevo, who was brought to European notice by his English tutor James Joyce, Gadda achieved recognition only at the end of his life, and only decades after most of his works had first been written. Since then Gadda has become established as a literary giant in the twentieth-century Italian canon, an author whose name is synonymous with linguistic experimentalism and the modern resuscitation of the Italian macaronic tradition.

The Language Question in Italy

The linkage of Gadda and the macaronic has been to a large extent the work of a single, eminent literary critic and philologist, Gianfranco Contini. The two first met in May of 1934 after Contini was converted to Gadda's cause by the poet Eugenio Montale (LGC 7). Contini's essay of the same period, "Carlo Emilio Gadda, o del pastiche," is laudable in its elevation of Gadda beyond the circumscribed Italian literary debate in the early 1930s of *calligrafismo* vs. *contenutismo* [roughly form vs. content] to a farsighted historical perspective that associates him with both the late-nineteenth-century Lombard and Piedmontese *Scapigliati* (Dossi-Faldella) and the erudite humanism of the Renaissance "pasticheurs" from the Italian macaronic poets to Rabelais (Contini 1989, 3–4).[2] The operation served a dual purpose for the philological Contini. It immediately lent to Gadda a canonical status, and it provided the critic with a contemporary pole around which the emarginated linguistic "irregulars" of the Italian literary tradition could be gathered. Contini would remain obstinately faithful to the coordinates of this macaronic lineage in all of his subsequent essays on Gadda, many of which were entries for encyclopedias or anthologies, thereby adding to their authority of peremptory declarations.

The most seminal and influential of these later essays is Contini's introduction to the 1963 edition of *La cognizione del dolore* (*in plenu* "caso Gadda"). Not only are the Scapigliati reaffirmed as Gadda's true "elective environment," but the association with the Renaissance macaronic is more emphatic still. With "typical disproportion between the inanity of the object and the extreme artfulness of the literary application," Gadda's "extraordinary *pezzi di bravura*" seem to issue "from the ancient and pacifying quills of the Renaissance Folengo or Rabelais." The result is that of a "macaronic art exercised on a Freudian material" (Contini 1989, 19). Contini concludes by locating Gadda within an exquisitely traced symphony of echoes and linguistic interests—from Pier Paolo Pasolini to Alberto Arbasino, from Beppe Fenoglio to Lucio Mastronardi, from *Roma, città aperta* to Ermanno Olmi!—at the center of which is C. E. G: "All around him there is in contemporary linguistic Italy a grand resonating chamber" (Contini 1989, 35).

Contini's approach also places Gadda squarely within the age-old normative language debate in Italy, the "questione della lingua." It begs the question of Gadda's "function" in the peculiar linguistic evolution of spoken and literary Italian, of which the historical macaronic is an illustrative episode.[3]

The Renaissance macaronic in its purest form is a northern Italian creation with its precedents in medieval burlesque, goliardic verse, and sacred parodies and with extra-Italian continuators and resonances in various European countries and in Rabelais.[4] Its origins lie in the late-fifteenth-century Benedictine athenaeum of Padua and specifically in the linguistic experimentalism of Tifi Odasi, whose poem *Macaronea* defines the genre. Its fame was assured in the first half of the following century by Odasi's Mantuan pupil and emulator Teofilo Folengo (pseudonym Merlin Cocai). Folengo's *Baldus* (four editions: 1517, 1521, 1534–35, and posthumously in 1552) is a mock-epic poem of giants and far-fetched chivalric adventures including the discovery of the mouth of the Nile and a final descent into Hell. *Baldus* is the genre's acknowledged masterpiece, and it enjoyed a notable popularity in the 1500s with over a dozen editions and reprintings. It was not without influence on Rabelais's *Gargantua and Pantagruel*, in which it is cited more than once. Such was the perceived connection that the first French translation of Folengo's works in 1606 bore the title *Histoire maccaronique de Merlin Coccaie, prototype de Rablais* (see Cordié 1977, xii–xiii; Tetel 1963).

The original macaronic is characterized linguistically by its vocabulary of Italian, dialect, and Latin words within a substantially Latin morphological, syntactic, and prosodic form. The hybridization is typically trilingual in the northern Italian macaronic poets involving Latin, Italian (Tuscan), and Po Valley dialects (Paccagnella 1983, 141). Not the natural or ingenuous product of a native plurilingualism, the Italian macaronic is a sophisticated caricatural artifice, a linguistic parody which exploits the situation of polyglossia experienced by the cultural elite (Paccagnella 1973, 363). The demise of the original macaronic is due precisely to the success of the Italian humanists in their philological recuperation of classical Latin which had made possible the complexity of macaronic verse in the first place. Latin as a literary language was frozen in a normative and chronological straitjacket as an eminently noble but irremeably ancient language. As a result, Tuscan Italian was finally able to assert itself fully as the contemporary national language of letters, and it underwent much of the same normative and chronological classicizing restrictions as had Latin. From a state of triglossia the linguistic and literary evolution of the Italian peninsula would evolve more clearly as a case of fragmented diglossia, with numerous epicenters of dialect in tension with written and literary Italian.

The contemporary rehabilitation of the term *macaronic* has consequently involved an extension of its classical definition to a broader category of literary works of a composite linguistic nature. Cesare Segre has argued that the determining criterion for the macaronic is not the presence of Latin and the vernacular, but the stylistic and diachronic "interference" among the various elements of the linguistic pastiche. This would separate a truly macaronic Italian line (Folengo-*Scapigliati*-Gadda) from other plurilingual writers such as Pasolini or Arbasino who engage in juxtaposition of language and dialect but without their mutual interference (Segre 1979, 173–74, 178). It can be added that the modern macaronic writers operate a specifically historical appeal to the parodic and archetypal features of the original Renaissance macaronic-Rabelaisian ribaldry.[5]

To understand the linguistic peculiarities of the Italian literary tradition, it is necessary to recur to the plurilinguistic anomaly of the Italian peninsula. This plurilingualism is largely the consequence of the precocious unification of a national literary language contrasted by the comparatively late social and political unification of the Italian nation. With the exception of Tuscany and certain elements of papal Rome, the "Italian" language remained for centuries an exclusively literary and in many ways archaic language. Fixed in its Trecento Tuscan and Florentine forms and Cinquecento normative prescriptions, Italian was a language with a latitudinally narrow scope, suitable for "high" literary expression while everyday communication continued to be carried out in local dialect, to the point that Italy's first king, Victor Emmanuel II, habitually used his native Piedmontese dialect even in meetings with his ministers (De Mauro 1979, 32). At the moment of Italian unification in 1870, the linguist Graziadio Isaia Ascoli observed that the centrifugal pull of the various dialects of the Italian peninsula had for centuries remained uncountered by the centripetal forces necessary to the establishment of a truly national language. The peninsula remained politically fragmented, ruled by local princes and occupying foreign powers long after the other major nations in Western Europe. There did not occur in Italy the demographic, economic, political, and intellectual concentration achieved by Spain, France, or England through national unification, and there was no capital city to serve as a national linguistic model. Nor had there been the cultural and linguistic unifying force of a religious Reformation as in the German states (De Mauro 1979, 16–17).

The consequences of this unusual evolution of the Italian national language are not as far removed from the situation of a twentieth-century author as one might at first suspect. This is especially true in the case of an author such as Gadda whose literary expressionism is firmly grounded in the historical anomalies of the Italian language, in the ongoing vitality of the nation's dialects after unification, and in the uniquely archaic characteristics of literary Italian.

As Contini notes, what ultimately distinguishes the expressionism of the Italian Gadda from that of the German expressionists, or Joyce, or Céline, is Gadda's abundant recourse to the reserves of dialect. This is linked to the elementary fact "that Italian is substantially the only great national literature whose production in dialect constitutes a visceral and inseparable corpus with the rest of the patrimony" (Contini 1989, 26). The dialectal literary lineage in Italy is diverse, with representatives in the great Roman and Milanese Romantic poets Giuseppe Gioachino Belli and Carlo Porta, in the Venetian Goldoni, in the multidialectal commedia dell'arte tradition, to name only a few. A heightened awareness of the defining patrimony of dialect and language can be traced to the beginnings of the Italian literary tradition in Dante's *De vulgari eloquentia* or in the thirteenth-century Sicilian school. Cielo d'Alcamo's parodic *contrasto* "Rosa fresca aulentissima," with which Francesco De Sanctis began his monumental history of Italian literature, is proof that "the bilingualism of *poesia illustre* and *poesia dialettale* is absolutely original and constitutive of Italian literature" (Contini 1989, 29).

Gadda's use of dialect is unique in several ways. He recurs to many different dialects, passing through Milanese, Florentine, and Roman "phases" with significant forays into Venetian and Neapolitan. He uses dialect—and foreign languages, especially Spanish, French, and Latin—in expressionistic and not merely naturalistic ways, through the macaronic interference between dialect and Italian, or dialect and dialect, through the mixture of Italian and dialect in free indirect discourse, through a recuperation of archaic forms, especially in his use of Florentine.

As concerns the evolution of Italian itself, the fact that for centuries it had remained largely a written language, together with the early triumph of highly conservative normative attitudes (Bembism, Accademia della Crusca), created a situation of near stasis up until and beyond unification in 1870. Its phonemes and variants in 1870 were essentially those of archaic Florentine. Its lexical and morphological innovations did not consist of substitutions and transformations but of the addition of new elements to the previous ones, and most of these came from Latin and not popular sources. Characterized by an extremely high incidence of morphological, lexical, and phraseological polymorphism, the Italian language over the centuries retained intact practically all of its lexical and morphological variants since they were not affected by the selective nature and economic tendencies of a spoken language in broad usage. Semantically, Italian was luxuriously polymorphous in the higher, literary registers but atrociously inadequate in the lower, spoken registers, since everyday communication was the realm of dialect (De Mauro 1979, 28–30).

Gadda's linguistic experimentalism hinges on his complete exploitation of this rich linguistic variance (phonological, morphological, lexical, syntactic) of literary Italian and its constitutive archaicism. He practices an aggressive "linguistic ecumenism" (Segre 1979, 178) and defends his right of access to the entire polymorphic treasure house of the Italian tradition:

> I want the doublet-doubloons ("i doppioni"), all of them, for the sake
> of my mania of possession and greed, and I also want the triploons, and
> the quadruploons, even if the Catholic King has not yet coined them,
> and all the synonyms, used in their variegated meanings and shades of

meaning, of current usage, or extremely rare usage. And so I say no to the proposal of the great and venerated Alessandro [Manzoni], who would want nothing less than to prune, etc. etc., in order to unify and codify: "within the laws, I removed the excessive and the useless." The excessive and the useless do not exist, for a language. ("Lingua letteraria e lingua dell'uso," VM 490)

Gadda's contribution to the "questione della lingua" can be characterized as an advocation of the entire gamut of the peninsula's vertical, diachronic, and geographical language heterogeneity. It is a position that evolves in the context of a series of eclectic influences including his technical formation; his preparation in philosophy, mathematics, and classical literature; his travels within Italy and abroad; and, most importantly, his insistence on viewing the writer's task as the creation of a "critical epitome" (MM 836) of reality's open-ended multiplicity, flux, and deformation.

Language and linguistic expressionism were key factors in Gadda's exaltation by critics and neophytes in the late 1950s and early 1960s, and his instant celebrity was connected in part to the widespread sense of restlessness with an exhausted neorealist legacy. Pier Paolo Pasolini accused neorealism of practicing a naive and falsifying "prospectivism." Giorgio Bassani rejected out of hand the wave of novels by "ex-truck drivers and ex-kitchen hands" for a Manzonian literature of the heart. Italo Calvino abandoned the last vestiges of his neorealist poetics and went into self-imposed exile in Paris where he embraced new scientific and combinatory paradigms. Neorealist cinema had yielded to a new Italian cinema d'auteurs in Fellini and Antonioni. Everywhere there were the manifestations of a sea change in the dominant literary and cinematic culture that paralleled the emergence of the new Italy of the "economic boom."

Gadda had preceded and never succumbed to the neorealist wave. He had criticized the school roundly for what he saw as its insipid social realism at the expense of any sort of Kantian "noumenal dimension" ("Un'opinione sul neorealismo," VM 629–30). When Gadda burst on the national literary consciousness in 1957 with his Roman novel *Quer pasticciaccio brutto de via Merulana*, he was seized as the example of an author in whom form and expressivity were one with the complexity and alienation of modern reality. There was an outcrop of literary followers and novelists in dialect whom writer Alberto Arbasino called Gadda's "nipotini," his nephews or grandchildren, including writers such as Giovanni Testori, Pasolini, and Arbasino himself. Gadda also became a rallying cry for the Italian "neo-avant-garde" Gruppo '63, which declared at its 1965 convention that the new experimental novel must take Gadda's *Pasticciaccio* as its starting point, though improving on it. Group member Angelo Guglielmi's anthology of the same year, *Vent'anni di impazienza,* reiterated this position by casting Gadda as the founding inspiration for the new experimental writers (Guglielmi 1965, 157). For the awkward and conservative Gadda his popularity at the hands of the new literary rebels was at times embarrassing, at times annoying. He even had to undergo the distress of defending his "bourgeois" attitudes to disillusioned young readers who assumed from his writings that he had to be a communist (Cattaneo 1973, 93–94).

During this same period, in December of 1964, the most passionate recent episode of the centuries-old language debate exploded with the publication in *Rinascita* of Pasolini's polemical essay "Nuove questioni linguistiche."[6] Pasolini's vision of Italy's postwar linguistic state was one of a renewed triglossia, with an impoverished "bourgeois," "bureaucratic," and "clerico-fascist" middle line of standard Italian contrasted from above by a high line of literary expressionism and from below by a low line of dialect and popular speech. Reviewing the relationship of contemporary Italian writers with this linguistic scenario, Pasolini declared that it was only the anomalous Gadda who fully exploited the expressive potentiality of the Italian situation. Gadda's use of a plurilingual free indirect discourse created a "serpentine line" which intersected all three horizontal lines—low, middle, high—of the Italian triglossia. Its power lay in its ability to absorb the "sublinguistic materials" of the lower languages and elevate them, not "to the level of everyday language in order to be worked out and objectified as a contribution to ordinary Italian," but to the very high level where they are "worked out in an expressive or expressionistic way" (Pasolini 1988, 8). For Pasolini, Gadda represented an extreme example of the possibilities of energizing the national language through a literary operation. But given the new linguistic situation in Italy this cultured operation was already impossible. Pasolini's provocative and apocalyptic thesis was that finally *Italian has been born as a national language,"* not via any literary operation but through the rise of an all-powerful technological and instrumental Italian with its origins in the industrial north. The vast power of homologation of this language was a "new spirituality" which was attacking the Italian language from deep within, threatening the very existence of both its expressive literary resources and its rejuvenating dialects (Pasolini 1988, 16–17).

Among those called upon to respond to Pasolini's dire scenario was Italo Calvino. The technological language which Pasolini feared was welcomed by Calvino as a positive and practical influx of precision and clarity against the "semantic terror" of the bureaucratic "antilanguage" (Calvino 1980, 122). It was an argument somewhat analogous to Gadda's own decades earlier in the 1929 "Le belle lettere e i contributi espressivi delle tecniche" (VM 475–88). For Calvino, the parties of the modern "questione della lingua" needed to turn away once and for all from the outdated polemic between an inadequate national language and the revitalizing power of Italy's dialects—"I have never thought that the dialects were health and truth" (Calvino 1980, 121)—and focus instead on the communicative competitiveness of Italian vis-à-vis the international community of languages. Italian would benefit from the confrontation with the possibility of finally being streamlined into an effective communicative instrument and modern language. Like the other modern languages it would concentrate itself around two poles, one of immediate "translatability" into other languages as part of a "worldwide international language on an elevated plane," the other around which would be distilled "language's special essence and creativity, untranslatable par excellence, and entrusted to diverse linguistic institutions such as popular *argot* and the poetic creativity of literature" (Calvino 1980, 125–26; see also Raimondi 1984, 3–4).

Pasolini had lamented the instant demise of Gadda as a possible standard of excellence for the national language. Calvino maintained a place for him as a standard of excellence for the national language's expressive pole, which was, in its own way, a new marginalization. Of the two scenarios for the national language, it was Calvino's which presented the Italian cultural establishment with a true praxis or plan of attack to influence positively the nation's linguistic and literary destiny. And certainly Calvino himself has been the contemporary Italian author who was able to best combine literary internationalism, "technological" precision, and language's secret essence. And so he became Italy's most respected and translatable author and its first literary postmodernist, all the while decrying the pernicious spread of the "antilanguage." For Pasolini, there was left only the rebellion of extremity of a modern Cassandra and a nostalgia for Gadda.

A nostalgia for Gadda was born at the moment of his eruption on the national literary scene. His arrival was too late. Not in tune with Calvino's lightness, nor with Eco's ironic revisitation of the past, Gadda's difficult macaronic prose makes him Italy's most untranslatable author (despite the noble efforts of William Weaver). His literature is a heavy and tangled knot or *groviglio;* his encounter with the past—his own, that of literature, that of humanity—is visceral, typically anguished. He is Italy's last great narrative modernist, Svevo and Pirandello being the first and only others. In the span of a few years Gadda had acquired the monumentality of an author who embodied a unique and centuries-long national legacy of plurilingualism besieged by a new postindustrial linguistic order. In a 1984 conference at the Roman Accademia dei Lincei on "Linguistic expressivity in Italian literature," Cesare Segre, the architect after Contini of the notion of a "macaronic tradition" in modern Italian literature, declared that Gadda represented a literary situation of a "not yet" and "never more." His expressionism seemed destined to remain an unrepeatable phenomenon, "and if there are still roads open to the novel, probably they are neither that of expressionism, nor that of polyphony" (Segre 1985, 194).[7]

ROMANTICISM AND SUBJECTIVITY

In the grandiose design of Italian literary history that is Francesco De Sanctis's *Storia della letteratura italiana,* the Renaissance is characterized by the struggle between form and content, Ariosto and Machiavelli. Ariosto's meticulously crafted *Orlando Furioso* is the triumph of ideal form over content. Machiavelli is the affirmation of a new and vital attention to a true human content, pointing the way to both a resurgent national spirit and the emergence of modern scientific thought. Between these two vertices of the Italian literary Renaissance De Sanctis dedicates an entire chapter of his history to Teofilo Folengo. It is an uncharacteristic indulgence toward a minor author whom De Sanctis locates at one of the most critical points in the *Storia's* unfolding saga of the Italian national-literary consciousness.

After two centuries of neglect, the rehabilitation of the Italian macaronic in the early 1800s was in large part the work of the German school of Romantic philology. De Sanctis appears to have first acquired his interest in Folengo during his thirty-two months in a Naples prison after the 1848 uprisings. Part of that time he spent translating Karl Rosenkranz's *Handbuch einer allgemeinen Geschichte der Poesie,* in which Rosenkranz had sketched a portrait of Folengo with all the requisite Romantic rebelliousness (Cordié 1977, xvi–xvii). De Sanctis would carry into his *Storia* elements of that Romantic iconography grounded on a largely apocryphal biography provided by the mocking jester Folengo himself, to which the critic, given the ideological thrust of his own opus, readily fell victim. The Merlino Cocaio of De Sanctis's *Storia* is a reckless daredevil and student of the freethinking naturalist Pietro Pomponazzi. His life was one of challenges, duels, and adventures, having fled the Benedictine order for a woman and lived for many years in a penniless and cynical vagabondage: "He treated society as an enemy, spit in its face, bursting forth in a laughter pregnant with bile" (De Sanctis 1973, 484). Underneath its parody, De Sanctis argues, Merlino's macaronic art excels for its satire of the beliefs, customs, and institutions, linguistic as well as political and religious, of a prejudiced and vitiated society. His verses possess a colorful and rapid realism reminiscent of Dante's, a language that is anathema to the horror of the particular and vague generalities of an age of rhetoric. Merlino takes the comic to an "extreme of humor" informed by an open-ended and cynical "universal negation." Confused glimpses of a new world can be seen but have no hold over his capricious fantasy (De Sanctis 1973, 487–95).

The subsequent attention to Folengo in the first decades of this century by critics such as Attilio Momigliano or Giuseppe Billanovich sought to correct the apocryphal inaccuracies of De Sanctis's portrait while moderating the Romantic features of his critical assessment. Cesare Segre in his reconstruction of the extended macaronic line from Folengo to Gadda sums up this reevaluation of the macaronic by concluding that the mockery of the macaronic writers is in the end incompatible with a reordering of the world. They are not revolutionaries but the purveyors of a "permanent contestation," one which goes beyond any specific political, religious, or moral polemic to "lay siege to the foundations of our comprehension and representation of the world" (Segre 1979, 183). Segre rises above the biographical peculiarities of his two macaronic end-point "planets," Folengo and Gadda, to offer an ontological essence of the macaronic literary enterprise. Yet to do so is perhaps to distort the historical and evolutionary dynamic of the modern macaronic, a dynamic that is played out in the autobiographical configuration of Gadda himself.

In spite of his inflated remonstrances to the contrary, Gadda's bilious satire is definitely linked as much to the "machinating liver" of the author as to that of reality (C 761). In his essays on language and literature gathered in *I viaggi la morte*, Gadda declares that the writer's task must be a vigilant identification and extirpation of fraud in the bowels of language. The macaronic is useful, he writes, when it "pulverizes and dissolves into nothingness every abuse . . . made of reason and language through the words of fraud" ("Fatto personale . . . o quasi," VM 496). This vocation goes beyond the macaronic to characterize the operation of the greatest writers of the Italian literary tradition. Boccaccio, Dante, Galileo, and Manzoni all "raise at times the edifice of judgment over a single phrase or word which is sagaciously borrowed and diabolically inserted into the text to the derision and confusion of the defrauders" ("Meditazione breve circa il dire e il fare," VM 452). This is the writer's "heroic operation," similar to that of the philosopher outlined in Gadda's 1928 speculative treatise *Meditazione milanese*. But for the "human residue" that is left behind there is often a different fate: "alone in the world, for no human can tolerate him, death alone awaits him" (MM 849).

The misfortunes of family, war, society, and a "tragic, useless life" had generated an "obscure illness" in Gadda, much like that suffered by his autobiographical protagonist Gonzalo Pirobutirro. The result is a linguistic and epistemological vigilance gone haywire: fraud is found everywhere and the resulting negation of universe and *self* is much more vicious than anything De Sanctis found in Folengo. Gonzalo knows that to deny the world is to deny himself, but for him the macaronic mockery becomes a destructive compulsion, one which Céline also experienced, and it bears within itself the threat of subjective annihilation.

The reader who peruses the pages of Gadda's World War I diary or his notes to his earliest manuscripts is struck by a rhetoric of great souls and tragic denial which bespeaks not only a youthful ingenuousness—and we are talking about a man well into his twenties—but a historical anachronism. Gadda has traditionally been seen as a creature more at ease in a nineteenth-century world than in the twentieth century, and it is not erroneous in his regard to speak of a Romantic spirit, or, as he preferred to refer to himself, of a Romantic kicked in the pants by reality and destiny ("Un'opinione sul neorealismo," VM 629). Lyricism and satire are the two poles toward which he declared that he gravitated, and his works have been criticized for their spastic evasions into a highly stylized lyrical sublime or, conversely, into a low sphere of ridicule and ridiculousness. The odd mixture of the ethereal sublime and low mockery is a trait of the original macaronic, but in Gadda, who sardonically traced his literary lineage in *La cognizione del dolore* to Jean Paul Richter, the macaronic grotesque merges with the Romantic grotesque and its crisis of subjective wholeness.

The resuscitation of the macaronic as an object of historical inquiry by the German Romantics was part of an overall reconfiguration of the classical division of the comic and sublime genres. Friedrich Schlegel's metamorphosis of irony from a rhetorical trope to a metaphysical implement for transcending from the worldly finite to the spiritually infinite marked the beginning of the modern quest for a transcendental integration of the comic into the discourse of the sublime. Jean Paul declared in courses six and seven of the *Vorschule der Aesthetik* that the ridiculous in its contrast of the finite with the finite was "the hereditary enemy of the sublime," whereas humor, or the Romantic comic, contrasted man's infinity with his finitude, ultimately in the name of the triumph of the infinite idea. Most successive elaborations on humor, irony, and the Kantian divide in the nineteenth century would be a reworking of the notion of the metaphysical split between the comic empirical self and the contemplative transcendent self.

Romantic humorism destabilizes the false sublimity of objective finitude within the framework of a continual teleological quest for subjective infinity. The Romantic text equates its own sublime nature with this subjective infinity. As such it calls unto itself the entire spectrum of subjective experience, including the comical ridiculousness of the empirical self. The operation of totalization is not without its dangers. What was previously the comic disembowelment of another's discourse in premodern parody and satire now becomes a necessary and purposeful self-mutilation. This is the reason behind what Bakhtin calls the transformation of the "joyful and triumphant hilarity" of the Renaissance grotesque into Romanticism's grotesque of "cold humor," its "melancholic" and "frightful" subjectivity (Bakhtin 1984b, 36–45). The comic becomes a source of pain in the Romantic text since it is inflicted on the subjectivity of the text itself. It is no surprise that Romantic humorism and its modern variants harbor a profound melancholy. Humor, Jean Paul stated, contains both pain and greatness; it walks with a tragic mask in hand.

Italy's foremost, albeit tardy, contributor to the European debate on humor was Luigi Pirandello. Pirandello's 1908 essay on humor, *L'umorismo*, is most memorable for its opposition of the traditional comic as a mere "perception of the opposite" on the part of the observing subject or reader vs. humor's generation of a subjective investment in the object via its "feeling of the opposite." Pirandello takes the example of an old woman who tries to make herself over as a young girl with ridiculous results. If we remain at the level of the traditional comic we merely perceive that the woman is the ridiculous opposite of what a good old lady should be, and we laugh. A humorous attitude requires us instead to reflect on the possible reasons behind the woman's grotesque maquillage; we thereby reach a higher state of awareness of and involvement with her inner drama.

Pirandello's argument is conditioned in part by his debate with Benedetto Croce over the role of reflection in art, Croce's position being that reflection (philosophy) in the work of art is alien to art's natural constitution as pure intuition. The appeal to reflection in Pirandello's theater is contained in his dismantlement of the mechanisms of theatrical fiction and his philosophizing characters in metaphysical crisis. These are also hallmarks of his modernity, and they condition his special relationship with the tradition of the commedia dell'arte.

As do other early modern forms of the comic, the commedia dell'arte undergoes a gradual transformation from the physical, obscene, and ridiculing black-faced masks of its early tradition to Goldoni's reform in the service of a new "commedia di carattere," to the dreamy or catatonic lunacy of the white-faced Pierrot (Celati 1975, 102–6). With its dialectic between the face and the mask, authenticity and form, Pirandello's theater completes the metaphysical transformation of the original commedia dell'arte's exuberance into the unhappy consciousness and frightening grotesque of modernity. The original commedia masks are barely recognizable. The characters imprisoned in their eternal masks of grief and pain in *Sei personaggi in cerca d'autore* communicate in a modern metaphysical language of alienation and relativity.

The Pirandellian character is often aware of the critical potentialities of buffoonish dismantlement. The eponymous protagonist of *Enrico IV* uses his feigned madness in a deliberate fashion to satirize the myth of subjective wholeness in others. At the same time he suffers their same anxiety of wanting to be whole and authentic, the satire becomes a self-mutilation, and the play ends tragically with Enrico's withdrawal back into the mask of madness.

In the years immediately following the student-worker upheavals of 1968, actor and playwright Dario Fo made an attempt to break away from the theater of subjective crisis through a politicized recuperation of the premodern tradition of popular comic performance. In his *Mistero buffo* shows of the early seventies, Fo sought, with the help of cultural historians, to reconstruct the tradition of the satiric medieval *giullari* and the precommedia dialect theater of Ruzante. The satirical and plurilingual *giullarate* were enacted by Fo himself, "*giullare* [minstrel] of the people in the midst of the people," and were interspersed with commentary and satiric puns on the contemporary Italian scene in an aggressive theater of "propaganda and provocation" (cited in Angelini 1978, 148). Fo's *giullarate* and contemporary farces also sought to do away with the Pirandellian discourse of subjective crisis as a bourgeois convention that was extraneous to popular theater. The contrast is evident in the comparison of the central figures of the fool in Pirandello and Fo. In Pirandello's *Enrico IV* the protagonist feigns a folly that illustrates modern man's crisis of alienated subjectivity and failed communication. Fo's madman or "Matto" in *Morte accidentale di un anarchico* embraces a schizophrenic madness of multiple personalities not as the metaphor of subjective alienation but as a tool to ridicule and subvert the oppressive institutions of the capitalist police state.

Fo's efforts at a politicized revival of a certain carnival tradition raise the question of the "liberating" quality of carnivalesque laughter. In reaction to Bakhtin's idealization of the carnival's revolutionary qualities, various respondents have criticized the carnivalesque as being ultimately more conservative than rebellious. Terry Eagleton has argued that carnival is "a *licensed* affair in every sense, a permissible rupture of hegemony, a contained popular blow-off as disturbing and relatively ineffectual as a revolutionary work of art" (Eagleton 1981, 148; cited in Stallybrass and White 1986, 13). Umberto Eco asserts that the moment of transgression of the carnivalesque "can exist only if a background of unquestioned observance exists" whereas the "feeling of the opposite" generated by Pirandello's humor discusses and questions the rules and therefore constitutes a "conscious and explicit" criticism (Eco 1980, 275, 277). But modern humor is also bound to the constraints or rules of the society and ideology in which it has flourished, modern bourgeois democracy. Democratic ideology sanctions the right to protest and criticize. Constant criticism is hailed in fact as the internal dynamism of its quest for overcoming and betterment, its mythos of progress. But in truth it is an ideology that can criticize only itself, for in its subjective infinity it sanctions only itself.[8]

Gadda is closer in spirit to Pirandello than to Fo, a confirmation that the carnivalesque in his works is subservient to a darker modern comic, André Breton's "humour noir." Gadda continues the Pirandellian discourse of alienated masks and subjectivity in crisis, although merged with what Gian Carlo Roscioni has called a Sternian humorism of autobiographical character (Roscioni 1994). Gonzalo Pirobutirro wears many masks, from those of Molière's *Misanthrope* and *Avare* to the "tragic mask on the metope of the theater" (C 682, 704; AWG 144, 171). What distinguishes Gadda's works in this regard is his amalgam of both the

Renaissance comic and the Romantic sublime. Gadda retains the languages of both carnivalesque parody and melancholic humorism, both the comic objectivity and the melancholic subjectivity, as in the following passage of young Gonzalo Pirobutirro's scientific curiosity at the expense of an innocent cat:

> Avendogli un dottore ebreo, nel legger matematiche a Pastrufazio, e col sussidio del calcolo, dimostrato come pervenga il gatto (di qualunque doccia cadendo) ad arrivar sanissimo al suolo in sulle quattro zampe, che è una meravigliosa applicazione ginnica del teorema dell'impulso, egli precipitò più volte un bel gatto dal secondo piano della villa, fatto curioso di sperimentare il teorema. E la povera bestiola, atterrando, gli diè difatti la desiderata conferma, ogni volta, ogni volta! come un pensiero che, traverso fortune, non intermetta dall'essere eterno; ma, in quanto gatto, poco dopo morì, con occhi velati d'una irrevocabile tristezza, immalinconito da quell'oltraggio. Poiché ogni oltraggio è morte. (C 598)

> [Since a Jewish doctor, in reading mathematics at Pastrufazio, and with the help of calculus, had demonstrated to him how the cat (from whatever drainpipe it falls) can safely reach the ground on all four paws, which is a marvelous gymnastic application of the theorem of impulse, he at various times hurled a handsome cat from the third floor of the villa, having become curious to test the theorem. And the poor animal, landing, in fact furnished him each time with the desired confirmation, each time! Each time! Like a thought that, through every vicissitude, never ceases being eternal; but, as cat, it died shortly thereafter, its eyes veiled with irrevocable sadness, made melancholy by that outrage. Because all outrage is death.] (AWG 39)

Pier Paolo Pasolini deliberately chose this unassuming passage from Gadda's *La cognizione del dolore* to analyze the reasons for his love of Gadda. Pasolini notes that there is a double literary "pastiche" at work: a modern imitation of an Italian Renaissance or Humanist adaptation of a well-crafted Ciceronian period (Pasolini 1963, 61). The passage also constitutes an understated imitation of a Rabelaisian scholastic parody, culminating in the comic exaggeration of the cat being scrupulously and repeatedly dropped from the third floor of the villa in the name of science. One is reminded of young Gargantua's scientific experimentation to find the perfect "torchecul" or "arsewipe." But in Gadda's novel the vehicle of laughter, the cat, does not remain a mere objective prop for the parodic mockery of official or scientific discourse as does Rabelais's well-downed goose. Gadda's cat retains this comic function, but it is also infused with an irrevocable sadness and melancholy. From comic object the cat is subjectified into both an empirical subject, "as cat," and a transcendental subject, "like a thought that, through every vicissitude, never ceases being eternal." Ultimately, the cat becomes a metaphor for the tragically sublime nature of the existential condition, subjected to outrage and death.

More than Gadda's well-crafted pastiche, it is this transformation into a painful subjectivity that is the true reason, Pasolini confesses, why he so loves Gadda. From the comic arises a deep-felt *pietas* for the poor cat, a "creature that neither knows nor asks for anything," and a hatred for himself the child, perpetrator of the world's atrocity. The verbal bravura is even more a self-defense, a mask behind which subjectivity's painfulness is distilled into language itself, since in reality it is not so much the little subject, the "kitty" or "gattino," as Pasolini puts it, that is thrown from the window but the big subject, "il Gaddone" (Pasolini 1963, 64–66). Subjectivity is both tormentor and victim in a melancholic ritual of self-mutilation, a ritual which Pasolini himself engaged in to an extreme degree in his last, desperate film, *Salò*.

The Modern Macaronic

> Zucca mihi patria est.
>
> TEOFILO FOLENGO, *Baldus* 25:649

The modern crisis of subjective wholeness receives its fullest expression in the *novel*, the genre of modernity. One of the most suggestive readings of this crisis continues to be that of György Lukács in *The Theory of the Novel*. For Lukács, the novel is the giving of form to a problematic modernity. The lack of a spontaneous totality of being in a modern society that still thinks in terms of totality becomes the problem of the novel form. Its epic story is that of the conflict between the soul and the fragmentary and out-of-joint structure of the world. In a later preface, Lukács stated that his immediate motive for writing *The Theory of the Novel* in 1914–15 was supplied by the outbreak of the First World War and his "vehement . . . and scarcely articulate rejection of the war and especially of enthusiasm for the war." This work was written "in a mood of permanent despair over the world" (Lukács 1971, 11–12). Lukács began writing the horrific lesson of the Great War before it had unfolded. For others the war had to be lived as the apocalypse of fragmentation that converted a generation of enthusiasts into disillusionists.

The nightmarish voyage of Céline's Bardamu begins with the war, "shut up on earth as if it were a loony bin, ready to demolish everything on it, Germany, France, whole continents, everything that breathes" (Céline 1983, 9). And yet Sergeant Destouches's valor had made him a national hero early in the war. Before Italy's 1915 entrance into the war, Gadda was a committed interventionist, and he volunteered to fight immediately. He saw the war as his final chance (at twenty-two years of age) to achieve both personal heroism and subjective wholeness. At the end of the war he was no hero but an abject and shattered man (and still very much a militarist). The "Racconto italiano di ignoto del Novecento" ["An Italian Tale by an Unknown Author of the Twentieth Century"] (written in 1924) was his first attempt at a novel. It was to have depicted a disintegrated, postwar Italian society. The book never advanced beyond a few scattered fragments. Reality had become for Gadda the hypertrophy of the part, "continual flux," "grotesque deformation," "deformed multiplicity," "impossible closure," "extreme decombination." The rest of his career was spent trying to give form to the fragmentation.

For Lukács there is a clear caesura in the history of "epic" fiction: an integrated civilization and a problematic civilization, a classical totality and a modern fragmentation, the epic and the novel. Other historians of the novel are less apocalyptic: they see evolution as much as rupture; they see a progressive evolution of mimesis, language, and dialogue. Auerbach's grand march of Western realism is the unfolding history of serious treatment of the humble and everyday. Its origins are in the early-Christian *sermo umilis* and its culmination in the great realist novels of the nineteenth century. In more recent years the study of the novel has shifted focus from the notion of its mimesis of reality to the Bakhtinian thesis of the novel as a forum for the dialogic exchange of competing ideologies and languages. At the origins of the modern tradition of novelistic discourse, there are for Bakhtin "laughter" and "polyglossia." The prehistory of novelistic discourse is the history of the "parodic-travesty-ing forms" that were found alongside every "straightforward genre" in the ancient and premodern world. Lukács's integrated word of the classical world finds its constant parodic countersong in Bakhtin: "It is as if such mimicry rips the word away from its object, disunifies the two, shows that a given straightforward generic word—epic or tragic—is onesided, bounded, incapable of exhausting the object" (Bakhtin 1981, 50–55). In the process, a linguistic consciousness is created that will make the modern novel possible.

Parodic laughter is raised to new artistic and ideological levels, Bakhtin argues, especially in historical conditions of polyglossia (the simultaneous presence of two or more national languages interacting within a single cultural system): "Only polyglossia fully frees consciousness from the tyranny of its own language and its own myth of language. Parodic-travestying forms flourish under these conditions, and only in this milieu are they capable of being elevated to completely new ideological heights" (Bakhtin 1981, 61).

This is where Bakhtin's arguments become crucial to the study of a macaronic tradition in the modern novel. The birth of what Bakhtin calls the great Renaissance novels, those of Rabelais and Cervantes, is occasioned by the breakthrough of the parodic-travestying word into the strict and closed straightforward genres. The prehistory of novelistic discourse reaches its apex in the hybrid compositions of the late Middle Ages and in the macaronic poets (Bakhtin 1981, 78–82). From that point on the discourse between languages was to become a dialogized internal hybrid within the stylistically "monoglot" new novels. The subsequent history of the novel would switch from one of polyglossia to one of "heteroglossia" within a national language, the problem of internal differentiation and stratification (Bakhtin 1981, 67). The macaronic is the preconscious of the modern novel. Hidden away in the forgotten folds of a prehistory, the macaronic would reappear in the novel's moment of ontological crisis.

The rise of the early novel is the story of a process of legitimation. The novel gradually establishes its credentials of seriousness, rationality, and realism which entitle it to become the new representative genre of a problematic modernity. The beginning of this process of legitimation involves discrediting the outgoing "epic" form of representation, the romance. Much of the early novel's premodern legacy of parody and satire is precisely in the service of this struggle: "In the sixteenth and seventeenth centuries, the aims of the satirist and the writer who wished to write realistic fiction coincided when both reacted against the chivalric and pastoral romances. Satire offered the first and perhaps the crudest kind of realism that contributed to the novel—a militant realism that establishes itself by destroying an illusion, by turning over a stone to expose the crawling things underneath. It attacks idealization by means of a counter-reality based on exaggerated probability, producing a travesty of the idealized world" (Paulson 1967b, 23–24).

The exemplar of this new realism, after Rabelais, is the satirical picaresque novel, the narrative form which leads to the greatest of the early novels, Cervantes's *Don Quijote* (Paulson 1967b, 24–33). In England the struggle of the novel against the romance assumes the form of the conquest of a statute of seriousness, rationality, and understanding for the narrative genre in prose (Celati 1975, 5–13). And it is in England that the rise of the novel is most closely tied to the rise of modern bourgeois culture in Europe, a culture which grounds itself on a discourse of reasonable seriousness and discussion. In early modern England new patterns of discourse were molded and regulated through the forms of corporate assembly in which they were produced. "Alehouse, coffee-house, church, law court, library, drawing room of a country mansion" were all significant "sites of assembly" and "spaces of discourse" requiring different manners and mores (Stallybrass and White 1986, 80). The coffeehouse was one of the most important of these sites, a "sober," "de-libidinized" and "democratic" space dedicated to fostering "the interests of serious, productive and *rational* intercourse" (Stallybrass and White 1986, 97).

The same was true to a minor degree in the less progressive nations of Europe. A dramaturgical case in point is the image of the coffeehouse in Goldoni's comic play *La bottega del caffè*. In the reactionary clime of the Venetian oligarchy, this site of a new discourse is more of an outpost in a still undemocratic and, in true commedia dell'arte fashion, libidinous society. The conversants of the new discourse are limited to a single character, the self-made entrepreneur and coffeehouse proprietor Ridolfo, a preacher of the new bourgeois sensibility in a realm of thinly disguised commedia masks. Nonetheless, Goldoni's theater of reform is a significant moment in the establishment of a representational culture of bourgeois modernity in Italy. This culture will find its epicenter not in Venice but in Milan, where the nascent tradition of civic discussion will flourish in the pages of journals such as the Enlightenment *Il caffè* (1764–66) and the Romantic *Il conciliatore*, a forum for the diffusion of literary and political discussion before its suppression by the Austrian authorities in 1819 after only fourteen months of publication. Gadda's own ethical formation has its roots in this Milanese civic tradition via the model of Manzoni, who shared the literary and political ideals of *Il conciliatore*, and in Gadda's education in the thought of other nineteenth-century civic Milanese intellectuals, perhaps the most significant being Carlo Cattaneo (see Vigorelli 1955).

The novel re-creates the "civilizing" trend of bourgeois culture, transposing the public "discussion" of the coffeehouses and other meeting places into the private sphere of domestic "conversation," a key element in the classical bildungsroman's "comfort of civilization" (Moretti 1987, 48–52). For that matter, the affirmation of the novel resembles that of the stumbling and youthful heroes of the Bildungsroman itself. Its official history is that of a gradual sublimation and education from comic rowdiness into serious and well-mannered sensibility. The other common denominator in the ascension of the novel as the genre of modernity is its increasingly confident engagement with the ideal of representational mimesis. The satiric exaggeration and metafictional commentary of the early novel gradually yield to the novel's self-constitution as the totalizing symbolic form of objective realism. The key to the novel's objectifying operation, Lukács argues, is its constitutive irony, "the sole possible a priori condition for a true, totality-creating objectivity" (Lukács 1971, 93). By ironizing all the subjective viewpoints within itself, the novel could create the illusion of objectivity, and thus mimesis, by claiming to remove all subjectivity from itself. It is the mimetic novel's technical coup and at the same time what has been called "the novel's worst moment of bad faith and self-deception where interpretation is taken to be representation, and fictional totalisation is identified with theoretical totalisation" (Bernstein 1984, 216).

> Because the objectivity of transcendental subjectivity could not be directly realised, the negativity of subjectivity was deployed to create a transcendental illusion, the illusion of objectivity. This troubling illusion could itself be dissimulated in a further ironic reflection, emphasising thus the dissonance and absence haunting the only partially figured represented world. Hence, the realist novel was torn in its recognition of transcendental subjectivity between irony as a means of generating an illusion of objectivity and irony as the affirmation of dissonance. (Bernstein 1984, 219)

The undisputed masterpiece of the use of negative irony to mask subjectivity within the guise of objectivity, through the technique of *style indirect libre*, is Gustave Flaubert's *Madame Bovary*. As Roland Barthes put it, Flaubert "never stops the play of codes . . . one never knows if he is responsible for what he writes (if there is a subject)" (Barthes 1975, 140). Yet it is precisely at the height of its affirmation as the genre of linguistic and representational objectivity in Flaubert that the novel begins to call into question that same affirmation. The novel's irony of dissonance quickly moves toward the satiric ridicule of its primordial origins. The opening chapter of Flaubert's *Madame Bovary*, with its rapid description of Charles's mediocre formation and education, is a satiric parody of a bildungsroman. It can even be read as a parodic rewriting of the history of the novel itself, a history which Flaubert transforms from a tale of comic affirmation as the new epic of a new era into a self-ridiculing satire.

Ridiculous in his mock-epic cap of Rabelaisian proportions, young Charles Bovary, "le nouveau," as he is referred to repeatedly, sets the school class to derisive laughter when he attempts to say his name. Le nouveau's repeated failures, his abnormally loud voice and hypertrophied mouth ("une bouche démesurée"), his disintegration of linguistic subjectivity into a jumble of syllables ("le même bredouillement de syllabes"), and the macaronic disfigurement of his name into an object of parodic ridicule—"Charbovari! Charbovari!"—all attest to Flaubert's recuperation of "parodic-travestying forms" in *Madame Bovary*.[9] Finally isolated from the others in the dunce's seat, the buffoonish nouveau is ordered by his exasperated master to declare repeatedly what he and the novelistic world he represents truly are, ridiculous: "'As for you the new boy, you will copy out for me twenty times the verb *ridiculus sum.*'" Charles's imposed self-denigration is not limited to himself. In the pedantic fashion of the elementary school Latin lesson he must write all the tenses and persons of *ridiculus sum*. It is not only Charles the object that is held up to ridicule and ridiculousness, it is the entire fictive world of the novel and the novel's own form-making status as a totality-creating objectivity.

Flaubert's near-sensual passion for the grotesque mixture of the sublime and the low and his admiration for ancient and Renaissance parodic authors such as Petronius, Apuleius, and Rabelais are well known (see Steegmuller 1968, 283–84 and La Capra 1982, 104–6). In *Madame Bovary* the novel's premodern legacy of parodic debasement of serious genres becomes a self-inflicted mutilation of ridicule within the novel's myth of the all-encompassing totality. Nothing and no one are spared as text, character, and author are all caught up in the self-destructive frenzy of subjective wholeness gone sour. In ridiculing Emma and her kitsch-inspired dreams of erotic or tragic transcendence, Flaubert's text likewise ridicules itself as the banal object of its own pretensions to lyrical sublimity and narrative totality. It also ridicules Flaubert's own yearning for subjective totality, an author who so identified with Emma Bovary's self-poisoning that he confessed to a similar sensation in himself: "I had such a taste of arsenic in my mouth and was poisoned so effectively myself, that I had two attacks of indigestion, one after the other—two very real attacks, for I vomited my entire dinner" (cited in Steegmuller 1968, 305). If certain readers of *Madame Bovary* were so incensed by the work that it was brought to trial, the obscenity they felt threatened by is also ascribable to its subjection of the myth of bourgeois subjective wholeness to a sado-masochistic exhibitionism of ridiculousness and ridicule.

At the heart of this frenzy of satiric mutilation, as Flaubert knew well, lies a linguistic double bind. For if the novel, as Bakhtin tells us, is unique and different from the poetic "single-voiced" genres because of its ability to engage in its internal dialogue all the languages of the world, this same linguistic totality places the novel in the predicament of having ingested all the ridiculousness of these languages as well. And while in premodern parody it was the incompleteness or stupidity of another's external language that was mocked, in the novel the mockery is directed inward, against its own component languages. Mutilation becomes subjectified, and it can only be so since the novel's enactment of the modern and essentially bourgeois myth of subjective wholeness rests on the "democratic" coexistence of languages, a bad-faith democracy in Flaubert. Spreading like a cancer through the conduit of the novel's celebrated free indirect discourse, stupidity infects every verbal element of the text. Any effort at correcting the grotesqueness only exacerbates it, just as Charles's botched operation on the footboy Hippolyte's lame foot only furthers his own ridiculousness and ridicule. The novel ends with the victory of human and linguistic stupidity in the triumphant figure of the word-mongering pharmacist Homais.

None of this means that the satiric novel of self-ridicule gives up its quest for sublime transcendence. Its subjective mutilation is nothing other than the direct result of this desperate quest. Perhaps no novelist ever strove so painstakingly to sublimate the novel as a form of art, and succeeded, as did Flaubert in writing ridiculous *Madame Bovary*.

Flaubert's disgust with the banal and ridiculous reality he so keenly depicted in *Madame Bovary* is well documented, and Gadda's *La cognizione del dolore* is an important continuator of the satiric novel of mimetic stupidity and self-deprecation. Only in Gadda, the subjective abuse, grotesque parody, and macaronic origins of the novel are exploited even more fully. *Cognizione* is a hall of mirrors in which there is a constant refraction of ridiculousness and ridicule. While the autobiographical protagonist Gonzalo continually heaps scorn on the inane inhabitants of the Lombard-like Néa Keltiké, and on his own forebears, he himself becomes the object of derision in the collective mock-epics of his avarice, indolence, and gargantuan gluttony. The reign of linguistic stupidity is opened up to the original macaronic hybridization of trilingual polyglossia (in this case Italian, Spanish, and the "vulgar" Lombard dialect). Gonzalo knows "very well . . . that the novel, bound to real characters and a real environment, was as stupid as those characters and that environment" (C 731; AWG 207). And he knows that the binding force between the modern myths of *mimetic* and *subjective* wholeness means that to deny and ridicule the illusion of mimetic reality is also to deny one's own self: "to deny vain images, most of the time, means denying oneself" (C 703; AWG 171). In the age of the myth of subjective wholeness, the satirist's attacks on his fictional world are also and above all a self-mutilation, a "laceration," as Gadda's puts it, of transcendent "possibility," comparable to the ripping up of a page of lies (C 703; AWG 171).

A European history of the modern macaronic traces its premodern roots to the original Renaissance macaronic and Rabelaisian comic, its amalgam of comic parody and melancholic subjective totality to the Romantic theorists, its crisis of mimetic realism to Flaubert (who becomes a veritable father of sorts in the encyclopedic parody of received ideas and bourgeois inanity of *Bouvard et Pécuchet*). It is by recognizing this broader European tradition that the occasional and intuitive comparisons of Gadda to other macaronic modernists such as Louis-Ferdinand Céline or James Joyce can gain in substance and justification. In these macaronic authors archaism is used to ridicule and overcome the myth of subjective totality and mimetic realism, not by going *beyond* it but rather *behind* it, all the way to the novel's premodern origins in satiric parody, grotesque realism, and macaronic pastiche.

All three of these authors share similar macaronic traits. Realism is exploded in the gigantism of physicality and the human body. Referentiality gives way to expressionism. Language tilts from its centripetal pole to the extremes of centrifugality. Narrative (plot) flies apart into fragments and episodes while subjectivity dissolves into a language stretched to the limits of its synchronic and diachronic elasticity.

Joyce is the most encyclopedic of the three, and linguistically the most experimental. In his study "James Joyce and the Macaronic Tradition," Vivian Mercier has cataloged examples from Joyce's works that correspond to the various categories of the macaronic outlined in Octave Delepierre's 1850 *Macaronéana*. They range from the schoolyard macaronic, "*Nos ad manum ballum jocabimus*" (*Stephen Hero*), to the "pedantesque," where the Latin word takes on the forms of the vulgar tongue and which Mercier finds to be "pretty much *passim* in *Finnegans Wake*" (Mercier 1966, 27).[10] Joyce is also the most genuinely Rabelaisian. "As great and comprehensive and human as Rabelais," Valery Larbaud gushed over *Ulysses* (Ellmann 1959, 514). Joyce shares Rabelais's robust love of language and style, his "comment by parody" of scholarship for which he nevertheless feels an instinctive affection (Cohen 1955, 18), his attachment to what biographer Ellmann calls the "dear and dirty" physicality of nature and human body (Ellmann 1959, 4).

The crisis of nineteenth-century sublimity of mimetic objectivity in Joyce has a Flaubertian genesis. We know from Joyce's friend Frank Budgen that Joyce greatly admired Flaubert, had read all his works, and had memorized entire pages from some of them (Budgen 1934, 176, 180–81). Certainly young Stephen Dedalus's ideal of the artist who "like the God of the creation, remains within or behind or beyond or above his handiwork, invisible, refined out of existence, indifferent, paring his fingernails" (Joyce 1966, 215) is consonant with Flaubert's that "[an] author in his book must be like God in the universe, present everywhere and visible nowhere" (Flaubert 1980, 173). In the modernist Joyce there is a constant tension between the spatio-temporal limits which condition objective mimetic literature and the urge to break through those limits to a new, all-encompassing subjectivity that is both synchronic and diachronic. The solutions he sought were based in language, the new subjective realism of the psycholinguistic flow of stream of consciousness, and, midway through *Ulysses,* the explosion of diachronically polyphonic and parodic narrative pastiches. In *Finnegans Wake* all the devices of polyphonic pastiche are still in place and have been concentrated into each semantic unit. The novel form yields to a macaronic musicality that attempts to say all at every moment and in every word. The inner subjectivity of stream of consciousness has been expanded to the historical and metaphysical flux and reflux of the linguistic sign. Freud and Jung, "the Viennese Tweedledee" and "the Swiss Tweedledum," are routinely ridiculed, their psychoanalytic shenanigans replaced by the metaphysical historicism of Giovanni Battista Vico's eternal "ricorso" and Giordano Bruno's "connexio oppositorum."

For Céline, France's great and vulgar modernist, language and style were everything. The core of Céline's linguistic revolution is argot. Popular slang belongs to the filthy, the abject, and the oppressed; it is the cry of despair and emotion, the language of hatred. But Céline's slang is at the center of a polyphony of other languages, of other types of French, which vary from the specialized languages of the vocations and sciences, medicine in particular, to the archaic French of the Renaissance and Villon. The languages rebound off of one another; the official meets the low. For every sanitized "rectum" there is a "trou" or a "cul" or a "fias" or an "oigne" (Godard 1985, 69).

Céline is macaronic and, of course, Rabelaisian—so much so, apparently, that Patrick McCarthy proffers that "the Rabelaisian style, realistic and refined, full of obscenity and of poetry, is Céline's great contribution to the technique of novel-writing," while Jean-Louis Bory feels at ease in calling Céline's earliest protagonist Bardamu, "the Pantagruel of the atomic era" (McCarthy 1975, 115; Bory 1960, 146). Céline went even further in his 1957 short essay "Rabelais, il a raté son coup." Céline is Rabelais and Rabelais is Céline: "Rabelais was a doctor and a writer, like me."—"I have had in my life the same vice as Rabelais. I too have spent my time getting into desperate situations. Like him I do not expect anything from others, like him, I regret nothing." Céline's paranoia and polemic with his academic persecutors draw him into a flawed analysis of Rabelais's language, which he associates solely with popular speech. Rabelais missed his chance because he was not able to pass on to future literary generations the true French tongue, the vulgar one. Plutarch's translator Amyot and the academics won the linguistic battle. Rabelais was too busy "spending his time trying not to get burnt," like Céline.[11]

Céline is macaronic, and an anti-Semite, a paranoiac, a madman. "La raison!" he sneers in "Rabelais, il a raté son coup": "Faut être fou." It is Julia Kristeva who has sought most to bridge the carnivalesque Céline and the abject and delirious Céline: "to the carnival's semantic ambivalences, which pair the high and the low, the sublime and the abject, Céline adds the merciless crashing of the *apocalypse*" (Kristeva 1982, 138). Like those of Gadda and Flaubert, Céline's crisis of mimesis exacerbates the abject in reality. His grotesque realism is vicious: vomit, sex, masturbation, excrement, and death, especially death. They all have an edge, they all are manifestations of the horror, of the apocalypse. Loathsomeness attaches itself to everything, from the most banal triviality to the most horrific outrage. Kristeva notes that narrative identity and the objective world that supports it become unbearable in Céline; narration is no longer possible; everything must be "*descried* with maximal stylistic intensity" (Kristeva 1982, 141).

Gadda falls between Joyce and Céline. With Joyce he shares the encyclopedism, the attraction to the scholastic comment by parody. His macaronic prose bears the peculiar characteristics of the Italian plurilingual and literary tradition. The codified formal origins of the Italian macaronic render Gadda's movement between the literary sublime and the physicality of dialect hilarious but always exquisitely philological. A radical sense of nineteenth-century Lombard "propriety" also renders Gadda the most prudish of the three in his use of low physicality. Sex and masturbation as physical acts are practically absent from his works, even though there is a massive presence of voluptuous servants and prostitutes, grotesque nymphomaniacs, and nasty voyeurism. Crapulous consumption and food fetishism are present, often as a symbolic exchange for the frustrated sexual act. But most typically failed sexual acts find their symbolic exchange in violent acts, symbolic matricides born of Oedipus-Orestes complexes. Defecation and feces—"merde" and "stronzi"—are abundant, especially in barnyard animals. What is obsessively present is death. Death for Gadda is the high-low amalgamation of metaphysical sublimity and biological physicality; it is the horrific regression from the possibility of heuristic combination to the residual lump of substance.

Words and death, to borrow Kristeva's terminology, constitute a first link between Gadda and Céline. They are accompanied by a shared sense of rage and abjection, of paranoia and schizophrenia, of suffering (*dolore*) and horror (*orrore*). In Gadda the rage is epistemological. It is born from the impossibility of a hypersensitive subjectivity to organize the multiplicity, flux, and deformation of an impossibly complex phenomenal reality, to forge "system" from "method." The result is a delirium, not the active nightmare of Bardamu's voyage to the end of night, but the "interpretative delirium" of a subjectivity irritated and outraged by the world's disorder and banality of evil. From this delirium is born Gadda's special abjection of ridicule and ridiculousness but also the possibility of a macaronic cure. This is Contini's thesis, that of the "unhappy syndrome which is cured through the classical prescriptions of erudite-plebean comic spirit" (Contini 1989, 19). The liberating laughter in Gadda is hilarious, even delirious, but never far is the melancholic subjectivity. This is the paradox of Gadda's poetics of the macaronic, what he himself more frequently referred to as his "grotesque" and "baroque" epistemology, his knowledge of grief. Gadda's premodern expulsion of evil and noxious gases through laughter is a robust, physical cure, but his modern melancholy is a metaphysical and mystified illness: a *"male invisibile,"* a *"male oscuro."*

Chapter 1

The Poetics of Polarity

Una confessione circa i problemi d'officina o le angosce o i ragnateli
d'officina, comporta di necessità dei riferimenti a una vita, a una biografia
interna ed esterna, si ingrana in una gnoseologia e in un'etica ("Come
lavoro," VM 427).

[A confession concerning problems of the workshop, or the dreads or
cobwebs of the workshop, necessarily entails references to a life, to an
internal and external biography, gets caught up in a gnoseology and in
an ethics.]

A tension toward polarity and paradox surrounds Carlo Emilio Gadda
and his work. Critics have tended to highlight two principal components
of Gadda's narrative: its linguistic expressionism and the complex philosophical "knot" or *groviglio* lurking behind the verbal pastiche.[1] Other
contrastive analyses spontaneously suggest themselves: the juxtaposition of lyricism and satire, subjectivity and mimesis, historical awareness and reactionary blindness. Biographers point to the schizophrenic
split between the timid and inordinately polite *gran lombardo* and the
alter ego of the sarcastic blasphemer.[2]

Gadda's awareness of his gravitation to paradox is apparent in his hesi-
tant overtures to the Italian literary community in the mid-1920s. Rome,
March 6, 1926: "Like a strange character, like a giraffe or a kangaroo in
your beautiful garden: that's what I can be" (AAF 43). An extravagant
oddity amongst the aloof belletrists of the fascist era is how Gadda markets himself to friend and intercessor Bonaventura Tecchi on the eve of
his first publication in the Florentine literary journal *Solaria*. The self-
effacing trepidation of his letters to Tecchi in this period are indicative of
Gadda's heterogenous relationship with the elite Italian literary establishment of the 1920s, located in the splendid Liberty cafés of Florence
and the cultured Europeanism of *Solaria* itself.[3]

In 1926 the electrotechnical engineer Carlo Emilio Gadda, at work on the planning and construction of synthetic ammonia plants for the Società Ammonia Casale in Italy and abroad, was still far from that select environment. Only in 1940 would Gadda definitively abandon his duties as an engineer and move to Florence. Yet it is precisely the qualities acquired in his workaday apprenticeship in the technological trades that the young engineer viewed as his possible contribution to *Solaria*'s genteel pages: "The only good thing I may possess is that, living outside of the literary camp, in a field of tedious and diligent actions, I can bring something of the boorish mentality of the trade into the province of the specialists and the refined: a curious pastiche will come of it" (AAF 44). Unfortunately, not even Gadda's ingenuous offer to purchase two additional subscriptions and buy eight copies of the issue in which his first contribution would appear was able to deter *Solaria*'s editors from rejecting his original submission "Manovre di artiglieria da campagna" [Field artillery maneuvers]. Eventually a more "literatoid" group of brief, lyrical prose pieces would be accepted (AAF 45–47). The episode is emblematic of Gadda's relationship to the Italian literary scene as an outsider looking in and of his assertions that his narrative weltanschauung of the "pasticcio" or mixture, mess, pastiche, was always sensed to be first and foremost an autobiographical truth.

The post–World War I decade of Gadda's literary formation was one of conflicting personal and professional interests, erratic travel, disappointment punctuated by facile enthusiasms. Raised in a family with conservative political and religious views and a strong sense of military tradition, Gadda was a fervent interventionist before the war and an early volunteer. It was, however, a disillusioned young Gadda who returned to Milan in January 1919. Embittered by Italian mismanagement of the war effort and the humiliating experience of capture and internment in Austria and Germany, Gadda was shattered by the news of the death of his younger brother Enrico, an aviator who had fatally crashed while testing a new plane a few months before the armistice (Sassi 1983, x). The moral imperatives and ethical nationalism that had occasioned Gadda's support for the war would become an obsessive topic in the author's writings in the twenties. With other disgruntled veterans he adhered early, 1921, albeit sheepishly to the National Fascist Party, "an ugly bit of news," as he prefaced the announcement of his enrollment in a letter to friend and former prisoner-of-war camp mate Ugo Betti (IF 58).

Gadda's career interests during the decade were torn between the fields of engineering, philosophy, and literature. In 1920 he received his degree

in electrotechnical engineering, having finished a program of studies at
the University of Milan begun in 1912 and interrupted by the war. After
an apprenticeship at a power plant in Sardinia, he left for a fourteen-
month position with the Compañia General de Fosforos (General Match
Company) in Argentina. Back in Milan in 1924, he temporarily with-
drew from engineering to compete for a literary prize offered by the publishing house Mondadori for a best new novel. The effort resulted in the
notebooks of the unfinished *Racconto italiano di ignoto del novecento*.
Subsisting on private lessons and substitute teaching in mathematics and
physics, Gadda resumed under the tutelage of Piero Martinetti the university program in philosophy he had begun in 1922 and would termi-
nate in 1928. Although he passed all the required examinations, the can-
didate never completed a projected thesis on Leibniz. In 1925 Gadda was
in Rome with the Società Ammonia Casale, having returned to electrotechnical engineering for financial reasons. The next several years saw
him at work in Belgium, Lorraine, the Ruhr, and Toulouse for Ammonia
Casale while contributing literary fragments, essays, reviews, and technical articles to *Solaria*, other journals, and the Milanese newspaper
L'Ambrosiano. In 1928 he composed the eccentric and unpublished philosophical treatise *Meditazione milanese* and began a second novel that
would never reach completion, *La meccanica*. Only in 1931 at the age of
thirty-eight would his first volume, *La Madonna dei Filosofi*, be published by *Solaria*.

A Philosophy of Systems, Polarity, and Deformation

> La mia monade e il mio io sono delle baracche sconquassate rispetto alle pure
> sfere d'acciaio di Leibniz e hanno mille finestre e fessure (MM 832).
>
> [My monad and my I are ramshackle shanties compared to Leibniz's pure
> steel spheres and they have a thousand windows and fissures.]

In approaching the reconstruction of Gadda's intellectual and literary formation, it is useful to begin with the philosophical construct of the
1928 *Meditazione milanese*. The treatise provides an essential speculative framework for understanding Gadda's world vision. We shall then
proceed backward to the early and problematic literary and autobiographical experiences of the *Racconto italiano* (1924) and the *Giornale di guerra
e di prigionia* (1915–19).

Presented as an erratic dialogue on the knowledge of self and reality,
Meditazione milanese pits a digressive and dilettante philosopher against
his vigilant and contentious critic. Despite this unorthodox and disper-

sive format, Gadda manages systematically to expound in its pages the obsessive speculative crusade of his narrative: the dismantlement of the hackneyed notion of reality and the human psyche as self-contained "postal parcels"; and its replacement with a vision of human and phenomenal reality as tangled, fissured webs of multiplicity, differentiation, and deformation.

Despite the consonances of this vision with the thought of Henri Bergson (Bergson is not mentioned in the treatise), Gadda's referents in *Meditazione milanese* remain obstinately archaic. Indicative of the circumscribed nature of his university studies in philosophy, the treatise is heavily indebted to the classical rationalism of Leibniz, Spinoza, and Kant and to Gadda's own mathematical and technical formation (see Roscioni 1974, xvi–xvii). Its interests reflect an idiosyncratic extension of Gadda's proposed university thesis on Leibniz's theory of knowledge in the *New Essays Concerning Human Understanding*.[4] Gadda's notes to his edition of the *New Essays* reveal a particular interest in Leibniz's monadism (Lucchini 1988, 32), and the critical thrust of *Meditazione* hinges on the dislocation of Leibniz's self-contained *monad* in favor of the *system*, a more permeable and open-ended universal building block. System is used, Gadda prefaces, with an extended sense of the meaning it has in mathematics and mechanics, "a set of entities that have common properties, even if only relative to a given cognitive moment. For example: a system of points, of lines, of curves. Deformable systems, rigid systems" (MM 861). But in spite of this mathematical grounding, the system as defined in *Meditazione* quickly assumes a nonlinear, organic, and chaotic nature. It is an unwieldy beast of continually changing contours and "impossible closure" (MM 740–43), and its substitution for the metaphysical essentiality of Leibnizian monadism will not pass unscathed by *Meditazione*'s resident critic:

> Your contrived concepts are anti-Leibnizian and reveal a crass ignorance of the elements of all true philosophy. Do you not recall that a monad or I is an absolute simple: and that the monad is the dark, windowless house? . . . It is the closed thought, pure I, that hasn't any need of the light from without, that has in itself the light? . . . A system is instead, according to your turns of speech, an indescribable monster, who gossips with everyone, like certain women servants who involve in their malefic curiosity all the building's tenants. And in this case, according to you, it is a question of the fellow tenants in the house of the universal world. (MM 804)

The critic's description of the system as a monstrous, malefic, and gossiping stairwell are anticipatory of the chaotic Roman universe of *Quer pasticciaccio brutto de via Merulana*, and they underscore Gadda's obsession with the messy interrelatedness of reality. Contrary to Leibniz's windowless and independently entelechial monads, even the simplest elements of reality for Gadda's philosopher are themselves complex systems within systems, "knots or nuclei or skeins of relationships, lacking entirely any polished contour" (MM 869). Identification of the minimal units that constitute a system is a hopeless endeavor, since those units are themselves constantly subject to division, like the perennially removable quantitative infinitesimal in mathematics (MM 713–15). Moreover, contrary to the synchronized preestablished harmony in which Leibniz's monads develop, Gadda's elemental knots of relationships are subject to a nearly opposite "preestablished disharmony" (Roscioni 1969b), an ongoing interaction of differentiation and deformation. Such is the degree of interrelatedness that each element in the system, no matter how seemingly distant from a given cause, is somehow effected: "to the extent that each one of them is a 'tangle or skein of actual logical relationships,' its actual logical value, its logical-historical essence, is changed through the activity of deformation. At times feebly changed" (MM 870). Gadda's vision of complex causality and his obsession with multiple and distant causes combines a Leibnizian vision of the conjunction of everything in the world with a Dostoyevskian ethos of the responsibility among all creatures. "If a dragonfly flies in Tokyo, it sets off a chain of reactions that reach me," Gadda writes in the 1953 "L'egoista," adding that whoever does not understand this precept has not meditated sufficiently on Leibniz's *Monadology* or Dostoyevsky's *The Brothers Karamazov* (VM 654–55).[5]

Gadda's system is a rejection of simplicity (MM 651). Each element, each monad, each "I" of phenomenal reality can be understood only in terms of its relationship to something else, a relationship that implies polarity: "the purely simple is a closed thing in itself and would not be able to represent anything, not even itself, not being able to refer to anything, not even to itself. For relation implies at least division or polarity" (MM 829). Having recurred to mathematics and mechanics to define the *system* as the elementary universal building block, Gadda employs analogies from magnetics and physics to posit *polarity* as the primary dynamic force in the universe (in opposition to Leibniz's independently harmonious monads). In a manner akin to the necessary coexistence of positive and negative poles in magnetism, polarity is the "intrinsic differentiation of being, implying logical coexistency" (MM 664). Polarity lies at the core of Gadda's vision of reality as a pulsating multiplicity determined by a plethoric web of coexisting causes and effects: "I wish to conclude here that causes and effects are a pulsation of multiplicity ensnarled within itself and are never thinkable in the singular. The simplest cause, a hammer blow, presupposes an anvil. Force is never unaccompanied: it manifests itself in a polar fashion" (MM 650).

The dynamics of polarity have far-reaching implications in Gadda's world vision and inspires his ethical, existential, and aesthetic thought, beginning with the vexing problem of the existence of evil. Rejecting any simplistic notion of virtue as a "fixed corpus" (MM 682), Gadda focuses on the intrinsic and necessary "coexistence" of good and evil, right and wrong, rather than their intrinsic natures (MM 691). Evil, "il male," exists in a "peripheral" relationship to good, "il bene." Good is characterized by a high polarity of relationships (reality) and evil by a low polarity of relationships. In a moral universe subject to the same laws of multiplicity as the physical universe, goodness is the coming together of as many relationships as possible. It is in effect a "more real reality" (MM 689, 691). Evil occurs with the diminution of relationships: "Evil is had in degrees proceeding toward the exterior or peripheral limit where the convergence of relations is ever smaller" (MM 689). It is the less real reality that constantly resurfaces in Gadda's narrative in the form of death and dispersion.

The association of good with the real and evil with the unreal are traceable to Gadda's reading of Spinoza through the interpretation of his mentor at the University of Milan, Piero Martinetti (Lucchini 1988, 22–23). In *Meditazione* Gadda argues that his theory constitutes a powerful reworking and modification of Spinoza's equation "virtue = power (reality)" and demonstrates that "the greatest reality or phenomenality is the greatest ethicality" (MM 691).

A Spinozistic analogy can also be found in Gadda's views of individual identity. In book 3 of his *Ethics,* Spinoza had refuted the notion of "man in Nature as a kingdom within a kingdom" by proposing to "consider human actions and appetites just as if I were considering lines, planes, or bodies" (Spinoza 1974, 127–28). Gadda sees the human condition as subject to the same conditions of system and polarity as the rest of the universe. This is another idée fixe that appears throughout Gadda's work. In the 1949 essay "Come lavoro" [How I work], Gadda wrote: "Each of us appears to me to be a lump, or knot, or tangle, of physical and metaphysical relationships: (the distinction is useful as an expedient). Each relationship is suspended, is kept in equilibrium in the 'field' that is proper to it: by a polar tension" (VM 428). The dismantling of the smug notion of an independent, integral, and selfsame ego, "the image-fetish of an I that persists, that resists, immanent to time" (VM 428), is the major catalyst for Gadda's scathing satire of society and self.

The concept of polarity is equally important for Gadda's epistemology since polarity characterizes our cognition of both the world and ourselves: "The act of consciousness is an act of polarization (at the least); it is a heuristic crisis or heuristic judgment juxtaposing something to something, even itself to itself" (MM 829). In fact, knowledge through polarization is the foundation for Gadda's mature poetics of subjective expressionism and grotesque distortion and is grounded in the crucial declaration in *Meditazione* that "the phenomenal stream identifies itself in a cognitive deformation, in a cognitive 'process.' To proceed, to know, is *to insert something into the real*, it is, therefore, *to deform* the real" (MM 862–63). The pervasiveness of the notions of the open-ended system and dynamic polarity in Gadda's thought and the resultant vision of reality as a tangled mechanism of differentiation, multiplicity, impermanence, and deformation become the obsessive nightmare in Gadda's biography and fiction. The Gaddian quest continually and tragically repeats itself as a doomed enterprise to impart order to the world's chaos. A similar frustration and resulting despondency can also be found in *Meditazione*, but in the philosophical treatise Gadda stresses that the "deformation" which governs both the world and human cognition is also a very positive organizational process of "invention," "creation," and "heuresis."[6] Gadda's philosophy denies any rigid finalistic teleology. The "heuristic process," he states, does not appear to proceed toward finalistic ends but toward that which is different, "verso il diverso" (MM 778); it is organized around a fundamental polarity between *being* and *becoming* (MM 833). Gadda defines this heuristic movement from "n" to "n + 1" as a "good of the 2nd degree (creative or inventive, or heuristic, or final)" in contrast to a first-degree good of mere preservation "good of the 1st degree (or physiological)" (MM 757). Gadda's ethicizing of the process of becoming, his association of it with a higher good, and his analogies of moral obligation and duty in describing it appear vaguely Kantian in inspiration and directed at an affirmation that the world does indeed make sense. These are some of the most impassioned pages of *Meditazione milanese* and contain numerous examples that echo the ethical and social moralism of Gadda's war diary and post–World War I narrative. The heuristic good is the triumph of the "superconscience" often implying "tragic renunciations" and "anguished and voluntary sacrifices" (MM 760). It is the man who overcomes his brutish attachment to his selfsame self, to his physiological "pause" in the universal flow; the man who sees himself not just as "body" but as "brother" and "father," not a citizen "adorned with rights" but "charged with duties and obligations" (MM 760). The heuristic evil (n - 1) is embodied instead in the military deserter, "because he denies in himself the country (a system implicating n + 1) to save his physical person (n)," the murderer, the corrupter, the man who is cruel without cause to animals, the man who sullies public places (MM 763)—characters of a heuristic aberration who will populate the world of Gadda's early narrative and satire.

THE GROTESQUE COMBINATION OF LIFE

> Il filosofo, indagatore ed escogitatore, è e deve essere la ragione pacatamente ed eroicamente integrantesi: non vanità, non grido cieco di dolore o di fame o di libidine, non piaggeria del pensiero comune e nemmeno preconcetta repulsa di esso, non ornatezza di atteggiamenti, ma quasi intrinseca concatenazione e flusso di posizioni reali, che interpreta e lega, che vede e ricerca, che constata e costruisce, che accumula e perfeziona (MM 849).

> [The philosopher, an investigator and inventor, is and must be reason calmly and heroically achieving integration: not vanity, not a blind cry of pain or hunger or lust, not an adulation of common opinion nor a preconceived rejection of it, not an ornateness of poses, but almost an intrinsic concatenation and flow of real positions, that interprets and ties together, that sees and inquires, that verifies and constructs, that accumulates and perfects.]

The reader in search of a systematic exposition of young Gadda's poetics will not find it in the pages of *Meditazione milanese*. If anything, as Roscioni points out, the ideas in Gadda's philosophical treatise are applied to literary creation in the nearly contemporaneous 1929 essay, "Le belle lettere e i contributi espressivi delle tecniche" (Roscioni 1974, xxiv). In that essay Gadda describes the writer's goal as the heuristic "co-ordination" of a given linguistic-cognitive reality. In a manner similar to the entelechial progression of real phenomenal systems, the good writer strives for the organization of a "supersignificance" that goes beyond the existing pause of the moment in the ever-evolving literary history of cognitive and expressive deformation. Like the progressive evolution of the reality it emulates, literary creation is guided by a forward-moving "expressive-coordinating impulse," but it must also be firmly grounded in an acceptance of a communal cognitive and linguistic reality; it must have a something, "un qualche cosa," to coordinate. For all their experimentation, even the futurists, Gadda argues, are forced to call rails rails and history history (VM 476–77).

The doubly mimetic inspiration of Gadda's poetics—literary creation as an emulation of reality's heuristic progression coupled with an attentive sounding of reality's pause of the moment—is related to his closing remarks on speculative method in *Meditazione milanese*. Gadda begins his discussion of method paradoxically, by underscoring its illusory nature: "1. *Skeptical proposition*. Method is an illusion. *Demonstration*. In fact, the real or heuresis precedes method and the latter can only be exercised as an ordering of real situations. And in this case it is itself heuresis or reality" (MM 835).

The philosopher, for Gadda, like the creative artist, follows a "coordinating impulse," and the method employed by each should entail a mimesis which, in Aristotelian fashion, goes beyond a mere mirroring of reality to an actual ordering or perfection of reality. As a consequence, method, which is used synonymously with mimesis in *Meditazione*, is the "summary or epitome" of the most recent phase of reality's heuristic process. Method is "destined to imitation," but it is also a "critical epitome." It affirms the optimal course taken by reality's heuresis or invention but also excludes and negates those paths abandoned by the heuristic evolution (MM 836–37). Like the multiple reality in flux it imitates, method does not admit of definite cognitive canons since "the actual point of observation," in Einsteinian fashion, "is perpetually changing." Method, like creative expression, must be anchored "in the consciousness of the best actual referent: it is a living sensation of present reality" (MM 839–40).

The third significant quality that Gadda demands from speculative (and narrative) method, together with its ability both to coordinate reality and change with reality, is its capacity to account for each and every aspect of reality. Method must be endowed with an exhaustive globality.

> There is a tendency to schematize in excessively impoverished ways, to abstract too arbitrarily from the monstrous knot of totality: and by reasoning in this way on the parts (that is to say, on logical regions) one reaches conclusions that are logically regionalistic which are dismissed and commanded to be repealed by the judgment of the supreme court of total reality.
>
> To overlook any one fact of life or of the world is a diminution of the force and of the certainty in the subsequent synthesis that will be made concerning this life or this world. (MM 842)

In Gadda's vision of reality as a universal web of inextricable relationships, no detail can be excluded in its speculative re-creation, nor in its narrative coordination. He burdens the writer-philosopher with a noble but impossible task.

The elaboration of the refractory methodological requisites of heuristic mimesis, shifting viewpoint, and globality is indicative of a speculative and poetic formation broadly consonant with contemporaneous modernist assaults on traditional notions of narrative and existential closure, that is, Pirandellian relativity, Svevian perspectivism, or Joycean encyclopedism. This same ambitious methodology, taken to its extreme, as Gadda will do, is likewise indicative of the dispersive and ultimately unattainable synthesis he aspired to in his early narrative. The impasse is quickly apparent in Gadda's first attempt at a novel, the 1924 *Racconto italiano di ignoto del novecento*.

Gadda's "cahier[s] d'études," as he entitles the manuscript notebooks of the *Racconto italiano* project, span sixteen months, from March 24, 1924, to July 15, 1925. The novel project was undertaken in response to a 10,000-lire literary prize offered by Mondadori, a considerable sum at the time for an aspiring writer: "The 1924 Mondadori prize entices me to try" (RI 391).[7] Despite the financial lure to focus on the novel itself, the dispersive quality of Gadda's efforts are manifest from the outset. Two days after beginning the project, Gadda has set aside the latter part of the first notebook for "pieces, ideas, inspirations, impressions jotted down at first thought, without restraint" (RI 575). Ample portions of the notebooks will be used to sketch projects, stories, and notes that have little or nothing to do with the novel itself. In his numerous "compositional" and "critical" notes, Gadda grapples with ideas such as polarity, combinatory multiplicity, heuristic evolution, the unreality of evil, and shifting cognitive moments that would receive more substantive treatment four years later in *Meditazione milanese*. If we also consider that Gadda's first notes in his editions of Kant and his manuscript outline of possible thesis topics in philosophy date to the final days of work on the aborted novel, the *Racconto italiano* emerges as an early literary treatment of seminal speculative interests simultaneously explored in other venues (Lucchini 1988, 24).

Gadda's design of the novel is ambitious in its attempt to fuse a traditional nineteenth-century realist narrative with the conventions of tragic drama and what Gadda refers to as his own irrepressible lyricism. The genre hybridization is necessary, he writes, to treat appropriately the novel's comprehensive study of "Italianism," entailing a global depiction of post–World War I Italian society with "lyrical-dramatic references" to the war and prewar periods (RI 395). From the "background of chaos" of this society are to materialize the story's central characters or "types": "type A . . . intimate tragedy, masked by an exterior accommodation" (RI 397); "type B . . . individual degeneration" (RI 398); "type C . . . humane, good, who triumphs calmly and sensibly over adversity" (RI 410).[8] Other characters will function as a dramatic "chorus" to which will be assigned "the conscience of the drama and its philosophical comment" (RI 395). Because of the time constraints imposed by the Mondadori competition, Gadda will not have time to engage in "historical studies"; the bulk of the novel's material will be autobiographical or semi-autobiographical, "my own personal material, lived or nearly lived" (RI 395). Finally, the novel is to be characterized by broad sweeps of *chiaroscuro* contrasts; it is "psychopathic and caravaggesque," and Gadda dedicates it to Caravaggio, his "great and unapproachable *maestro*" (RI 411, 580).

The complex story, of which Gadda wrote only a few incomplete episodes, is an odd pastiche of romance-novel motifs with scenes of contemporary political and social strife. At the novel's core are twin, ill-fated love stories. A volatile young fascist, Grifonetto Lampugnani, loves Maria de la Garde, whose family opposes the relationship and wants Maria to marry a local viscount. Carletto, a young socialist, loves Nerina, also from a socialist family but of more middle-class origins and aspirations. Nerina prefers to read novels of young girls swept off their feet by gallant marquises, and the jealous Carletto suspects her of flirting with the fascists. The protagonists and the other characters who surround them—the alcoholic philosopher-mathematician Gerolamo Lehrer; the traveling salesman Cesare Manni hounded by the jilted Emma Renzi, mother of his child; the engineer Morone at work on a hydroelectric project—are all variants of characters who will resurface in Gadda's early fiction. The novel's action takes place against the backdrop of Gadda's ubiquitous "Italian work" motif, narrative site of violent clashes between the socialist and fascist partisans.

Gadda's diagnosis of the postwar Italian crisis in the novel is one of disintegrated ethos and political irresponsibility. In an early note of March 25, 1924, he delineates the personal and literary sources of this view. The novel is to bear witness to the autobiographical motif of the suffocation of individual achievement and greatness by an inadequate Italian environment: "One of my long-standing concepts (the two nations) is the ethnic, historical and economic insufficiency of the Italian environment for the development of certain souls and intellects that stand too far above it. My foundering in the Brianza bog. Adolescent longings for a better life. Serious militarism, etc." (RI 396).

This traumatic consciousness of Gadda's own trampled potentiality, which he universalizes as a constant in Italian cultural and intellectual history going back to Dante (RI 397), is elaborated in an intertextual dialogue with the political moralism of Alessandro Manzoni's *I promessi sposi*. Gadda posits Manzoni's novel as an ethical yardstick from which he will effect a *"continuation and dilatation"* to fit his own interpretation of post–World War I Italian reality (RI 396–97). Manzoni is described as chastising society's upper echelon, which fails in its civic duty: "men and authorities who violate their office and are the cause of evil in a society that is fundamentally good." Gadda extends this failure to all classes of society: "not just persons in authority, but also plebs and the entire populace that profanes the interior inspirations of life, its sacred and innermost laws, and perverts itself" (RI 397).

Manzoni's explanation of the misused authority of Milan's seventeenth-century Spanish overlords reflects his moderate, Catholic critique of the city's nineteenth-century benighted Austrian governance. It is a critique accompanied by a commitment, common to much of the civic patriotism of post-Napoleonic Italian intellectuals, to the creation and education of a civic-minded "popolo," people capable of constituting a true Italian citizenry. Gadda's extension of blame for the post–World War I Italian civic disintegration to all social classes reflects instead the rejection of what he sees as a naive and mistaken nineteenth-century legacy of idealized populism, the "base love affair with the people" that he resented in his father (IDM 10). In a late narrative sketch of July 15, 1925, Grifonetto Lampugnani launches into a particularly virulent, semi-autobiographical diatribe against what he calls the socialist and Catholic "criminal arcadia of the 19th century," which idealizes the lower class as the repository of all that is good: "To hear some of them, the lower class has the attributes that priests usually attribute to the all-perfect God: it's pure, it's beautiful, it's healthy, it's saintly, it's worthy, it's wise, it's intelligent, it's sensitive, it's heroic. It's the entire uni[verse]. The rest is shit. The rest is a lie" (RI 566). Against this falsely idealized proletariat, Grifonetto asserts that the lower classes are merely the "primary matter" or *rohstoff* of history and not history's dynamic of becoming (RI 566).

Grifonetto's sarcastic ire is representative of the disillusionment of disgruntled middle-class veterans such as Gadda and their angry reaction to the perceived defeatism and class agitation of the socialists, Bolsheviks, and Catholic Popolari. Giuseppe Antonio Borgese had explored the theme three years previously in his prophetic novel *Rubé*, and in many ways Gadda's twin protagonists Carletto and Grifonetto are politically polarized manifestations of Borgese's sociologically and psychologically more complex Filippo Rubé. The rhetoric of disenchantment and adherence to violence of Gadda's hotheaded Grifonetto, who professes faith in the machine gun alone and draws inspiration from D'Annunzio's *Laus Vitae* (RI 563–64), mirrors the classic profile of the first recruits to the postwar fascist cadres.

Fascism had been idealized by Gadda as a forceful and realistic way to deal with the nation's ills. Even Grifonetto's aggressive fascist neophytism is expressed in Gadda's rhetoric of a politics of constructive pragmatism. The regeneration of the Italian social reality, Grifonetto argues, cannot be based on the humanitarians' "fanciful mania of chimerical palingeneses" but must be based on a real method steeped in reality itself: "it means to look at the enormous mass of real work and design a real method to develop a better reality from the present reality" (RI 566). In an earlier note in which Gadda lays out the political critique he will present in the novel, he contrasts the "lack of critical ability" of the socialists and Catholic Popolari to the pragmatism of the Italian fascists: "All of this will demonstrate the Italian reaction in fascism. A clear, practical, human reaction against the Gordian knot of ideological nonsense accumulated from the 18th and 19th centuries. 'Life must be LIFE, not a victim of chatter'" (RI 417). The final sentence on life as LIFE—the quotation marks indicate Gadda's intent to use it, probably uttered by Grifonetto, to close the first part of the novel—indicates the D'Annunzian rhetorical matrix in Gadda's early approach to fascism that he grafts onto his Spinozist association of good and evil with a more or less real reality. Years later Gadda would base his vicious satire of Mussolini's fascism on its total detachment from "real reality," but for the moment Gadda's "Italian tale" is grounded ideologically in the political "Italian reaction" against the popular "threat" of the masses and their organizers.

Many of the speculative constructs of *Meditazione milanese* are contained *in nuce* in the political theses of *Racconto italiano*. There is an even greater confluence in Gadda's notes on character and plot. Outwardly averse to avant-garde movements in general, with never a kind word for futurist experimentation, Gadda admires the ability of the classic nineteenth-century novels to link characters through plot: "To tie the characters to one another: for now this is for me the greatest difficulty: 'the plot' of the old novels, which the new ones often disdain'" (RI 460). Replicating the traditional plot becomes difficult in *Racconto italiano* because of Gadda's rejection of simple cause-and-effect scenarios. Like all of Gadda's fiction, *Racconto italiano* is at bottom a detective story, an attempt to understand an aberrational act within the universal order (in this case, Grifonetto's murder of Maria de la Garde and his suicide at the novel's end). Understanding is complicated by Gadda's rejection of the hereditary determinism of the positivist and naturalist schools for a more open-ended combinatory paradigm: "In short, I want to affirm that even immoral or criminal actions enter into the universal law and more than on determinism-heredity (Lombroso, neurology, experimental psychology, biological studies) I base this on my idea of combination-possibility" (RI 406).

Determinism, Gadda appears to imply, is cognitively circumscribed by its linearity. He calls it the reading of the curve of fate but not its explanation. His vision of causality is instead nonlinear and organic at the same time. "The instinct of combination is in the universe" (RI 407), he declares, and unlike the trajectory of closure of determinism, combination-possibility is imbued with an almost mystical open-endedness: "As long as there exists a possibility, as long as there exists a combination, the eternal will want it manifested in the dazzling forms of activity" (RI 406). The universal "instinct of combination" is the innovative combinatory paradigm on which Gadda will attempt to construct an epitome of reality that accounts for all of its complexity and aberrations. It is also the weak point upon which the novel will collapse.[9]

The expression "instinct of combination," together with Gadda's notions of multiple causes and systemic equilibrium, is not as original as the young author appears to claim. Beyond the allusion to Leibniz's *ars combinatoria*, it indicates the influence of sociologist Vilfredo Pareto's 1916 *Trattato di sociologia generale* (Lucchini 1988, 25–29; Roscioni 1974, xviii–xxi). The outspoken Pareto had died in August 1923, and his importance in the Italian intellectual and political landscape during this period was substantial. His disdain for parliamentary government, his theory of self-perpetuating elites, and a series of favorable pronouncements on the early fascist movement had caused Mussolini actively to court his approval and later claim him as a founding influence on fascist ideology. All of the above could have contributed to an interest on Gadda's part in Pareto, along with Pareto's application of mathematical analyses to economic and social phenomena and his stylistic influence on what Gadda called his "logical-rationalistic, Paretian" manner (RI 396).

In the *Trattato di sociologia generale* Pareto uses the term "instinct of combinations" to describe the drive for adaptation and change in human beings which brings about new cognitive, moral, and sociocultural forms (see Lopreato 1980, xxxii–xxxiii). In *Racconto italiano* Gadda borrows Pareto's term without much concern for its original context and adapts it to his ideas on good and evil and the etiology of criminal or immoral acts. Anticipating his argument in *Meditazione milanese* four years later, Gadda notes that good, which he calls here the "norm" or the "law," is "the conscious affirmation of combination," while evil, called here the "abnormal" or "*ex-lege*," is the "uncombinable," the "unreal," the "mistake" (RI 407). The norm and the abnormal necessarily "co-exist" in a state of polar equilibrium (RI 407). From this polarity Gadda derives what he calls the core idea or "idea-base" of the novel: "that the abnormal has its mysterious (for now) justification . . . and that . . . in life the antisocial person also has his place" (RI 407). The mystery of evil, the necessity of the abnormal—this is the prelude to the novel's final component, the inevitable final catastrophe and comprehension:

> I thought this morning to divide the poem into three parts, the first of which is *The Norm*, (or *the normal*)—second, the Abnormal (with the episode of the fighting, etc.) third, Comprehension or the Vision on life. . . .
>
> In the first part there could be assembled germination, springtime, sentiments, the good aspect of life, with a *latent* preparation of the evil that is already poisoning and ruining that goodness. In the second part the leitmotif of the abnormal and of the monstrous and grotesque combination of life,—in the third part exhaustion-catastrophe and comprehension (action and self-consciousness as in Hamlet). (RI 415)

These three elements—norm (normal), abnormal, final understanding—are the blueprint for all of Gadda's narrative fiction, including *La cognizione del dolore* and *Quer pasticciaccio brutto de via Merulana*. The schema also contains the organizational "flaw," so to speak, which leads to the rapid unraveling of the *Racconto italiano* project and the "impossible closure" of all of Gadda's novels: the association of *combination* with the *abnormal*. The transfer of the "instinct of combination" from the moment of normal "germination" to the antithetical moment of abnormality transforms it into something "monstrous and grotesque." In the more abstract formulations of *Meditazione milanese*, "combination," which is used rather infrequently, perhaps indicating an attenuation of Gadda's Paretian encounter, is synonymous with the positive heuristic process of creation and becoming $(n + 1)$. In *Racconto italiano* "combination" is synonymous with the negative historical moment of the disintegration of postwar Italian society (n - 1) and its disastrous effects on its most promising and consequently most disillusioned individuals: "The moment n_1 can be more baroque, inconclusive and wretched than n. The series can be involutive instead of evolutive" (RI 472).

The combinatorial aberration affects the construction of the novel itself, since "method" in Gadda is "mimesis" and must adhere to the nature of the reality that is the object of its critical epitome. This is evident in Gadda's note on his difficulty in duplicating the coherent plot structure of the nineteenth-century novel. Life itself is a "plot," Gadda continues in that note, "and a very muddled plot" (RI 460). *Racconto italiano*'s plot becomes hopelessly muddled because it replicates the mysterious dissolution of reality into its individual elements: "The plot must not be one of forced events, but should correspond to the 'institution of combinations,' that is, to the profound and obscure dissociation of reality into elements, which sometimes (ethics) lose sight of the unitary nexus" (RI 460). With a revealing slippage in his Paretian terminology, what Gadda had described earlier as the quasi-providential "instinct" for combination in the universe has become "institutionalized" in the monstrous "abnormality" of a dysfunctional historical universe. The dissolution is "physiological," but it is "also moral" and "also theoretical" (RI 460). The good of the civic whole (n + 1) is sacrificed to the involuted egoism of the individual part (n - 1): "one could say that there is dissolution in an organism when one of its parts acts on its own, for its own (supposed) advantage or pleasure and not in harmony with the whole" (RI 460).

The evil or abnormal is the grotesque hypertrophy of the part over the whole. Relationships dissolve, combination yields to disgregation, and society becomes anarchic. Grounded in its methodology of mimetic epitome, *Racconto*'s project of a heuristic rational synthesis is doomed to disintegrate in accordance with the grotesque and monstrous reality it would seek to imitate and understand. "Baroque is the world," Gadda would claim some forty years later in defense of this same poetics in *La cognizione del dolore*, "and G. has perceived and depicted its baroqueness" (C 760).

WORLD WAR I

Era troppo evidente che l'arsenale della gloria aveva rifiutato di prenderlo in carico (C 632).

[It was too obvious that the arsenal of glory had refused to place him on its roster] (AWG 144).

Racconto italiano and *Meditazione milanese* are attempts to provide a sublimated literary and philosophical structure to a panoply of concerns that are not abstract but desperately experiential for the young Gadda. Gadda's war diary, the *Giornale di guerra e di prigionia*, documents many of these experiences.

Gadda kept a private journal throughout his participation in the First World War, from his arrival in the Val Camonica on the Trentino front in August of 1915, to his transfer to the main Isonzo front and capture at Caporetto on October 25, 1917, to the bitter experience of his imprisonment in Germany and return home to the devastating news of his younger brother's death.[10] His final entry on December 31, 1919, reveals the profound disillusionment and abjection Gadda felt as a result of his shattered aspirations. Paradoxically, the war from which he had sought to begin truly living had concluded leaving him feeling more dead than alive: "My life is useless, it is that of an automaton that has outlived itself, who because of inertia does some material things, without love or faith" (GGP 867).

In "Impossibilità di un diario di guerra" [Impossibility of a war diary], one of several essays on his war experience included in the 1934 *Il castello di Udine*, Gadda recalls his fervent interventionism on the eve of Italy's entrance into the conflict: "I participated with a sincere spirit in the demonstrations of 1915, I yelled Long Live D'Annunzio, and Death to Giolitti" (CU 142). University students were a driving force of the 1915 prowar agitation (Mack Smith 1959, 300), and Gadda, a third-year student in engineering at the Istituto Tecnico Superiore di Milano, apparently distinguished himself for the fervor of his commitment by mockingly referring to himself as "that dog of an interventionist Gaddus" (LAM 16). On May 22, 1915, two days prior to Italy's entrance into the war, a letter entitled "Una legittima protesta di studenti" [A legitimate protest by students] was published in Mussolini's interventionist newspaper *Il popolo d'Italia*. Its authors, Gadda and friends and classmates Emilio Fornasini and Luigi Semenza, took issue with a directive of the Ministry of Education to permit early examinations for engineering students given the imminence of war. They argued against any delay whatsoever in their participation, declaring that "it is intolerable for honorable men of twenty to languish in a state of civil apathy, in order to attend to school affairs that involve no kind of military preparation." The letter continued, with a rhetoric most probably of Gadda's composition, decrying the shame these students felt in their civilian clothes while their brothers in arms rushed to the supreme defense of the country. The authors demanded their real participation in the war as a sacred right (cited in Ungarelli 1991, 24).

Letter notwithstanding, what little testimony we have of Gadda's interventionist position at the beginning of the war pales in extremism when compared to the incendiary call for a "hot bath of black blood" by a futurist fellow traveler such as Giovanni Papini or to D'Annunzio's own "obscene and unquotable" language on Giolitti's neutralism (Papini 1914; Mack Smith 1959, 303). Gadda was far from having a futurist vision of the war as a disinhibiting liberation of instinctual drives. He justified it instead as a trial of discipline, order, and abnegation of the self for the nation.

Politically, young Gadda's vision of the war as both "necessary and holy" (GGP 533) was most consonant with the platform of the Italian Nationalist Association, of which he was a member until 1921 when he joined the Fascist Party.[11] The Nationalist assertion that the war was a necessary struggle of poor but vital nations against rich nations is echoed in Gadda's "Darwinian" view of the war in the *Giornale* as a test of Italy's adaptation to the new industrial age and its fight for life against German aggression (GGP 594, 617, 770). In his notes to *Racconto italiano* Gadda refers to the polarity between rich nations and poor nations and the struggle between different races (in particular the Italian race against the Germanic race and, after the war, against the Anglo-Saxon race) (RI 408, 416). The Nationalist vision of the war as a consecration of a sense of Italian national identity and pride is likewise echoed in Gadda's diary. This vision is repeatedly betrayed, however, by the behavior of Gadda's countrymen. An incident in which an Italian officer lets himself be insulted after he is caught stealing a pair of pants from some fellow French prisoners is seen as emblematic of national ruin: "That's how national catastrophes happen" (GGP 674). Many of the young lieutenant's most intense moments of shame and irritation with his fellow Italians are felt after the Allied victory and the release of his camp mates in Germany: "Annoying boorishness of two Italian officers; a hideous Milanese lout, who wanted to play the would-be wit with a servant girl (banal interjections in dialect which she did not understand), extinguished his cigarette butt on the ground: the girl showed him the ashtray on the table and said to him: 'you do that in Italy, not here'; and we are the victors and we want to be a great people!" (GGP 839).

The war is also a proving ground for Gadda's evolving thoughts on the triumph of the common good over the individual self and his ethos of pragmatic reality. A recurring motif in his often harsh criticism of the

Italian war effort is the unbridled egoism of Italian soldiers and officers and their lack of self-sacrifice for the benefit of the nation. An egoistic attitude toward the war had been sanctioned as national policy, so to speak, by Prime Minister Antonio Salandra's realistic but unfortunate reference to Italy's own "sacred egoism" in her war objectives of territorial gains from the Austrians (Mack Smith 1959, 305). The personal egoism of his countrymen was sadly manifest to Gadda shortly after his arrival in 1915 at the Trentino front: "I have realized that egoism is the only law for many" (GGP 472). It is an observation that is repeated again and again in the *Giornale:* the egoistic individualism that destroys all cooperation, common ideas, and spirit of sacrifice (GGP 481–82); the cowardly attachment to the self which extinguishes any heroism, "personal fear, fear of me, fear of I, fear of that very same I, of one's own I, of one's own I-me" (GGP 575); the vainglory of the Italians who turn everything into a personal quarrel (GGP 579); the selfishness of his prison camp companions whose fear of personal hardship causes them to invoke peace at any cost (GGP 673).

Gadda, with his "German spirit" of military discipline, feels himself to be different and estranged from other Italians. At the beginning of the war he had sought to elaborate Giuseppe Mazzini's grand lesson of "thought and action" (GGP 461) into a military ethos of analytic pragmatism firmly grounded in the heroic action of self-sacrifice for the common good: "the individual soldier must disappear before the requirements of duty and country" (GGP 597). Unfortunately, these are qualities that he finds lacking in the Italian character and war effort, distinguished instead by "moral unworthiness" and "ideological error" (GGP 482).

Gadda's disillusionment with the Italian military command leads to a particularly irascible outpouring of disdain. He would later declare that his own militarism was "*in signo rationis*" (MM 696) and that the good officer must possess a broad and pragmatic sense of analysis and reality (CU 131). In the *Giornale* there is no tolerance for the badly planned military action. A colonel who decides to die a hero's death after having poorly located his troops elicits not admiration but criticism: "the country, oh stupid ass, doesn't want your life for the pleasure of listing yet another brave soul: it wants your constant vigilance, your thought, your reflection, analysis, calculation" (GGP 458). Harsher invective-laden criticisms are launched at the strategic ineptitude of the Italian high command: "Asses, asses, stupid oxen, Grand Hotel, Havana and beach-resort big shots; but not warriors, not thinkers, not creators, not builders; incapable of observation and analysis, ignorant of psychological matters, incapable of synthesis" (GGP 468). Other targets for disdain are profiteering military industrialists and Victor Emanuel himself, "that imbecilic stammerer of a king" (GGP 467).

In the general yearning felt by so many prowar European intellectuals to experience a Bergsonian élan or Nietzschean will to power, the young Gadda, who absorbed many of these sentiments through his avid reading of D'Annunzio's poetry, saw the war as a last chance to overcome what he felt to be the "deviation" of his life and "waste of marvelous faculties" (GGP 645). The fighting becomes a desperate attempt to avoid a bleak personal fate, and throughout the war Gadda continually seeks frontline action with the most exposed units of the Italian Alpini (GGP 515). Any news of a possible end to the war fills him with sadness that the "heroic" part of his life may soon be over (GGP 657). This struggle to live a glorious heroism with energy is countered by a much more frequent sense of despair and abjection. Heroism is hampered not only by the apathy and egoism of Gadda's comrades in arms but by the obsessive presence of his own traumatic personal history. Too often the days pass by "boring, squalid and inglorious" while the "sad events" of his life create a debilitating "paralysis of the will" and thoughts of suicide or death in the field (GGP 470, 484, 486, 503, 507).

The feared destiny of indistinction finally catches up with Gadda with the national ignomy of the rout at Caporetto. After his capture, the tendency toward abjection precipitates atrociously. Capture, he writes, has spelled the end of hope and the annihilation of his moral and interior life (GGP 664, 671). Extreme physical hunger and profound feelings of shame plague him during his imprisonment in Germany, but worst of all is his tragic exclusion from the sublime and heroic deeds of the battlefield: "This is my gnawing and terrible pang, this is the sorrow of sorrows. The war will end, let us hope that it will end, and I will no longer have been there . . . no divine moments of danger, sublime actions of battle. . . . This is my rage, this is my obsessive grief, which leads me to madness" (GGP 784–85).

Spirit, body, and senses have degenerated into a state of "stupidity" and "automatism"; "dream and reality are confused in a single, indistinct greyness" (GGP 779). Imprisonment is the humiliating negation of Gadda's greater and personal vision of the war as thought and action in reality. The regression into inactive dreaming is the denial of all the war had promised him. The end of the war only increases Gadda's abjection.

The experience of Caporetto, imprisonment, and the death of his brother, who is idolized throughout the *Giornale* as the "better and dearer" part of Gadda himself, fuse into "a single wave of atrocious agony" (GGP 850, 867). What will become the psychological catalysts of Gadda's autobiographical fiction, "dolore" [grief] and "rabbia" [rage], only increase as the months pass (GGP 854). The diary ends with a final reiteration that its author's life is useless. Any "possibility of action" has given way to "vain and sterile dreams" (GGP 867).

The Gaddian Psychoneuroses

> Era, forse, un timido. Ma piú spesso veniva ritenuto un imbecille.
>
> C 412

> He was, perhaps, timid. But more frequently he was considered a fool.
>
> AWG 203

No biography of Gadda can ignore the psychoneuroses, phobias, and ailments that pervade his correspondence, autobiographical essays, and fiction. No Italian author better managed to cultivate the persona of the neurotic author, or author because neurotic. Among the more notable of these neuroses were his hypochondria, excitability, lethargy, depression, paranoia, sense of guilt and persecution, timidity, rage, and, in general, debilitating hypersensitivity. Friends jokingly referred to Gadda's quirks, his fear of automobiles and electric razors, his misogyny and obsession with being collared into marriage, the symptoms of homophobic homosexuality, the hatred for the family villa, his troubles with landladies, his need for mathematic precision in everything, his other-century gallantry with women colleagues. As Gadda grew older and more feeble, the eccentric quirks degenerated into frightful phobias. His letters acquired a viciously bitter or pathetically apologetic and whimpering tone. His reclusiveness increased in the final years as he spent his days between his armchair and his bed. He broke into tears easily. The world was darkened by a perpetual melancholy. Clinically, Gadda would probably have been diagnosed as a manic-depressive. His enormous unhappiness, Contini wrote, was punctuated by intervals of an equally enormous hilarity (LGC 9).

The *Giornale di guerra e di prigionia* is the first and, given its "private" and nonliterary format, perhaps Gadda's most reliable analysis of his neuroses and their etiology.[12] At war's end Gadda arrives in Milan for a brief reunion on the 14th and 15th of January 1919 with his mother,

Adelaide, and sister, Clara. Here he is told of Enrico's plane crash. On the 16th of January he is in Florence where he undergoes debriefing with other officers captured and interned during the fighting, and on the 20th he is in Livorno to be interrogated by a Commission of Inquiry. With typical scrupulousness, Gadda provides a detailed written statement of his capture at Caporetto and a summary of his imprisonment in Germany, including the bribery of German soldiers to acquire a compass, maps, and civilian clothing for an aborted escape with Bonaventura Tecchi (see Ungarelli 1991, 24–47). Gen. R. Gigli, in his review and personal report of Captain Gadda, praises his superior responsibility, solid learning, sense of military duty, alert perception, and elevated sentiments. Gadda could continue to be an officer of the highest caliber, "if he will be able to put his nerves in absolute calm, which are now somewhat shaken by the special conditions of his family" (Ungarelli 1991, 47).

As he confirms in his diary, Gadda's nerves are indeed shattered by Enrico's death and difficulties at home between his mother and sister. But what he refers to in the *Giornale* as his debilitating "general neurasthenia" (GGP 792) is a psycho-physical constant which predates these latest developments. Its origins lie instead in his "beastly hypersensitivity" and "childhood terrors" (GGP 603, 786):

> September 25, 1916. . . . The battle I have fought in life has been terrible, exhausting; it has been atrocious because of the superiority of the enemy, who mocked my efforts. It has cost me my spirit and now I am nothing but a vegetable. The atrocious and villainous enemy is called *sensitivity, excitability;* cerebral excitability, of my enquiring mind that imagines future sufferings, future struggles; my morbid sensitivity that is terrified by every obstacle, every test. Truly the trials I sustained in my childhood have been such, due to family circumstances, that would upset any nervous system, let alone mine, my own, I who was afraid to greet on the street a schoolmate or my teacher, I who turned melancholy and fearful at the approach of evening! (GGP 629)

The linkage between Gadda's nervous condition, hypersensitivity, and childhood traumas is a obsessive motif in the *Giornale.* It was a condition which was apparently shared by his sister, Clara.[13] "Continual and congenital" (GGP 503) hypersensitivity occasions a series of physical ailments in the young officer, including a nervous heart, painful gastrointestinal disorders, and insomnia (GGP 547). It has left him sorely unadapted to his environment and is the cause of his excessive reaction to disorder and his heightened perception of the grotesque. This environmental hypersensitivity is underscored in the autobiographical *La cognizione del dolore*. At the Patrufazian (Milanese) carnival, the child Gonzalo is terrified to the point of anguished collapse by the stench, music, sideshows, and disorder of confetti, peanut shells, and orange peels. The adult Gonzalo, in a relapse of his "lifelong obsession with crowds" (C 728; AWG 203) suffers an "infernal rage" at the sight and smells of the filthy peasants who bring an offering to his mother of "dead, fetent fish" and "mushrooms that smell like feet" (C 727; AWG 202).

For all the torment it causes him, Gadda does take great pains to associate hypersensitivity with a heightened understanding and artistic creativity. "Cerebral excitability" is a by-product of the "enquiring mind," and in Gadda's case the excitability becomes, in typical Romantic fashion, "a precious gift . . . which allows me to perceive to a greater extent, and thus live to a greater extent, even if suffering" (GGP 755). In the lives of great men there is often something "fatally excessive" that constitutes the "biographical counterweight" to their "victorious hypercognition" ("I grandi uomini," SD 979). And it is the abnormally sensitive individual who, in a fragmented and alienating world, is best able to fathom the depths of his own neurosis and, consequently, of his own humanity:

> In reality, the difference between the normal person and the abnormal person is the following, and the following alone: that the normal person is not conscious, does not have even a metaphysical inkling, of his neurotic or paraneurotic states. . . . His puerile certainties immunize him from the deadly danger of any uncertainty, from any attempted escape, from any temptation to establish relations with darkness, with the unknown infinite. The abnormal person, on the other hand, achieves, sometimes, a reasonably clear understanding of reality, and of the causes, origins, first shape, development, final sclerotization and cessation, with his own death, of his neuroses. ("Come lavoro," VM 440–41)

Hypersensitivity bears in its wake a series of other personality "defects" which the young Gadda finds in himself: his lack of will, his excessive timidity, his exaggerated sense of compassion. His inability to express himself leads, in Pirandellian fashion, to a continual misunderstanding by others of who he truly is. During his final days at the Cellelager prisoner-of-war camp, Gadda reflects on how embittered he is by the fact that he alone has argued with more people than anyone else. The reason, he concludes, is because he does not know how to express his "good" qualities: "My good qualities are hidden in my reserve; my tantrums, my noisy and sorrowful uproar, to deaden myself to my deep grief, my quickness to laughter and joking causes most people to take me for a child and a trivial person" (GGP 834). Gadda's manic-depressive bent causes him to don the tragic mask of melancholy or the vulgar mask of the loudmouthed fool as he enacts and writes his biography of alienation.

Misunderstanding of the self by others is a central theme of Italian modernism, and it pervades the works of Luigi Pirandello and Italo Svevo. One finds scenes in the tormented biography of the *Giornale di guerra e di prigionia* that appear almost to have been lifted from the pages of those two authors, such is the convoluted interaction of failed communication and the resultant misunderstanding:

> It is not something new for me to be poorly judged in life. I recognize in myself very serious defects, negative qualities: (hypersensitivity, timidity, laziness, neurasthenia, distraction to the point of ridiculousness). But too severe and too superficial are the judgments passed on me by many who think they know me to the core. My beloved mother herself has not always understood me. This is also because I am essentially deficient in demeanor and expression. The only vivid and correct expression, for which I can be answerable, is expression through written thought. I remember when, kneeling before the bed of my dead father, I cried out in my tears: "I'm hardly fifteen years old!," meaning to say: "Only for this short time have I been close to you, oh father." This phrase was interpreted, and perhaps reasonably, in its egoistic sense: "Oh father, you have left me at an age when I needed your help." It must be recognized that this was the thought that corresponded to the utterance, but that the utterance did not respond to my thought. This is one example out of a thousand. So it has often happened in my life, I admit it to myself, that I have passed for a fool, or for someone haughty, or for an egoist, or for a madman, while I was distracted, timid, reserved, tired. (GGP 789)

The misinterpretation of the son's words at his father's deathbed, the resultant sense of guilt and search for exoneration through dubious self-justification, the exaltation of written expression over the insidiousness of verbal expression—these are all typical motifs in the literature of Italo Svevo. The scene itself is strikingly similar to the misunderstanding of Zeno Cosini at his father's deathbed in *La coscienza di Zeno* (written a few years after Gadda's war diary). There is an important difference, however. Svevo dismantles the contorted acrobatics of Zeno's arguments through the patient and ironic dissection of their discursive devices. Gadda instead is desperately earnest in his efforts to fill the chasm between the feelings in his heart and their misinterpretation by others. Svevo seeks the rhetorical deconstruction of Zeno's consciousness, of his modern madness of misunderstanding. Gadda seeks to justify the madness, to communicate the reasonableness of the thought while ascribing the painfulness of its incomprehension to the inadequacy of its expression. Ultimate awareness is achieved in a much more "spastic" way in Gadda than in Svevo, through the violent confrontation between the hypersensitive protagonist's misunderstanding of reality and reality's misunderstanding of him. It is this misunderstanding that leads to the tragic catastrophe and the knowledge of grief that haunts both Gadda's fiction and his autobiography.

"Disorder is my continual *cauchemar* and it causes me moments of unspeakable rage and desperation" (GGP 597). Of all of Gadda's obsessions and phobias, the vehement outrage at disorder occupies a central place. It is, perhaps, the primal force in his narrative. Order in Gadda is always associated with rationality and sublimity. Disorder is the realm of the irrational and the filthy. Gadda's militarism is born precisely from his mania for order. He is attracted to the "lived discipline," "military duty," and "motivated obligation" of army life (CU 136, 138, 150). His heroes are the great military organizers from Caesar to Lord Kitchener (CU 128–29; GGP 535). His description of the well-organized military operation as a "method" or a "machine" to be judged by its "output" and "economy" attest to his engineer's sensibility for the orderly quality of military duty (CU 127–28). Even the simplest trappings of military order such as the uniform and the razor-short haircut cast a fascination over him (GGP 578, 649, 865).

Paradoxically, the chaos of war becomes the opportunity for the exertion of methodic discipline and rational order. The chaotic blizzards of the Adamello front or the haphazard arrangement of a mountain camp are described as manifestations of a larger natural order and picturesque spirituality. These are the only occasions, Gadda writes, in which his nerves are not upset with the sight of disorder (GGP 570–71, 581). But such occasions are rare, and the war diary will become a paradigmatic battleground between the young officer's repeatedly frustrated aspiration to rational method and discipline and a disillusioned reaction of rage and invective.

Nightmarish disorder is, to Gadda, yet another national defect of his fellow Italians. He describes Italian soldiers as lazy and dirty (GGP 546). Their encampments are surrounded by vast quantities of "merde" [shits] of "all dimensions, forms, colors, of every quality and consistency" (GGP 650). Their desks, uselessly cluttered with every sort of object, excite expressionistic fits of condemnation in the young officer:

> What goddamn rage, what filthy Italians. When is it that my lurid compatriots of all classes and stations will learn to keep their own writing-table in order? and not pile up their office papers together with letters from their mistresses, with their lunch basket, with the portrait of their granddaughter, with the newspaper, with the latest novel, the train schedule, the shoemaker's receipts, the paper to wipe their ass, their dripping hat, their nail scissors, their private wallet, their picture calendar? When, when? When is it that this race of pigs, of swine, of beings capable only of dirtying with the disorder and prolixity of their incoherent actions, will rise to the aptitudes of builders and doers, will be capable of giving a logical connection to the train of their actions. . . . But we have disorder: it's here, always, everywhere, with everyone: oh, it's here all right, and what a horrendous, corrosive, disorder! It is the Sargassi Sea for our ship. (GGP 574–75)

This and similar explosions of rage in the *Giornale* are indicative of the power of disorder to move the narrative of Gadda's war diary away from its "serious," "human," and "Manzonian" (RI 396) expression toward a very different rhetoric of excess. Highly oratorical in construction with its use of repetition, exclamation, enumeration, and rhetorical questions, Gadda's outbursts strain the conventional limits of these figures. This is especially true in the case of chaotic enumeration. The long list of disparate objects that clutter the desktops moves the narration beyond mimesis to a distorting deformation. The lower body imagery so typical of Gadda's later "grotesque" and "macaronic" prose is underscored here through the juxtaposition of letters to mistresses, lunch baskets, toilet paper, nail scissors, picture calendars. Excrement, food, sex, family, money, literature, and more converge and mix promiscuously in a disorderly pile. The narrative focus becomes muddled as the argument against bureaucratic inefficiency yields to grotesque's "temporary reign of the senses" (Harpham 1982, 17).

Disorder, however, is not only a social aberration of *"italianità"* for Gadda. It is also a personal nemesis that conditions his behavior, saps his strength, and impedes his creative vigor. He dares not wash his hands in his basin or take a sip of grappa for fear of disturbing the alignment of his possessions in his tent. Dripping water is a particular scourge, "because that damn whore water is out of place," as are the accursed flies: "I am now beginning to outline a sort of novel, in which I would like to capture some of the ancient visions of my soul, but nothing will come of it. I write letters and damn the flies, another of the most slutty, whoring, sowlike, shitty, swinish, thieving and damned forms of creation" (GGP 571).

Disorder is a prime reason for the would-be author's feelings of abjection and abulia, leaving him with strength only for invective and not for positive or heroic action. It annuls his aspirations to the artistic sublime, the novel project repeatedly mentioned in Gadda's war diary with its registration of the "ancient visions" of his soul. Disorder collapses rational synthesis and the literary sublime into irrational invective: the classical birds of augury become the transgressive flies of base reality; literature yields to the more modest epistolary alternative.

The conflict between an obsessive will to order and its continual defeat at the hands of prolific and destructive disorder will become a constant motif in Gadda's life and work. In his ideal resolution of the conflict in *Meditazione milanese*, Gadda links the idea of analytic "method" to "an increase of order" and "a greater richness of relationships," qualities which he admires in well-executed military organization. Method achieves this greater order/reality through critical selection and elimination: "The system that has a method is not the same as one which does not have one: it is a different system, richer, endowed with countless relationships pertaining to a critical selection. Endowed with logical phagocytes. The phagocytes of the organism and the cats that devour the mice in the house-organism are the critical relationships in the system that houses them. The house that has cats is an 'elegantius' with respect to the same house where the mice rule. The two systems are different" (MM 836).

The goal of rational method is to impose order on reality. But when the system cannot be rid of mice, when the shelter cannot be rid of flies, then method gives way to the terror of contamination, to the abjection of will, to the exorcism of invective. When faced with a world that no longer seems subject to order, reason, and method, Gadda abandons himself to a rhetorical exasperation of reality's disorder, not so much in a mimetic project of perception and portrayal, but in a desperate effort to remain in some way reality's "arbiter and author" (Roscioni 1969b, 161).

THE LITERATURE OF RETRIBUTION

> Le mie naturali tendenze, la mia infanzia, i miei sogni, le mie speranze,
> il mio disinganno sono stati, o sono, quelli di un romantico: di un romantico
> preso a calci dal destino, e dunque dalla realtà ("Un'opinione sul
> neorealismo," VM 629).

> [My natural tendencies, my childhood, my dreams, my hopes, my disillusionment have been, or are, those of a Romantic: of a Romantic kicked in the pants by destiny, and therefore by reality.]

Within Gadda's personal and narrative quest for rational analysis and order there lies a matrix of irrational emotivity, an existential neurosis, a textual psychosis. Nowhere is this paradoxical coupling more dramatic than in the tragic issue of the Gaddian quest, in which philosophy merges with paranoia and textual awareness necessitates a retributory ritual of mutilation and holocaust.

A case could be made for the similarity of post-Cartesian philosophy and paranoia, or as Freud put it in *Totem and Taboo*, for "paranoiac delusion [as] a caricature of a philosophic system" (Freud 1938, 846). In both, interpretative frenzy issues from an existential perspective in which everything is related to the thinking self. Descartes and Spinoza both suffered, Gadda wrote in *Meditazione milanese*, from a "fixation" to make the multiple derive from the one (MM 881, 1364). The emblematic literary enactment of this modern philosophical paranoia is Kafka's *The Trial*. Joseph K. is desperate in his attempt to fathom a system, the Law, which has decided mysteriously to accuse and persecute him. The process of understanding in Kafka's novel becomes synonymous with the defense of one's own case (a duality which the German "Prozess" captures well). In Gadda there is a similar relationship between understanding and persecution.

"I am incriminated," Gadda wrote to Bonaventura Tecchi in 1946; "I am on trial, by an infinite number of people. . . . I am always on trial. Just as in Kafka's 'trial'" (AF 150). Gadda's mind was populated by imaginary enemies (Gadda Conti 1974, 13). In his war diary he writes of holding everything in suspicion (GGP 604), and he endowed his autobiographical protagonist Gonzalo Pirobutirro with a similar "mania of persecution" (GGP 604; C$_2$ 541). This paranoia and sense of persecution would increase steadily over the years in Gadda's private life. In his narrative it is played out in a tragic cycle of transgression, retribution, and guilt.

Born from a desire to document Gadda's last chance for a heroic new life, the *Giornale di guerra e di prigionia* concludes, after his imprisonment and Enrico's death, as an unremediable tragedy: "Tragic horrible life" (GGP 849). In the first entry of his 1924 *cahier d'études* Gadda returns to this tragic vision in explaining his decision to embark on the *Racconto italiano* project: "Before the last glimmer of light in my soul is extinguished, I want to rescue these desperate memoirs of [my] tragic, terrible life" (RI 391). The traumatic remembrance of things past fused with a story of tragic agon becomes the core of Gadda's novelistic fiction which reaches its fullest development in *La cognizione del dolore*.

Like his countryman Cesare Pavese, Gadda constructs himself in the modern mold of "the artist as exemplary sufferer" (Sontag 1962). His writing is the exegesis of a painful and tragic reality, a "gnoseological" quest. At the core of this tragic knowledge or *cognizione* lies *il dolore* (pain, sorrow, grief). In *Meditazione milanese* Gadda posits *il dolore* as the necessary coefficient in the heuristic movement from being to becoming: "for it is nature's law that every action encounters obstacles and each becoming is rent by the pain and torment of its being, like the chick from the egg or the babe from the breast of the mother" (MM 791). The example of the detachment of the newborn from the womb or breast is a personally relevant one, since the autobiographical roots of Gadda's literary tragedies always involve a violent detachment from the mother. But beyond this existential *dolore* there exists an epistemological *dolore*—not surprising given Gadda's view of speculative method as an epitome of reality's becoming—in which the cognitive results of the heroic philosophical quest become confused with the tragic process of the quest itself. *Meditazione milanese* closes with just this confusion between the tragic humanity of the philosopher-poet and the heroic nature of his search:

> "Persevere" is his motto. Alone in the world, for no human can tolerate him, only death awaits him. But his work is not in vain, and so he takes courage and without terror will trod the funereal avenues where walk silence and invisible evils. Beyond every road, in the blond light lies sweet death.
>
> The critic: "Not evil but redemption. Not death, but life is the kingdom of thought."

I answer: "Yes. I evidently became confused. In a moment of ill humor I exchanged the person or human residue with the heroic undertaking." (MM 849)

Gadda's slippage is perhaps an ironic revision of Spinoza's affirmation in book 4 of the *Ethics* that the man who "lives according to the dictates of reason alone . . . thinks, therefore, of nothing less than of death, and his wisdom is a meditation upon life" (Spinoza 1974, 237). Wisdom and knowledge are not born from reason alone for Gadda but issue from and leave in their wake a broken and neurotic human residue. The linkage between *conoscenza* [knowledge] and *dolore* [suffering/grief] in the Western tradition has been a dual one: "Knowledge produces or increments suffering," and "suffering generates and develops knowledge" (Bodei 1983, 5). The two had been linked in tragedy where they appeared through the tragic devices of peripeteia and recognition. But it is only with the philosophical tragedy and tragic philosophy of the German Romantics that the tragic, with its tow of conflict, grief, and knowledge, fully penetrates into philosophy culminating in Hegelian dialectics and Schopenhauerian pessimism (see Bodei 1983, 8–18).

In Gadda this tradition of tragic philosophy is borne by the autobiographical Romantic protagonist, isolated in his quest for knowledge and condemned to proceed along the funereal avenues of death. His literary referent is Shakespeare's Hamlet. Modernity's first enigmatic and speculative antihero, Hamlet was to be the model for *Racconto italiano*'s climactic "catastrophe" with "philosophical commentary" (RI 410, 415). In a 1952 theater review, "*Amleto* al Teatro Valle," Gadda described Hamlet's conflict as emblematic of the passage from intellectual being to pragmatic becoming: "Hamlet investigates and expresses the mechanism of the notion that becomes *prâgma*, pragmatic reason, not without devastation of the sacrificed heart" (VM 543). The autobiographical Gonzalo Pirobutirro enacts this modern tragedy of the idea that becomes deed, and his folly of revenge is meant to be one of deliberate and lucid neurosis rather than blind psychosis (VM 543). But Gadda/Gonzalo's tragedy is also archaic and psychotic; it is a classical tragedy of one man at odds with an omnipotent and hostile destiny. If tragedy is dead because "God's . . . shadow no longer falls upon us" (Steiner 1961, 353), Gadda's mythical self-constructs seek to reinstate that ancient mystery in the modern clothing of the Freudian Oedipus complex.

Gadda's attacks against the excessive narcissism of his companions in the *Giornale di guerra e di prigionia* and his "antisubstantialist" assault on the ego or "io" in *Racconto italiano* and *Meditazione milanese* are generically pre-Freudian. Explicitly Freudian imagery and terminology only begin to surface in his writings in the mid-1930s, precisely in the gestational period of *La cognizione del dolore*, the "future novel" in which Gadda sought to merge the social and metaphysical satire of his early fiction with his own traumatic biography.

The first glaring example of the newly adopted Freudian schema can be seen in the 1936 "Una tigre nel parco" (MI 74–79). In this biographical *divertissement*, Gadda attributes his infantile "narcissistic delusion" and "Oedipus complex" to a traumatic episode in the Parco Sempione in Milan. Narcissistic delusion was triggered when the small child Carlo Emilio, fancying himself to be a regal tiger, crawls on all fours into a hobo's excrement: "the no of the cosmic I suddenly manifested itself" (MI 76). The Oedipus complex fully kicks in when the already traumatized and outraged infant sees his nurse courted by soldiers (a traumatic episode to which Gadda also attributes his "military mania") (MI 77–78). More generally, Gadda observes that his biography is most rich in "delightful preconfirmations" of the "analyses" and "complex doctrinal systematizations" of the psychoanalytic specialists (MI 74). The discovery that his own traumatic infancy lent itself so well to a Freudian elaboration was no doubt of use to Gadda in structuring the tragic family tension of *La cognizione del dolore*. Already in "Una tigre nel parco" Gadda declares that from the Freudian coordinates of narcissistic delusion and the Oedipus complex was born "the entire repertory of the future novel, so worthy of psychic analysis, of the most terrifying analysis" (MI 77).[14]

Gadda's recourse to psychoanalysis occurs in the official cultural climate of "fascist Italy's rejection of Freudian ideas, intellectually at the hands of Crocean and Gentilian neo-idealism . . . and, culturally, according to the popular notion, strengthened by fascism, of Latin purity and decorum" (Dombroski 1984b, 137). The fascist rejection of Freud took on more sinister tones in the late thirties as the regime moved toward official anti-Semitic policies and enactment of the infamous 1938 "racial laws." Freudianism is attacked in the fascist press as a particular example of the dangerous Jewish depravity.[15] In "Una tigre nel parco" Gadda pokes fun at official pronouncements that Freud's focus on the infantile, sexual origins of neuroses and psychoses undermines "the moral imperative of Goodness (sic) on the human collectivity" (MI 74). He will jeer the lingering official resistance to Freudianism after the war in the 1949

"Psicanalisi e letteratura" (VM 455–73). By the time *La cognizione del dolore* begins to appear in *Letteratura* (1938–41), Gadda had grown increasingly critical and bitter over Italian fascism, a stance that would precipitate into open animosity as the peninsula and Carlo Emilio are plunged into untold hardships during the Second World War. Gadda would later blame the war for his inability to finish the novel (C 759).

If the representation of Gadda's autobiographical tragedy assumes a consciously manipulated Freudian form from the mid-1930s on, the classic symptoms of a narcissistic delusion and Oedipus complex are already in evidence in the author's pre-Freudian period. There is a tortured resentment for his father, Francesco Ippolito. In his 1968 interview with Dacia Maraini on his childhood, Gadda recalled that his father's bad business moves and construction of the family villa at Longone had kept the family in a humiliating poverty (motifs which also appear in *La cognizione del dolore*). He blamed many of his childhood problems on the fact that his father had remarried (to Gadda's mother) late in life because he did not want to give Gadda's half sister Emilia a new mother: "my consanguineous sister had, so to speak, captured with her affection my father's entire attention" (IDM 10–11). Feelings of abandonment and disapproval by Gadda's father—and, by extension, his mother, progenitors, family, clan, society—first appear in several autobiographical reminiscences in the *Giornale di guerra e di prigionia*. These repressed feelings come to the surface in the diary entry examined earlier in which Gadda writes of the misunderstanding of his words at his father's deathbed, "I am barely fifteen years old!," which are interpreted by those around him, "and perhaps reasonably," he adds, as an egotistical reprimand to his father for having abandoned him at such a tender age (GGP 789). The father's negative influence on his son is evoked repeatedly, and Gadda felt that Francesco Ippolito held a disparaging opinion of him (another link to Svevo's Zeno Cosini). The often-lamented inability to function in life has its self-fulfilling prophecy in his father's disapproval: "It's true; I don't know how to live. My father used to tell me: 'You'll never do anything good in life.' So far that gracious prediction has proven true" (GGP 834). Gadda's "military mania" in the *Giornale* often takes the form of a frustrated search for a positive paternal/filial relationship he never had as a youth. Continually disappointed, frustrated, and angry with the Italian military high command, Gadda complains that his own commanding officers are never men of intellect and spirit that can help him in his life and career (GGP 621, 650). When he does come into contact with an officer who could serve as a positive paternal figure, the encounter sours into a nightmarish regression to the tormented relationship with his own father.

On August 10, 1916, a Captain De Castiglioni visits the position of Gadda's division in the Val d'Assa. Decorated with numerous ribbons and three medals for valor, the captain is not only the true war hero young Gadda has been seeking to emulate but the long-sought father substitute as well. He even takes on the physiognomy of the father, "making some slight shoulder movements just as poor papà used to do" (GGP 587). The captain takes Gadda under his wing with a "gentle cordiality" that becomes outright effusion when he learns that he is the brother of Enrico Gadda. After the captain's inspection of the troops, he dismisses the other officers but asks Gadda to remain. "And, when we were alone, once again he inquired about me, about my studies, about my brother, and he told me to say hello to him. Such a man!" (GGP 587). From that moment on, however, another characteristic misunderstanding of the young officer who does not "know how to live" turns Gadda's joy into humiliation and abjection:

> Speaking of my brother he exclaimed: "We shall soon make him a lieutenant!" I, who am both impudent and awkward, impertinent and timid, advanced the question of whether I, too, might hope for a promotion, to which he did not even deign to respond, leaving me humiliated. . . . He left me with less effusion than when he had greeted me, almost as if I had disappointed him, after having heard me speak. With a voice which seemed to me to have a slight intonation of sadness and sternness, he said, shaking my hand: "So long Gadda, and stay on the ball! Okay? Please give my warmest greetings to your brother." And with this last sentence his voice become more affectionate. I was hurt, disappointed in myself. It seemed to me that those words were meant to say: "I thought better of you, given what your kinship to the other Gadda would have led me to believe." In addition, the expression "stay on the ball" could easily have been interpreted in two ways. The more kindly as a wish that he was making to me: "don't let the Austrians get you"; the sterner as a reprimand: "don't be afraid."
>
> Me afraid? afraid of what? What gesture or tone could have given him such an idea? Perhaps the fact that instead of walking next to him I followed him? I did that as a sign of respect. Perhaps the tremor in my voice when I found myself alone with him? That was the result of

the deep emotion that envelops a heart prone to esteem and respect when honored by the special attention of an illustrious or authoritative person. . . .

The afternoon was a series of spiritual crises, since Captain De Castiglioni's visit had upset my inner equilibrium; then, bitterness, humiliation, dejection, etc. at all of these thoughts. (GGP 587–88)

Gadda's cursed hypersensitivity causes him to inflate a momentary reaction on his interlocutor's part into a traumatic reenactment of his childhood complex as the defective son, "the sad offshoot of the good plant" (GGP 784), especially in the light of brother Enrico's "handsome and strong" alternative (GGP 488). Gadda's adoration of his younger brother in the *Giornale,* his constant fear for his brother's safety, his repeated prayer that the war take him and not Enrico, and his lifelong despondency at Enrico's death might be interpreted by an analyst as bordering on the pathological. Elio Gioanola takes pains to underscore the Freudian obvious, that all the affection, care, worry, and grief are the reactive manifestations of a repressed hatred toward the more promising and loved offspring (Gioanola 1987, 22–36). As with all his family members, Gadda's affections for Enrico are ambivalent, and the dead brother is often superimposed in his fiction onto the person of the young and handsome other man who receives the affection and sexual favors of women. By all testimonies Enrico was the happy Gadda, carefree and with a witty spirit. These are qualities which Gadda admires in his brother, but not without moments of resentment, in particular concerning the latter's spendthrift ways. Enrico saves nothing. He asks for money from his brother while riding around on a new motorcycle (GGP 628). In a compositional note for *La cognizione del dolore,* Gadda reminded himself to explain the causes for Gonzalo's rage toward his siblings and to include the "scene of the wrench thrown at his brother's face, irritability: scene of the chessboard thrown to the ground after having lost a game" (Mazotti 1987, 169).

The scenario of the less loved and jealous son is developed to painful degrees in *La cognizione del dolore.* Both Gonzalo and his mother, the only survivors in the isolated Pirobutirro family villa, display a pious cult of adoration for the brother and son killed in the war, but for *la Señora,* in the hallucinatory narration of her grief, the son that survived was the defective one: "Her first son. The one in whose little body she had wanted to see, oh! days! the defective proof of nature, a failed experiment of her womb after the received fraud of the seed, reluctant at having suffered, at having generated what was not hers" (C 271–72; AWG 138–39). Gonzalo's pathological reaction to this denial of love is to lash out at anyone who receives the mother's affection, all of whom in the Oedipal economy of the text become surrogates for the dead father or the dead brother.

Adelaide Lehr Gadda, commonly known as Adele, is the other central figure in Gadda's family trauma. She was an extremely strong-willed and patriotic woman who instilled a "national feeling" in her son from his earliest childhood (SA 874). In the *Giornale* she is revered for her continual sacrifices for the family and resented for her refusal to sell the family villa at Longone in the Brianza region north of Milan. "I was nasty to mother," Gadda writes on September 10, 1919, after one of their many fights, "and I foresee that I always will be because we diverge on too many things. . . . And because, I say, she loves the walls of Longone, the chairs in Milan, more than me, more than sick Clara" (GGP 863–64). In a 1972 television interview with Gadda and Clara, both complained about their mother's severity when they were children, especially concerning their school studies. When asked why he did not rebel, Gadda replied: "One rebels if one has the power to rebel! If, for example, one is physically weaker than he who forces him to do that thing, he cannot rebel!" (Gadda 1973, 367).

The mother in *La cognizione del dolore* is a feeble, white-haired woman who is repeatedly threatened by her angry son, but the memory of her monstrous refusal of her child remains strong. In an unincorporated narrative sketch the narrator argues that the mother should have strangled Gonzalo after eight days (C$_2$ 532), grafting onto Freudian Oedipus a tale from classical tragedy and myth. This link to classical tragedy reappears in the contemporaneous biographical elegy "Dalle specchiere dei laghi" (1941; "From the mirrors of the lakes"), in which Gadda elaborates his family romance of the unloved, defective, and denied son in reference to the ending to Virgil's Messianic fourth eclogue: "I had worked on translating the eclogue in *terza rima*: oh! I had it memorized. Oh! the world to come. But, in closing the Messianic, Virgil had lacerated the theme, abruptly: the prediction of the painted sheep: 'He for whom his parents had no smile, nor will a god deign to have him at his table, nor will a goddess deign him her bed. Nec dignata cubili est'" (GA 229).[16]

The abandoned and unloved Gaddian protagonist is equipped for future greatness but tragically denied by social environment, by nature, and by those who should have loved him most, his parents, and, by extension, the parents of mankind, the gods. The inexplicable abandonment and denial can only be interpreted by the child as a sort of punishment for an unknown and distant fault, a tragically fatal transgression of a severe and unfathomable law that brands the infant with an unmedicable sense of guilt:

> [M]y land. It should have been a mother to me too, if the Lord's commandment was not vain, as it was to everybody, to the poorest, to the most destitute, and even to the deformed, or to those incapable of discernment. But the gentle slopes of those hills could not mitigate the extraordinary severity, the unnatural refusal, with which each semblance of the world would gaze back at me. I was then at fault, even if against my own knowledge. In the common light, undoubtedly, I had not observed my obligations, the infinite obligations; I had neglected the law, the law that terrifies, that punishes, that kills. (GA 228–29)

Gadda/Gonzalo's grief goes beyond tangible causes to a mysterious original sin of transgression and its punishment. It is both tragic and mythical, the "obscure" and "invisible" malady of Inca legend (C 690; AWG 154). The metaphysics of distant causes pushes the Freudian explanatory matrix in *Cognizione* toward these sacred and tragic sources. Gonzalo's is "an impious sentiment" that seems to come "from a deep, inexpiable zone of shrouded verities: from a torment without confession" (C 690; AWG 154). From an analytical point of view, the attempt to move beyond Freudian Oedipus to a tragic Oedipus can be explained as a further instance of repression. What results, in any case, is a literature of repressed rage and revenge: "In my 'humiliated and offended' life, narration has appeared to me, at times, to be the instrument which would allow me to restore 'my' truth, 'my' way of seeing, that is to say: the instrument of vindication against the outrages of destiny and of its human projectiles, the instrument, in an absolute sense, of redemption and revenge. As such my narrative manifests, many times, the resentful tone of one who speaks while holding back his ire, his indignation" ("Intervista al microfono," VM 503).

At the heart of this narrative of revenge lies *invective,* or more properly, *blasphemy.* The distinction is important, since blasphemy, a transgression against the sacred, moves beyond the verbal assault against reality to a mythical and tragic agon against divine authority. In Gadda, as in much of modern art, blasphemy becomes the frustrated manifestation of sacredness; transgression becomes "a displaced religion in the very vehemence of its blasphemies" (White 1982, 64).

Already in the *Giornale di guerra e di prigionia*, Gadda's tattered nerves, hypersensitivity to disorder, and family problems frequently drive him to frightful blasphemies. These, in turn, plunge him into an even greater sense of abjection, guilt, and remorse (GGP 770, 789, 804, 835, 838, 856). Years later Gadda confessed that his Catholic education had had a strong effect on him because he took the ideas of sin, remorse, and confession very seriously. It was remorse that continued to cause him the greatest anguish (IDM 12, 20). The *Giornale* is punctuated by Gadda's oscillations from fervent prayers to blasphemous outbursts. Similar to Freud's obsessive Rat Man, Gadda cannot stop the blasphemous from entering into the sacred, and this only increases the cycle of unresolved guilt. Upon seeing a fellow prisoner at Celle Lager pray, Gadda remarks: "I bear toward him, as toward all my religious companions, the heavy and black remorse of my horrendous blasphemies, which in moments of nervousness and madness issue forth horrible, atrocious, abominable" (GGP 804). The blasphemous urge only heightens Gadda's isolation from his companions and his sense of guilt and shame. Excluded from the divine legions of fallen heroes, Gadda can only evoke their example in an elegiac prayer that is the confession of his own guilt and acknowledgment of his punishment:

> What must I do? When I walk, it seems to me that I shouldn't. When I speak, it seems to me that I swear; when in the noonday sun every plant drinks in the warm light, I feel that guilt and shame are with me.
>   Forgive me!
>   I have tried to imitate you and to follow you, but I have been rejected. Certainly I committed very grave errors, and thus I was not permitted to join your Legion. ("Preghiera," MF 38)

A lifelong superstitious phobia that Gadda associated with his blasphemous outbursts was the fear of an inevitable retribution of the cosmic law that terrifies, punishes, and kills: "Concerning artillery shells, I note a strange and invincible superstition or suggestion of mine, according to which when blasphemies slip from my lips I think and fear that, as punishment, shells will strike me or land nearby" (GGP 607). The blasphemous rage of the Gaddian protagonist can never be anything more than an impotent rebellion against a much more powerful foe, against God the father, cruel deity and authoritative promulgator of the severe law: "Impotent anger was in him, in the son; a pretext having been offered, it immediately was freed in words, tumultuous, vain, and wicked:

in fierce threats—like a madman's scream from the depths of a prison" (C 668; AWG 152).

Gadda's personal mythology and vicious circle of divine negation, blasphemous revenge, and divine retribution reach their ultimate (perhaps cathartic) elaboration in the hallucinatory pages of *La cognizione del dolore*. In *Cognizione* the impotent rage of the frustrated Gaddian protagonist, excluded from the sublime and forced to live in a world of grotesque mediocrity, is directed, ultimately, against God the Father: "He would have repeatedly held up to shame the villa, cursing it along with the furniture and the chandeliers, with the memory of his father who had built it; crowning with obscene vituperations all the fathers and all the mothers who had preceded him in the series, back, back to the procreator of Adam" (C 686; AWG 149). The memory of the father is repeatedly desecrated by the son Gonzalo, who, in his outbursts, not only crushes the father's portrait under his feet but desecrates other mementos of paternal authority—a watch, a pen, the obscene church bells of Lukones financed by money denied to the son, and, especially, the cursed country villa. But the father, and the whole ancestral lineage of Gadda/Gonzalo's "eternalfather family" (MM 778), are merely surrogates for a higher sadistic order in Gadda's discourse of subjective wholeness, which, in Romantic fashion, strives toward the cosmic.

In the *Giornale di guerra e di prigionia* divine retribution against the rebellious blasphemer was meted out in the form of artillery shells. In *La cognizione del dolore* shells give way to Zeus's thunderbolt. The thunderbolt, a punishment traditionally reserved for the blasphemous, strikes ominously close to the protagonist Gonzalo. Its victims are the very descendants of that noble cast of giants, who, according to Vico, had founded piety and civil society at the first sight of lightning.[17]

Bertoloni, Trabatta, Pirobutirro—these are the families entrusted in *Cognizione* with the sacred institutions of home, marriage, religion, and paternal authority. Yet these institutions and the entire postwar bourgeois world of Gadda's Brianza have degenerated to such a tyranny of stupidity that they become the obsessive butt of Gadda/Gonzalo's satire.[18] There is a complicity of codependence between blasphemy and divine retribution in the novel. The severe law is a necessary construct of the subjective self in Gadda. It is needed to rationalize the frustration of subjective sublimation and to punish the resultant blasphemous rebellion. The punishment serves in turn to perpetuate the same cycle over and over. Moreover, the same punishing law is also the instrument of subjectivity's rebellion against the real-world surrogates of divine authority: family and bourgeois clan. The divine law punishes not only the rebellious subject but its surrogates, confirming their status as extensions of the subject's frustrated ego ideal. The punishment is a self-mutilation.

The vicious centripetal/centrifugal circle of punishment and satire in the novel is enacted at the social level through the relationship between Italian fascism and the degenerate bourgeois aristocracy of which Gonzalo is the "last hidalgo." The fascist *Nistitúo de vigilancia para la Noche* thrives on the inanity of the residents of the Néa Keltiké and in particular on their maniacal attachment to their villas. In the mafialike protection it provides them against assault, it asserts its tyrannical hold over this social class and its prompt punishment of any defiance. The grotesque triple assault of the errant thunderbolt on the innocent villa Giuseppina in the first part of the novel is a textual epiphany of the retribution that the Nistitúo, in the guise of the omnipotent deity, will mete out to the rebellious cavalier Trabatta in the second half:

Now, God is great.

Like the Thina of the ancient Tuscii, the God we have is one of those who knows his business well: with certain pigs, he isn't in any hurry; he lets them have their way, and even pretends he hasn't noticed a thing; he looks in the other direction, because in the meanwhile he is taking care of others, for as far as troubles are concerned, if you start looking for them, you find more than the fleas in a dog's coat. And the other goes on, goes on believing that all is going his way: then He, all of a sudden, wham, flings at his balls the prima manubia, which is a warning thunderbolt: a zigzag whore of a yellow flash, terrifying, with a blinding burst of flame and then a sharp report, that makes your flesh crawl.

The other, ha ha, acts nonchalant . . . yes, he assumes an I-don't-care attitude . . . but meanwhile, at heart, he's already begun to realize that his legs are wobbly. And sometimes he also feels a certain damp warmth in his drawers, and, when he has changed his clothes, the laundress later enjoys that jam. After a while, however, since he sees everything is proceeding as before, he starts up again, the louse. And this is the very time, then, when Thina flings the second trump at him, the peremptorium, and keeps the third in readiness for immediately afterwards, namely the annihilating thunderbolt, headlong. This is the definitive thunderbolt that leaves, where the crook was, a blackish spot on the ground, singed, which sometimes gives off a brief smell of sulphites and ammonia: and nothing else. Nothing else, you understand? Nothing else, nothing else except a brief smell of sulphites and ammonia, which a gust of wind annihilates in the air. Nothing else.

And thus, more or less, it had befallen Trabatta, guilty of wickedness toward the Nistitúo para la Noche. (C 718; AWG 191–92)

The Nistitúo is the ultimate instrument of the deity who is so malevolent toward the Gaddian subject yet is also an extended construct of that same subject. Gadda's early faith in fascism is confirmed by his 1921 enrollment in the Fascist Party (IF 58), his active participation in the directorate of the Buenos Aires fascio all'estero [Fascist cell abroad] during his 1922–24 stay in Argentina (LAS 86), his admiration for the Fascist *squadristi* and marchers on Rome, and his awe at Mussolini's international prestige (IF 72, 77, 90). The pragmatic justification for fascism that Gadda had espoused in his notes to *Racconto italiano* in 1924 had gradually withered over the years. In *La cognizione del dolore*, written between 1938 and 1941, fascism has itself become the ultimate symbol of the unreal evil, of "the lying kiss of Appearances," which Gonzalo must deny along with everything else, even though to do so means to deny himself (C 703; AWG 171). Both the hidalgo and the fascist Nistitúo carry forth the novel's nihilistic impulse, leaving nothing in their wake. Gonzalo's politically blasphemous *non credo* against the Nistitúo guard and against the volcano god Mussolini—"I don't believe in the guard, just as I don't believe in the omniscience of the volcano Akatapulqui" (C 653; AWG 109)—results in the third and most devastating episode of divine retribution: the "annihilating thunderbolt" that leaves Gonzalo's battered mother on the verge of death.

In Gadda's notes to a final, unwritten chapter we learn that the mysterious assault on the mother was committed by the Nistitúo guard Pedro Mahagones, called by some Manganones in allusion the "manganello" [club], which the fascist *squadristi* used to beat their adversaries into submission. When Gonzalo is brought in to see his mother, she reels back in horror thinking that it was he who had assaulted her. She dies, and he is left with *il dolore eterno* [eternal grief] (C$_2$ 554–55, 563). The mother is drawn into error by the irascible and threatening behavior of her son and by similarities of appearance between Gonzalo and Mahagones (C 563). The confusion is not casual. Gadda's early faith and complicity in the regime are brutally betrayed when he finally comes to recognize fascism's manifest unreality, but the guilt of complicity and sense of responsibility remain. The son's horrific dream of the black force that rises from him to extinguish his mother, his object of sublime desire, has a political as well as psychotraumatic origin. In *Cognizione*'s sadomasochistic circle of guilt, blame, and punishment responsibility for Manganone's murderous assault on the mother ultimately falls on the son. Once again the severe deity of retribution and the blasphemous subject intersect.

Sadistic punishment is not just the work of a malevolent deity within Gadda's autobiographical narrative. It is linked to the Gaddian textual enterprise in its entirety. Elio Gioanola has tied Gadda's obsession with the sadistic thunderbolt to a sadistic-anal obsession in which the original attraction to dirt or "lo sporco" is masked by a reactive impulse toward order (Gioanola 1987, 91). The attraction/repulsion impulse to dirt and the anal is the primary figurative vehicle of Gadda's self-defined hypersensitivity to disorder, which manifests itself in the recurring motif of feces or their numerous surrogates, the fetid *croconsuelo* cheese of *Cognizione* being the most obvious example. The punitive thunderbolt enacts the desperate attempt to recover sublime order through the sadistic assault on the disorder to which Gadda's neurotic hypersensitivity obsessively gravitates. The thunderbolt that falls on the "female" villas Giuseppina, Enrichetta, and Antonietta, "when it realized it could no longer resist the call of nature" (C 587; AWG 24), caroms through a clogged latrine under repair in one villa and ends its journey in another villa in the dry tub of the maidservant. The metaphorical thunderbolts that fall on the cavalier Trabatta leave him first with shit in his pants only to annihilate both him and his feces, leaving behind only a faint smell of sulphites and ammonia. The thunderbolt becomes the omnipotent form of the destructive-purifying impulse, able to satisfy fully the sadistic drive without finding resistance of any kind. It annihilates all enemies, eliminates every mess, and reestablishes order (Gioanola 1987, 115–16). It is the symbol of the necessary ritual holocaust of disorder in the Gaddian text.

In *Meditazione milanese* Gadda attributes the "pleasure" a sadist experiences "to extreme wrongs occasioned at the genesis, even distant genesis, of that abnormal individual by the fabric of reality. . . . He demands from reality a restoration or reinstatement and he demands it in a spastic, anguished, mad, deadly and monstrous form" (MM 799). In Gadda's textual universe sadism belongs as much to the victim as to the cruel deity. The attraction to grotesque disorder and the desperate attempt to eliminate it become a spastic enactment of the struggle between repression and the repressed that links the figural systems of both the unconscious and literature (F. Orlando 1978, 137–60). The sadism of the Gaddian text toward its own grotesque "reality" is a monstrous attempt at a narrative restoration, a solution that is alluded to in Gonzalo's hallucination of a sadistic annihilation of disorder:

> Scendeva: le scale di casa sua, scendeva. La sala era piena di gaglioffi. Si piazzava allora sul terrazzo, ritto, a gambe larghe sul terrazzo di casa sua, con la pistola a mitraglia, come tenesse un bel mandolino, da grattarlo! da grattarlo ben bene, quel mandolino. Tatrac: la molla, il nottolino, il gancio. Un caricatore lucido, un pettine. La canna del mandolino infilava la sala. Oh! che bella romanza, che manduline, checcanzuna, che marechiare, nella casa liberata! disinfettata! (C 736)

> He went down: the steps of his house. He went down. The room was full of louts. He took up his position then on the terrace, erect, legs apart on the terrace of his house, with the machine pistol, as if he were holding a lovely mandoline, to scratch it! to scratch that mandoline good and proper. *Click-clack:* the spring, the pin, the catch. A shining loader, a comb. The barrel of the mandoline stuck into the room. Oh! what a lovely song, what a mandoline, what a *sole mio,* in the house, freed! disinfected! (AWG 213)

Gonzalo's "machine pistol" is a barely disguised metaphor for the divine thunderbolt, and the sadistic pleasure he experiences is heightened by the sardonic reference to the Neapolitan musical tradition emblematic for Gadda of Italy's negative culture of vulgarity and disorder. The elimination of the oafish entourage that surrounds his mother in his own house (there is a mock-epic Homeric echo of Odysseus's massacre of Penelope's suitors) is the sadistic enactment of the rational method of order prescribed in *Meditazione milanese:* the cat that eliminates the rats in the house organism. But the mice always run wild for Gadda; the cat becomes a sadist and engages in a destructive frenzy.

Satiric blasphemy and sadistic punishment are the two sides of a single coin in Gadda's works. Punishment is a common motif in satire, especially punishment of the innocent (Paulson 1967a, 10–11). The Gaddian text subsists on an extreme instance of this latter form of punishment: the murder of a "loved" one. The theme has its biographical origins in the death of Gadda's brother in the First World War. Gadda's repeated prayer is that the war take him and not Enrico. But the prayers are not answered: "And who died? God knows with what purity and fervor I prayed to him or destiny to take me, so wretched, and to leave my brother, out of compassion. Tragic fate has been different than my wish and my most virile and sincere hopes: it has left me to suffer for him and for me in a world that is now dull in my soul, in a society toward which I have only disdain" (GGP 853).

The prayers of the blasphemous Carlo Emilio are not heard; Enrico is taken, and his brother is left to suffer in the wasteland. A sacrificial victim is necessary to the poetics of abjection, guilt, and grief in Gadda. In *La cognizione del dolore* guilt over the mother's death is also a transposition of guilt over the brother's death. Both victims have the same eyes that fix upon the horrible void; both are marked by identical streams of blood that flow from their nostrils (C 728, 752).[19]

In Gadda's narrative universe it is the "mother"—Dejanira Classis in *Novella seconda*, Liliana Balducci in *Pasticciaccio,* la Señora in *Cognizione*—who is offered up to the textual deity. The disorder or pasticcio eliminated through their immolation is couched in the sexual metaphor of incest. The object of the subjective desire for sublime integration and wholeness is a prohibited and frightful one. "Gonzalo must exist separated from his mother only because he is so absorbed in her. To accept integral relatedness with her means passing from a 'neurotic' identity, characterized by uncertainty and fear, to a 'psychotic' union with the *other*. It is this fullness, expressed through longing,—we repeat—that is terrifying" (Dombroski 1984b, 131). The repression of the incestuous transgression occurs through the tragic distancing of the object from the subject. The sadistic retribution that strikes these women is the text's way of sublimating illicit desire into mournful nostalgia. The textual awareness of the premeditated necessity of this sublimating carnage generates the sense of guilt which pervades the Gaddian text. Indicative of this guilty knowledge is the provisory ending Gadda sketched for the novel: the mother's suspicion that it was her son who viciously attacked her and the anguish of the son who thinks that his mother could have suspected him (C_2 555). Tragic knowledge in the Gaddian text remains enshrouded in its internal dynamics of "misunderstanding." But what is misunderstanding within the text points to the possibility of a greater understanding at the level of textuality itself. Gadda appears to hint at this duality in another annotation to *Cognizione* in which Gonzalo is declared innocent from the perspective of "physical realty" but guilty within the broader realm of the "imaginary":

Gnoseologically:
Perhaps aside from physical reality, mechanical reality, meanly stereo-

metric and historical reality = there flows a frightful and real plot, a frightful thought. And the contemplated thing or act is more real than the thing which has occurred or the act which has been executed. And God sees thought, fantasy. And even if He didn't see, if He refused to see (for God can do anything), the fantasy and the delirium would remain and the soul is lost by imagining, not by doing. (C_2 570)

The "gnoseological" dilemma posed by the duality of the "imaginary" and the "real" can be extended beyond the autobiographical character to the text in its entirety. The sins of the imagination are ultimately those of the text. The testimony of God, be he malicious or benevolent, is no longer important. The text is self-sufficient in its imaginary delirium: it generates its own sin, guilt, and punishment.

But what is the great sin of the Gaddian text? The answer strikes at the heart of the text's poetics of sublimity, of its quest for rational synthesis. To borrow an insight from Theodor Adorno, "the unity of *logos* is caught up in a complex of blame because it tends to mutilate what it unifies" (Adorno 1986, 267). The Gaddian poetics of the "critical epitome" claims to embrace the manifold multiplicity of reality, but its literary method is, in its frenzied imposition of narrative order, the opposite of the drive toward union with the manifold other. To truly unify the other, to incorporate the other into the desired wholeness, would mean the explosion of the textual enterprise, the perdition of the text itself. Mutilation ensures that the text's destructive desire will never achieve fruition. The imagination is free to hack away. The neurotic and hypersensitive Gaddian text is acutely aware of the paradox. It manifests its awareness through the spastic tension between its contrastive but complicit poetics of rational wholeness and satiric mutilation.

The modern dilemma of a frustrated textual sublimity based on an "ordered" disorder is enacted in *La cognizione del dolore* through its incest/matricide motif. The sublime union of mother and son, the height of natural order, is also the most monstrous disorder. Mutilation prevents this ultimate disorder; yet it also seals the impossibility of ever achieving the sublimity of desire. The text, having committed its sin and inflicted its punishment, is left to ponder its guilt.

Chapter 2

In Search of a Necessary Style

Costruire, definire le proprie modalità espressive: raggiungere lo stile necessario: è il dramma di chi da prima ignora, poi percepisce, poi rompe i vincoli che avevano legato la sua "forma" insorgente ("Arte del Belli," VM 548).

[To construct, to define one's own expressive patterns; to reach the necessary style. This is the drama of he who at first does not know, then perceives, then breaks the chains which had bound his insurgent "form."]

Gadda, it has been said, is the author of a single work. Themes, images, character types, fixed ideas, obsessive metaphors, and linguistic tics recur with a frequency that would be intolerable in a writer of less afflatus and breadth (Roscioni 1969b, 49–50). Statistical analyses would only corroborate in an excess of data what even the most casual reader can attest in comparing two of Gadda works written decades apart. The major changes in Gadda's themes and language occur late in his career and are occasioned by the irremeable cataclysms of history and migration. World War II and the moves to Florence and Rome lessen the obsessive Milanese and First World War elements in Gadda's early production. They are replaced with Roman and Florentine pastiches and the relentless execration of Mussolini.

Gadda's apprenticeship as a writer in the 1920s and 1930s is a struggle between inspiration and form. It is a period rich in stylistic and linguistic experimentation as he seeks to forge a style not merely adequate but *necessary* to his vision of the tangled muddle of existence and his own psyche. The necessary motivation behind Gadda's stylistic choices becomes a constant refrain during this period, often as a defense against allegations of caprice and triviality. The experimentation is not always a felicitous development of innate potentiality. It bears the imprint of repression and regression, the effort to find a stylistic compromise acceptable to the purist *calligrafismo* of the official literary establishment or to the political vigilance of the fascist regime.

The "fragmentary" nature of Gadda's literary production is in part a result of these pressures. The failure to forge a novel based on a combinatorial model coupled with Gadda's stylistic heterogeneity transformed the *Racconto italiano* project into a series of sketches. These would constitute the nucleus of his first publications in *Solaria* and his first book, *La Madonna dei Filosofi* ("Apologia manzoniana," "Preghiera," "L'antica basilica," "Manovre di artiglieria da campagna"). Gadda's other interwar attempts at a novel—*Dejanira Classis* (*Novella seconda*), *La meccanica*, "Un fulmine sul 220" (from whence *L'Adalgisa*), *La cognizione del dolore*—underwent a similar process of publication as fragments in journals.[1] Stylistic heterogeneity is seen as an impediment to publication. Gadda proposes to Bonaventura Tecchi that he could "facet" his work, according to style, into "a satirical book, a lyrical one, a fantastic one" (May 1, 1932; AAF 109). The impossibility of editorial integration and closure contributes to the continual recycling of images and themes, to an endless restatement of the author's obsessive metaphors.

There were also problems of time and money. Gadda came from an extended family of engineers and was forcibly nudged into the profession by the insistence of his mother and the expectations of clan and environment.[2] In the positivistic Milan described so sardonically yet nostalgically in *L'Adalgisa*, engineering is a cultural, almost biological inheritance. Even the humble Roman prostitute Ines Cionini declares with assurance that "[l]i milanesi, be,' se sa . . . quelli so' tutti ingegneri" [Well, the Milanese, everybody knows . . . they're all engineers] (P 179; TAM 248). The 1920s and 1930s were spent in a constant struggle between the desire to write and study philosophy and the constraints of Gadda's merry-go-round positions as an electrotechnical engineer and on-site worker in Italy and abroad. Waves of writing activity rose and fell according to the rigors of his assignments. There were interludes from engineering during which Gadda sought a supplemental income via an eclectic production of essays, reviews, technical articles, and short fiction.[3] In one spurt of activity in 1931–32, Gadda published twelve literary reviews, nine travel and leisure essays, seven technical essays (on metal alloys and the industrial uses of nitrogen and lignite), five World War I memoirs, four short stories, a music review, and a poem (see *Opere* 5/2:19–22). Beginning in the mid-1930s this diversified production is accompanied by a series of translations, most of which bear Gadda's name but were translated by

Lucia Rodocanachi and "reviewed" by Gadda.[4] Uniquely Gadda's own, however, are the stupendous 1941 translations in a macaronic Florentine expressionism of *Siglo de oro* satirists Francisco Quevedo's *El mundo por de dentro* and Alonso Jerónimo de Salas Barbadillo's *La peregrinación sabia.*[5] When these translations were executed, Gadda had written and published significant portions of *La cognizione del dolore* and *L'Adalgisa.* He was in firm command of his necessary style.

The Sublime and the Comic

> Il forte senso della mia personalità . . . mi traeva a riuscire un lirico, piuttosto, o un satirico ("Intervista al microfono," VM 503).

> [The strong sense of my personality . . . led me to be a lyricist, or, rather, a satirist.]

Gadda's double vocation as a lyricist and a satirist is responsible for the wide divergence between sublime and comic tonalities in his works. No contemporary Italian author plumbs the extremes of high and low discourse as did Gadda. The shifting tonality was felt to be a problem from his earliest compositions, and much of his early fiction reveals the effort to harness the stylistic and personal excesses of the sublime and the comic.

"La passeggiata autunnale," Gadda's first extant narrative, was composed, by his own account, from August 22 to 30, 1918, during his internment as a prisoner of war in Germany (Isella 1989b, 1296). The story is striking in its inclusion of the essential features of Gadda's mature epistemology of muddle, grief, and autobiography, elaborated in an uncharacteristically simplistic style of monotonal uniformity.

"Passeggiata" traces the tragic triangle of three elect souls—Stefano, Nerina, and Rineri—caught in the grip of conflicting passions and an inexorable fate. Rineri, in his timidity and troubled cynicism, is the first of a long succession of autobiographical Gaddian characters, and certainly the most psychologically complex figure in the "La passeggiata autunnale." Yet even in his case, Gadda stumbles in trying to find an authentic voice, and the character can describe his "illness of solitude" only in a Romantic iconography reminiscent of Ugo Foscolo's histrionic Jacopo Ortis, and with analogous Petrarchan resonances: "'I constantly wandered, alone, as if cursed by an evil spell. I endured the company of others like branches that whip the face when walking in the valleys, with the desire to leave them as quickly as possible, in order to scrape and toughen myself against the mountain crags, the more exposed the better, the higher, the more deserted, the better'" (RD 945–46).

The story's flat characters and lack of the ironic and baroque complexity of Gadda's later works can be ascribed perhaps to the ingenuousness of the traumatized prisoner of war who viewed writing as an escape from base reality to an ideal realm of noble sentiments. Whenever authorship is mentioned in the *Giornale di guerra e di prigionia*, it is in the sense of sublimity: the registration of the "ancient visions" of Gadda's soul or the fantasized sublime battalion Retica (GGP 571, 784). The spatial coordinates of Greek *hypsos* and Latin *sublimis* are constantly evoked in Gadda via a series of anachronistic Romantic archetypes: ancient trees, distant mountains, flashes of lightning, transiting clouds, gusting winds, lofty castles, towers, and hermitages. The temporality of this sublimity is elegiac: a beyond of elect souls that has been closed forever to the excluded subjectivity. The distant, sublime landscape is the site of community for Gadda's fallen comrades in arms, for his dead brother, a community from which he is excluded: "But I think of you, my dead comrades. There are distant, terrible mountains; and the clouds rise, like dreams, or like thoughts, from the mountains and the forests" ("Preghiera," MF 38).

Elegiac heroism renders the Gaddian sublime impervious to irony and binds it to tragedy. The Gaddian mythos of tragic denial and exclusion at the hands of an inexorable fate has its psycho-figural etymon in what has been termed Gadda's "Palinurus complex" (Pedriali 1990, 33). In "La passeggiata autunnale" the autobiographical Rineri sees in himself the shipwrecked and besieged Palinurus, "madida cum veste gravatum prensantemque uncis manibus capita asperi monti" [burdened by my sea-drenched clothing, my hooked hands clinging to a jagged cliff] (RD 938; *Aeneid*, book 6, verses 359–60). Even more poignant are Palinurus's words upon his momentary sighting of Italy which Gadda quotes as a preface to the books of his war diary: "Prospexi Italiam summa sublimis ab unda" [raised aloft on a wave's crest I saw Italy in the distance] (GGP 530, 655, 775, 822; *Aeneid*, book 6, verse 357). Gadda's Virgilian self-construction models itself not on triumphant Aeneas but on tragic Palinurus. Palinurus espies Italy but is murdered by native barbarians shortly after; Gadda fights in the war to create a "real" Italy but is crushed by the insufficiency of the Italian environment. Sublimity for the subjective self in Gadda is an impossibility: the distant community of the elect is an unreachable beyond; there will be no transcendence. Aeneas's purposive heroism cannot be appropriated, only his elegiac *pietas*.

The figural and epistemological expansion of Gadda's category of the sublime is influenced in the years following the war by his contact with French symbolism and Kant. In his analysis of Rimbaud and Baudelaire

in the 1927 "I viaggi la morte," the "Palinurus complex" is countered by
a more contemporary and decadent imagery of voyage, reverie, and dissolution. The symbolist poets, Gadda writes, transform the notion of sublime distance into a "spatial immortality," a "topographical beyond" of
"infinite experience" (VM 564). The operation is decadent in that it binds
the notion of voyage with that of death and dissolution: "The migration
of the symbolists is a determination of new spatial fortunes, new discov-
eries of knowledge and new sensations disengaged from the coordinating
impulse of the I, it is to lose oneself in oceanic chance; to die is to enter
into a vaster dissolution, a more boundless chance, where each hindrance
of the chains of every teleology is removed" (VM 581).

Death as a sublime dissolution will be a recurrent topos in Gadda's
fiction, especially in the "dissociation of a panic nature" and "return to
the Indistinct" of Liliana Balducci in *Quer pasticciaccio* (P 105; TAM 138).[6]
The abandonment of any finalistic teleology for Gadda the man of order
is, however, a frightening sublime, and the author's women achieve their
transcendence of dissolution only in the horrific outrage of their physiological beings. The horror is not without effect on the contemplating
subject. It involves an evolution from Gadda's early "Palinurus complex"
of exclusion to a broader, metaphysical "knowledge of grief."[7]

This is where the Kantian coordinates of the Gaddian sublime come
into play. During the same period of "I viaggi e la morte," Gadda was
undergoing his examinations in philosophy at the University of Milan
with Piero Martinetti. Gadda's personal library contained several annotated volumes of Martinetti's work on Kant, and the professor had given
his pupil an autographed copy of his *Antologia kantiana* (Lucchini 1988,
17–18). Although Gadda never refers to Kant's *Critique of Judgement*,
he would later declare, as "a reader of Kant," that literature must possess
a "noumenal dimension," a "mystery" or "tragic tension." It must point
beyond surface appearances to "a more real 'thing'" (VM 630).[8] Know-
ing the "thing-in-itself" is the ultimate quest of Gadda's rational or cognitive sublime. Most often the quest becomes a painful failure of reason
faced with a horror beyond its powers of logical understanding. What it
can know, in Kantian critical fashion, is its own tortured process of human cognition, its own grief.

The tragic sublimity of this knowledge of grief is the guiding force, as
the title indicates, of *La cognizione del dolore*. In Gadda's earliest works,
published in the pages of *Solaria* and later gathered in *La Madonna dei
Filosofi*, there is, instead, a studied avoidance of the tragic excess, griev-
ing autobiography, and blasphemous rage already present in Gadda's war

diary. Guido Baldi, who has remained Gadda's harshest critic, argues that *La Madonna dei Filosofi* rarely rises above the comic or humorous sketch, "il bozzetto umoristico," and that it purposely eschews any true tragic tension (Baldi 1972, 63–75). Guido Lucchini, who has executed meticulous studies of both Gadda's early philosophical formation and *La Madonna dei Filosofi*, concludes that the latter does not appear to constitute a natural derivation from the narrative or speculative constructs of the *Racconto italiano* and *Meditazione milanese*. He classifies it instead as a retreat to Gadda's humorous-ironic manner of Dickens and Panzini (RI 396), attributable perhaps to his contact with a Florentine literary environment very different from his own more eclectic formation (Lucchini 1988, 53–54).

In the early reviews of *La Madonna dei Filosofi* and the 1934 *Il castello di Udine*, the definition of Gadda as a "humorist" recurs with insistence, beginning with Carlo Linati's "Un umorista. Carlo Emilio Gadda" (*L'Ambrosiano*, May 10, 1931). The reviews are mixed in their assessment. Gadda's humor is effective when motivated and sober, Alfredo Gargiulo wrote, but too often in *La Madonna dei Filosofi* it degenerates to "un cincischiato e molto letterario esercizio di Penna" ["a mangled and very literary exercise of the pen"] (Gargiulo 1958, 553).

Often upset by the reviews, Gadda sought to explain his choices to critics in an apologetic tone laced with a none-too-veiled satire of their own literary pretensions: "I understand how much there is in my belabored writing that is not so acceptable to you; perhaps, if I had the strength to free myself from my obsessions, your suggestion could guide me to a purity and chastity of lofty tone" (letter of September 14, 1934, to De Robertis; TLI 28).[9] The most sardonic rebuttal to these early appraisals appeared a few years later in the opening chapter of *La cognizione del dolore* in Gadda's self-chastisement as an author who took advantage of the tragedy of the war "per cincischiarne e sottilizzarne fuori i suoi ribòboli sterili" [to mangle and squeeze out of it his sterile witticisms] (C 579; AWG 13). The baroque *cincischiare* is squeezed, of course, not from Gadda's pen but from that of Gargiulo.[10]

Gadda was well aware that the excessively bizarre qualities of his own temperamental humors ran the risk of incompatibility with the literary norms of the times. Already in his 1926 letters to enlist Bonaventura Tecchi's assistance in getting published in *Solaria*, he worries that he is and may be judged too "crude, trivial and peevish" for the "splendor" of the Florentine journal (AAF 43–44).[11] The link between Gadda's stylistic humor and his temperamental humor is not casual. Gadda's early use of humor, irony, and caricature serve not only as an antidote to the wooden monotonality of "La passeggiata autunnale," but as a means for channeling the blasphemous impulse of his native invective into more acceptable artistic forms. Caricatural humor refashions the pathological impetus of Gadda's literature into the innocuous eccentricities and quirks of an anachronistic comedy of manners.

Whereas the characters of "La passeggiata autunnale" were serious and flat, Gadda's early works in the twenties are populated by a panoply of humorous and moody characters. The most developed and autobiographical of these is the engineer Cesare Baronfo of the story "La Madonna dei filosofi." Baronfo is similar to Gadda in his interest in philosophy, his neurasthenia and his environmental hypersensitivity, his incessant travels, and his desire to abandon his career. Baronfo, however, never succumbs to the disturbing and tragic manifestations of pathological excess of Gonzalo Pirobutirro. His explosions of outraged invective are immediately neutralized in a slapstick comedy of corrective bumps and knocks, as when he receives a blow to the head by a rude chap from Calabria after Baronfo had called him a "calabrese" (MF 82).

Never an author dedicated to the creation of the "rounded" characters dear to E. M. Forster, Gadda's irritated pen more often sketched caricatural character types marked by their physical and behavioral tics: generals given to Napoleonic temper tantrums, absentminded and alcoholic philosophers, aging and cackling nymphomaniacs, slavering Milanese patriarchs, terrorized Milanese matriarchs fearful for their jewels, voluptuous servants, overprotective mothers, awkward large-nosed and nose-picking youths, hypersensitive downstairs neighbors. In "Intervista al microfono" Gadda declared that the gestures and opinions of others did not excite him to write: "Thus a painter turns without a special vocation, or even with a certain repugnance, to a particularly ignoble or squalid model, or one without 'signs' of personality, that is to say, 'insignificant.' (It is true that pure color itself attracts him)" (VM 503).

Many of the most entertaining of these colorful but insignificant types are the ubiquitous comic bystanders in Gadda's works, characters not directly involved in the central narrative action but whose reactions cast it in a comic perspective. These humorous bystanders function as a deflating and digressive technique against any tragic or pathetic sublimity. When the unfortunate Dejanira Classis returns by train from the gravesite of her lover killed in the war, she is offered whisky to overcome her convulsive chills. Eventually she throws up, scattering two nuns and other "horrified" passengers, among whom is a well-dressed fellow from Rome:

"'*Mannaggia*, curse it . . . ,' he said under his breath, shaken, making his way through the crowd with his suitcase and examining himself, twisting his chest and head and lifting a leg with that elegant movement with which one looks at oneself sidelong, examining his new, pressed pants, if by bad luck any drops of ex-cognac had made a stain" (RaI 1059–60). Any pathos in this scene for the unfortunate Dejanira, who was destined in the never-completed homonymous novel to be brutally murdered, is dissolved in the elegant sidelong glance of a Roman bystander.

AB INTERIORE/AB EXTERIORE

> Io voglio essere io, e non il pappagallo d'alcuno (LGC 12).

> [I want to be myself, and not the parrot of anyone.]

The problems of tone and character in Gadda's early works are accompanied by a related one of narrative voice.[12] This is especially true when Gadda confronts the extended form of the novel, with its requirements of a sustained plot; multiple, rounded characters; and the depiction of a variegated society. Story and discourse undergo a high and erratic degree of confusion in these early efforts. There is an intrusion into the story of authorial voice and parodic stylization.

The issue of voice is addressed at length in a series of notes in the *Racconto italiano* concerning the choice between a narration that is "*ab interiore*" or "*ab exteriore*." The former, in Gadda's terminology, entails a "lyricism of representation through the characters," the latter, "a lyricism through the 'author'" (RI 461). Gadda habitually associates the character's or author-narrator's "point of view" or "world vision" with his lyricism. The sensation of lyrical expressionism, a peculiarly intensive propensity to the pole of subjectivity in language, is especially strong in Gadda and becomes a counterforce to the unfolding of narrative plot in his novels. Serious and reasoned discussion is rarely developed in his works, as it is, for instance, in those of Thomas Mann. World vision tends to be conveyed instead through an oneiric and sublime lyricism or the satiric ridicule and parody of another's discourse.

Gadda inevitably feels drawn to the *ab exteriore* mode of narration. Narration *ab interiore* is difficult to sustain, he writes, since "it is instinctive in the author to superimpose his own representations and comments on those of the protagonists" (RI 462). Gadda's solution to the *ab interiore/ab exteriore* problem entails grafting the author's lyricism onto that of the characters. To do so the author must position himself within the text to create adequate "terms of reference" with his character's lyricism and to generate reader interest in the author's viewpoint (RI 476). In the great poets such as Homer, author and reader viewpoints harmoniously merge with those of the character in our common universality as sentient members of the "societas humani generis" (RI 476). When an author does not possess this unifying lyrical genius, he must create for himself an authorial "potency" that will cause the reader to become interested in his lyricism and voice. Very much aware of the psycho-sociological reality of the author-reader relationship, Gadda declares that to generate reader interest the author must endow himself either within the text or in his personal and historical self-construction with a strong personality. This can be accomplished via his "expressive lyrical *genius*" or "historical importance" (the example of Caesar is offered), or, in more mundane ways, through the author's "sexual potency, deriving from beauty and youth . . . *Dolcestilnuovo* works well when one is twenty," or through similar equivalents: the author as snob, aristocrat, bohemian, delinquent, etc. "Then he is the golden mouth, and he's interesting" (RI 478).

If these expedients fail, two final alternatives remain: the substitution of a universal or potent term of reference with a nonuniversal "fashionable term"—"common representations," "things in vogue," "topics of the moment or ambience"—or the direct insertion of the author's lyricism into the text as a counterpoint that will interest the reader through its dissonance with the characters' lyricism (RI 479–80). Both of these techniques imply a shift from a lyrical consonance of voices to an ironic or satiric dissonance. The first technique results in what Gadda calls an "ironic embroidery" in which "the character measures the fashionable idea, and the fashionable idea measures the character" (RI 479). Of the second he notes: "I relate to my historicity and humanity the [character's] idea and with my created human person I counterpoint it. Then my commentary or my irony or my anger or my judgment generally have a flavor, they make sense, they have a justification" (RI 480).

The double penetration into the story and the characters' thoughts of an authorial voice based on either a lyrical consonance or an ironic or satirical dissonance results in a high degree of promiscuity of voice and tone in Gadda's fiction. The structures of ironic dissonance are set in place through the constant parody of received ideas, but often the ironic structure is arbitrarily dropped and the mental life of a character is indiscriminately invaded by a direct and unparodied authorial lyricism. This is apparent in Gadda's most ambitious early attempt at a novel, *La meccanica.*

Most of *La meccanica* was written between October and December

1928, during an extended fourteen-month period in which Gadda's stomach illnesses forced him to leave Rome and the Ammonia Casale for a cure in Milan. During this Milanese sojourn the author was actively engaged in the composition of the *Meditazione milanese, Dejanira Classis, La meccanica,* and various pieces for *Solaria* (Isella 1989a, 1173–75). In keeping with Gadda's early Manzonian and Balzacian vision of a sweeping "Italian tale," *La meccanica* seeks to trace a broad portrait of the mores and attitudes of Milanese society in the period immediately prior to Italy's entrance into the First World War. Its immediate plot is that of a romantic triangle focused around the voluptuous and enticing Zoraide, a young bride whose hardworking but naive Socialist husband Luigi Pessina has been sent off to war suffering from tuberculosis. During Luigi's absence, Zoraide has an affair with a handsome young "mechanic" from the bourgeois class, Franco Velaschi. The novel concludes when the gravely ill Luigi discovers Zoraide and Franco in bed together. He dies shortly thereafter, an event to which the couple remain nearly oblivious, immersed as they are in their erotic and vitalistic passion.[13]

The novel is punctuated throughout by the intrusion of authorial discourses ranging from the civic indignation and satirical excoriation of prewar bourgeois hypocrisy and Socialist defeatism, to indulgent (and misogynistic) descriptions of Zoraide's voluptuous sexuality, to the sublime lyricism of the lovers' motif and Gadda's war motif. The contrasting satirical and lyrical poles of authorial voice find their way into the narration and story through a process of parodic stylization in which the lyricism of the characters is continually at the mercy of that of the author. A case in point is the narrative treatment of Donna Teresa Velaschi. Having used every means and connection possible to keep her son Franco from serving his country, the Velaschis, husband and wife, are the target for the author's satire on bourgeois hypocrisy and false values. When the inevitable occurs and Franco is conscripted, Donna Teresa is enveloped by an equally hypocritical pride at the thought of her son as a hero. The shallowness of her character, ambience, and values is mocked in the parodic description of her conversation with other Milanese matrons. But as the narration of Teresa's inner thoughts continues, the stylized parody of her lyricism gradually yields to a more genuine lyricism:

Ritornavano, come un sogno, le dolcezze dei sereni anni, dei salotti, dei drappi: (le amiche ed i giovani parlavano, eleganti, con ardenti pensieri): delle maioliche, dei fondants. O in villa, aurore meravigliose dal crinale dei lontani monti, come ne videro dentro la lor notte gli occhî del poeta paradisiaco; con topazio liquido e oro, con nimbo di tenui nuvole rosa; e sul declivio e nelle rugiade de' prati prossimi era come il presagio e l'anticipato riverbero della splendidezza imminente.

Dolci anni! La Grigna risfavillante contro il tramonto, quando la dolomia pareva tutta un rubino. Il giovane marito, arrivando, la stringeva come un amante fervido. Dal freddo specchio del lago la parete rupestre balzava selvaggiamente; cupe e fonde, le valli rimandavano l'ululato de' loro torrenti e nei dirupi dove s'annidano i falchi erano torri, ed èremi, nel tramonto, rossi. Ed erme, come un pensiero: antiche erme sotto i platani e i mormoranti faggi, negli antichi giardini. Le generazioni passarono! E dalla terra esalava l'antico anelito, l'antica preghiera. (M 557–58)

[They returned, like a dream, the charms of the happy years, the drawing rooms, the draperies: (her girlfriends and the young men spoke, elegant, with burning thoughts): the majolica ware, the fondants. Or at the villa, marvelous dawns from the ridge of the distant mountains, as the eyes of the celestial poet had seen them in their night; with liquid topaz and gold, with the halo of tenuous pink clouds; and on the slope and in the dew of the nearby meadows there seemed to be the presage and the anticipated reflection of the imminent splendor.

Sweet years! The Grigna gleaming against the sunset, when the entire dolomite seemed to be a ruby. Her young husband, arriving, squeezed her like an ardent lover. From the cold mirror of the lake the rocky wall bobbed wildly; dark and deep, the valleys echoed the howl of their torrents and in the crags where the falcons nest were towers, and hermitages, red in the sunset. Secluded hermitages, like a thought: ancient hermitages under the plantains and the whispering beech trees, in the ancient gardens. The generations passed. And from the earth was exhaled the ancient yearning, the ancient prayer.]

The flexibility of free indirect discourse to evoke either a sympathetic consonance or ironic dissonance of voices is fully exploited in Gadda's parodic stylizations. The ironic contextualization of Donna Teresa's remembrances is present in the "false notes" (Cohn 1978, 117) that appear early on in her mental language: the "burning thoughts" of her young friends, the sublimation of the bourgeois salon or country villa. These thoughts are soon invaded, however, by an authorial lyricism, as is apparent to the reader familiar with Gadda's obsessively repeated repertory of sublime images (distant mountains, whispering trees, lofty towers, and hermitages, etc.). No longer a mere parodic stylization of Teresa's thoughts, the exaggerated lyricism of these images belongs to the emphatic excess that Gadda recognized in his own "symbolistic" and "puerile" manners (RI 396). The price of these transitions along the sliding scale of lyrical consonance and paradoic dissonance is the sacrifice of character identity and integrity. Not only do Donna Teresa's thoughts undergo a rinsing in the Gaddian sublime, so do those of almost all the other characters in the novel. Zoraide dreams of going with Franco "nell'ombra fonda di lontane selve o giardini" [in the dark shadows of distant forests or gardens]; Luigi envisions "foreste immense, su di cui trasmigrano le nubi sognanti" [immense forests, over which migrate the dreamy clouds] (M 494, 529). As Guido Baldi comments, behind the supposed parody in *La meccanica* of the bovarism of the characters through free indirect discourse lurks the genuine, first-person bovarism of the author himself (Baldi 1972, 45).

The massive presence of parodic stylization is also crucial for the evolution of the "ideological function" of narrative voice in Gadda's works (Genette 1980, 256). Not an "artist of the idea," as is Dostoyevsky (Bakhtin 1984a, 85), Gadda is an artist of the expression of the idea. The distinction is substantial. In Gadda's works one does not find the swarming parley of thoughts, ideas, and outlooks found in an author such as Dostoyevsky. To the contrary, ideas and *ideologies* are confined, in a neurotic fashion, to an obsessive core that is repeatedly reworked and hypertrophied into a grand linguistic edifice. As Gian Carlo Roscioni remarks, "the pluri-articulated complexity of structures and ornamentations often hides stimuli and motivations of a disconcerting simplicity" (Roscioni 1975, 170). Centrifugal and schizophrenic in form, Gadda is highly centripetal and paranoiac in content. There rarely appears in his works a neutral delegation of "other" ideas to competent spokespersons. Ideological difference exists only within the debasing framework of tendentious parody.

The characters of *La meccanica* become focal points for the dismantlement of other extratextual discourses through parody. Zoraide is a maquette for "a late-blooming D'Annunzian" (M 471), the Velaschis for bourgeois doublespeak, the motorcycling Franco—"il guidatore, dattilografo e lynotipista vertiginoso" [the driver, a vertiginous typist and linotypist] (M 561)—for the futurist celebration of speed. But the principal parodied discourse in *La meccanica* is that of socialism and social humanitarianism. Gadda's parodic ridicule of socialist discourse revolves around two characters, the serious and hardworking Luigi Pessina and his nasty and repugnant cousin Gildo. Gildo is the demonized caricature of what Gadda saw as the socialist hooliganism nearly responsible for the destruction of the Italian war effort and nation through fomented disorder and defeatism. Physically loathsome and morally base, Gildo takes to "plagiarizing" the socialist newspaper *Avanti* (M 473) to justify his own cowardly draft dodging and later desertion. Only at death's door, after he is shot in the back running away from a patrol, does he evoke a moment of authorial *pietas* (M 580–81).

The theme of the military deserter, ultimate symbol of the heuristic regression from n to n - 1, was an obsessive one for the interventionist Gadda. In his discussion on narration *ab exteriore* in *Racconto italiano*, Gadda wrote that he could position his authorial presence in the novel as that of a soldier who has made sacrifices for the ideal of country in order to counterpoint the "idea of the deserter" (RI 481). This is what he does in *La meccanica*, both in the novel and in an introductory note with which he intended to preface its publication in *Solaria:* "The above mentioned novel is the expression of my exasperated bitterness as an Italian, a nationalist, and a soldier, for the 'evil' which preceded our intervention and stagnated the war" (cited in Isella 1989a, 1197).

This authorial persona erupts in bouts of sarcastic parody against socialist rhetoric when his exasperated bitterness can no longer be contained within the confines of narrative story. Such is the case when the description of Luigi Pessina's reaction to the antiwar socialist press is abruptly abandoned for a direct authorial attack on that discourse:

> Banner headlines, titles, captions, columns, cartoons: it was, for months and months, a joy for the ears, a feast for the eyes. Every attempt was made to stop "the event." And if the heavy artillery was aimed against "the sugar manufacturers," the "iron manufacturers," "the Lybians," "Salandra's uniformed jackals," the "beastlike criminality of the evil Carabinieri," the "scoundrels of San Fedele," the "nationalist brothels," concerning the physical or metaphysical entities of which it would be difficult to pass judgment, certainly however the true fear was one, and in the end it was the most logical: the fear that the real aspect of the country might unveil itself to the hearts and consciousnesses of the humble, that is to say of the afflicted, the delirious, the illiteratoids; the fear that Italy might appear to them no longer a neoclassical allegory or a Metternichian geographical expression, not a fissured pot from which to wrench antimilitarist conscripts toward stinking barracks, but finally a fact, a living nation. That's when the apostles risked retirement. The "tragic event," the "slaughter," were deprecated not so much

in themselves, as for the presumable political consequences: first and most odious the necessary adherence of the masses to the idea of country. (M 517–18)

Luigi, the other pole for the parody of socialist rhetoric in the novel, reads the *Avanti* diligently but remains untouched by its tendentious meanspiritedness. Luigi is a studious but gullible "autodidact" who spent his youth between "work and thought," a socialist variant of Mazzini's "thought and action" (M 495–96). He embodies a worthy but also disingenuous and anemic idealism that finds its biographical metaphors in his unsuspecting cuckoldry and his tuberculosis, a disease Gadda once feared he had contracted at Cellelager (GGP 769–70). This naive and nonpragmatic socialist idealism is mocked in gentler fashion in Gadda's parody of the Milanese *Società Umanitaria*, the charitable institution where Luigi underwent his professional and cultural formation.

Gadda's excursus on the *Umantaria* is by far the longest and most researched parody in *La meccanica*, occupying most of the second chapter. The laudatory rhetoric of three lengthy tomes on the *Umanitaria* is quoted and parodied in the novel's ironic reproduction of the organization's history and culture of philanthropic idealism (see Isella 1989a, 1188–94). The operation bears an unmistakable debt to Manzoni's procedure of historical documentation, citation, and ironic commentary in his reconstruction of superstitious attitudes toward the 1630 Milanese plague in *I promessi sposi*. Despite the satire, Gadda's depiction of the *Umanitaria*, and of its socialist product, the young Luigi Pessina, is tinged with a nostalgic sympathy—so much so, it seems, that Gadda worried over how the regime would react if *La meccanica* were ever to be published.

When word began to circulate in 1929 that Gadda was working on a "book on the third Italy," publisher Leo Longanesi, known for his fascist sympathies, asked Gadda's cousin, Piero Gadda Conti, for more information (Isella 1989a, 1176). Gadda wrote to Gadda Conti that the novel did not express a flag-waving patriotism but a love of country which was revealed in his polemic against deserters and his description of battle scenes. He also expressed his concern that Longanesi's interest should not result in his being subjected to the fascist repressive policy of the *confino*, the forced residence in isolated southern villages, since he did not spare the misdeeds of the Italian military command in the novel and demonstrated "some touches of human sympathy for the *Umanitaria*, etc." (LPGC 12). Certainly there is much in the novel that would have appealed to the regime. Gadda's interventionism, nationalism, and anti-socialism expressed in *La meccanica* were consonant with the official rhetoric of the party, and he was not beyond adapting his own ideological bêtes noires to the greater glory of the regime. His long-standing polemic against the "Franciscan" exaltation of the humble, an attitude he shared with Pareto and D'Annunzio, seems to find its resolution precisely in the advent to power of the fascists in the early twenties: "The adjective humble is typical in the history of Italy until all of '22–'23: the humble worker and the humble servant were the tasty morsel for the tender hearts that abound in Italy, like its stockings of false wool and its catarrh" (M 589). And yet one of the problems of voice in *La meccanica* is the lack of a character who serves as a spokesperson for the ideological function of the narration. Grifonetto Lampugnani, the young fascist protagonist in *Racconto italiano*, shared several biographical traits with Gadda and was a mouthpiece for some of the author's own political ideals. There is not a similar nationalist or protofascist character in *La meccanica*. There is no one in whom the autobiographical pain and rage of the Gaddian authorial voice can be fully lyricized. The character in the novel closest to Gadda and his ethos is in fact the socialist Luigi Pessina. He is also its most sympathetic character.

The omission of the autobiographical protagonist in *La meccanica* is not casual, I believe, but is motivated, at least in part, by political considerations. Already in Gadda's 1924 projections for the *Racconto italiano*, Grifonetto's fascist idealism and *squadrismo* were to be marred by his "knowledge of the vile motives that led to the first punitive mission" (RI 469), one of a series of disillusionments responsible for his climactic murder-suicide. In Gadda's notes to his other unfinished 1928 novel, *Dejanira Classis*, he rails against the false moralism of the times and the inexcusable political instrumentalization by the fascist magistrates of the Renzo Pettine murder case, which was to serve as the real-world model for the novel: "The trial was tragically intimate, psychological, a family affair, and there is no justification for political grandstanding, not even in a roundabout way" (cited in Isella 1989c, 1316).

The sway of satirical parody and self-abnegation in Gadda's authorial voice consistently subjects his autobiographical protagonists to an ironic and often derisive ridicule of self-critique. Such a procedure must have been felt to be impossible in the fascist Italy of 1928–29 in a novel as overtly political and satirical as *La meccanica*. It is an awareness manifest in a manuscript note of January 2, 1929, concerning the "third revision" of the *Umanitaria* chapter: "The delicate political argument lies in my hand like a coin that cannot be spent: I cannot treat it with that freedom and open-mindedness that perhaps would make of it a work of a certain merit. . . . With an acrid manner, which is the one I prefer for myself, I would like to depict all of the senseless life of useless words and passions characteristic of our people. . . . And, then again, this is not a propitious time for a manner that would perhaps offend, even unintentionally, the dogmas of the moment" (cited in Isella 1989a, 1195).

Gadda's published works were never censured by the regime, although a lengthy delay in the 1934 publication of *Il castello di Udine* because of the Florentine censor's objections to certain obscenities caused the author no small amount of humiliation and grief (LS 508–15; LGC 12). Gadda did feel pressured to change the nature of his discourse during the fascist years, to impose a muzzle on the ideological function of his native and necessary style. Later he would lament bitterly in the words of Tacitus that he had arrived at old age under the gag of silence, "per silentium ad senectutem pervenere" (VM 508; EP 225). One can only speculate on the extent to which this perceived political pressure curtailed Gadda's aspirations to become a modern poet of civic rectitude and eliminated forever from his narrative horizon the Manzonian ideal of a measured civic discourse. Writing of *La cognizione del dolore*, Piero Pucci has argued that Gadda is an extreme example of a repressed civic consciousness during the fascist years. Unable to project a possible reparation for the evils of the world, nor resigned to that evil, he redirects his fury to the microscopic objects of the physical world, rendering that fury both "demented" and "comic" at the same time (Pucci 1967, 51). This frustration in Gadda is present long before fascism, appearing repeatedly in his war diary. It is a native temperament that is nourished, however, by the regime, especially in light of Gadda's early belief that fascism would offer a pragmatic solution to Italy's ills. When he would be able to write "freely" after the fall of Mussolini, Gadda's long-repressed civic cry remained obsessively trapped in the coordinates of the fascist *ventennio* issuing forth in the bilious spew of invective and obscenity of *Eros e Priapo*.

GADDA *milanese e scapigliato*

> Dio liberi!, uno scrittore: uno scrittore arzigogolato e barocco, come Jean Paul, o Carlo Gozzi, o Carlo Dossi, o un qualche altro Carlo anche peggio di questi due (C 26).

> God forbid! a writer: a baroque and labyrinthine writer, like Jean Paul, or Carlo Gozzi, or Carlo Dossi, or some other Carlo even worse than these two (AWG 13).

The concept of a history of Italian literature as the affirmation of different regional traditions interacting across space and time has become a foregrounded paradigm in Italian criticism.[14] Certainly one of the strongest regional traditions in this sense is the "Lombard line," dating back from Gadda and his more recent emulators to the medieval Bonvesin de la Riva, the author, Gadda recalled, of the "sinquanta cortesie" or "fifty courtesies," among which the prohibition of wiping one's nose on the sleeve of one's table companion ("Cinema," MF 62). That the fiercely Milanese Gadda occupies a defining position in the Lombard line is without question. This is especially evident in his early period, characterized by the constant backdrop of Milan and its mores, from "San Giorgio in Casa Brocchi" to the sketches of *L'Adalgisa,* from *La meccanica* to *La cognizione del dolore.* The problem lies in establishing Gadda's relationship with the other main coordinates of the Lombard line: the use of Milanese dialect by Carlo Maria Maggi and Carlo Porta, Manzoni and founding narrative exemplar of *I promessi sposi;* the political-ethical school of Milanese thought from the Enlightenment to Carlo Cattaneo; the linguistic expressionism of Carlo Dossi and other writers of the Scapigliatura (Cavallini 1977, 106–7).[15]

Two elements bind the disparate threads of the Lombard line which have profound echoes in Gadda. There is the pronounced "bourgeois" structure of Lombard and Milanese society (whether adulated or execrated, or both, as in the case of Gadda) that has informed the ethos of its writers (Isella 1984, 4–5). Bourgeois Milan is ubiquitous in Gadda's early works, in its dual allegiance to "famiglia e lavoro" [family and work] (A 467), to community (clan), and to the pocketbook: "the legitimate desire for gain, for prosperity, a cordial and civil brotherhood" ("Milano," SD 1075). The Lombard line has also been characterized by the notion that the representation of reality in literature can only be pursued through a captious attention to both a regional and a national linguistic reality (Siciliano 1970, 283–84). It is this language tension, regardless of its various resolutions (Porta's use of dialect, Manzoni's option for a Florentine monochromaticism, the studied and exquisitely literary Lombard-Tuscan expressionism in the Scapigliati), which is Gadda's great inheritance from the Lombard line and his great contribution to its definition.

Despite Gadda's own strong sense of affinity with the early nineteenth-century civic and literary tradition of Manzoni, Porta, and Cattaneo, the early reviews of his work invariably linked him to the Scapigliati, not to the "macabre" and scandalous Scapigliatura of mummies, disease, and postunification *bòheme* (Emilio Praga, Igino Ugo Tarchetti, Arrigo, and

Camillo Boito) but to the bon-mot satire and literary extravagance of Carlo Dossi and the "second" Scapigliatura (Gian Pietro Lucini, Carlo Linati, the Piedmontese Giovanni Faldella). A spiritual bond between Gadda and Dossi was proclaimed immediately upon publication of *La Madonna dei Filosofi*. In his review of the work, Alfredo Gargiulo characterizes Gadda as a writer who ridicules every object that befalls him with "an acrid literary satisfaction" reminiscent of "the most authentic Dossi, the extremely literary bizarre spirit" (Gargiulo 1958, 549). Gargiulo's association of Gadda with Dossi has much to do with the linguistic and conceptual gamesmanship of *La Madonna dei Filosofi* and Gadda's other earliest published works: the relish of paradox and conceptual oxymorons for their own sake (Roscioni 1969b, 75), the mixture of bizarre humor and temperamental humors, the indulgence in an eccentric literary expressionism. Gargiulo criticizes the "gratuitous" element in the literary eccentricity of Dossi and Gadda that is unable at times "to translate itself into artistic realizations sufficiently motivated in their links and developments" (Gargiulo 1958, 550).

Gianfranco Contini broadened the link between Gadda and the Scapigliati and anchored it to a positive "post-Romantic avant-garde" patrimony of linguistic expressionism. In his 1934 essay "C. E. Gadda o del pastiche," Contini moved beyond Gargiulo's Gadda-Dossi linkage to trace a more extensive parallel between Gadda and the expressionism of authors such as Lucini and Linati (Contini 1989, 3–4). But it was especially in his 1963 introduction to *La cognizione del dolore* that Contini explicated the literary affinities between Gadda and the linguistic Scapigliati. Returning specifically to Dossi and the Piedmontese Giovanni Faldella, Contini argued that the "aristocratic" Scapigliati are, like Gadda, "anarchistic conservatives who want reserved for themselves a total freedom of the laboratory." Parodoxically, they both derive the authorization for their linguistic preciosities, Gadda's self-declared "ribòboli sterili" from Manzoni's search for a Florentine "zero degree" language, a search that resulted instead in a language connoted by a "differential affectation" for the vast majority of Italians and consequently open to parody (Contini 1989, 30–31).

Despite Contini's and later Dante Isella's efforts (1984, 238–39) to distance the Gadda-Scapigliatura expressionism from any sort of indolent aestheticism, Gadda himself retained a defiant attitude toward the association. To begin with, there were his repeated denials of any familiarity with the Scapigliati confirmed by the testimony of friends such as Giulio Cattaneo and Carlo Linati and substantiated by the presence in Gadda's personal library of only one book pertaining to the movement, Linati's 1944 *Dossi* (Cattaneo 1973, 79; Linati 1982, 82; Lucchini 1988, 57). The Scapigliati receive almost no mention in Gadda's essays and fiction, apart from a 1949 radio presentation commissioned by the RAI and entitled "La scapigliatura milanese" (SD 970–73).

"La scapigliatura milanese" provides the official testimony of Gadda's attitude toward the Scapigliati. In preparing it, Gadda had lamented to Contini, of all people, that it was an "incredible waste of time" and poked fun at the "disheveled" movement while bowing ironically to Contini's definition of them as Gadda's forerunners: "If only these louse-infested fellows had had their hair cut! They would have saved us this hairdressing chapter. On the other hand, they are dear and respectable prodromes and one must love them. Prodromes of our discharges" (LGC 66). The essay itself has a mechanical and unexpressive sense of duty about it, with a de rigueur Gaddization of the movement: "A certain propensity toward the search for a freer expression, where language and dialect end up contaminating one another with bizarre results: a certain humor, a certain whim, grief, delusion, hope, physical illness, social evil . . . they react to a certain conformism, to a certain mushy Manzonianism, between conservative and sanctimonious. . . . There is in them a dual motive of interest: the moral question and the philological question. . . . Disbelievers, and, on more than one occasion, blasphemers" (SD 970–72).

Gadda's comments on the movement are guarded. Their derision is "marginal" and lacks the "firm hostility" of the much admired Carlo Cattaneo while their splintered prose is far from Cattaneo's "classical granite." Only occasionally does their "second-hand *maledettismo*" compensate for their empty virtuosity or "academia" (SD 972).

Underlying this less than enthusiastic evaluation was Gadda's feeling that the satire and expressionism of the Scapigliati authors, unlike his own, was artificial, unmotivated, and aristocratic. Dossi had declared in his introduction to *La desinenza in A* that in art he was "aristocraticissimo," but for Gadda it was the aristocratic origins and wealth of several members of the Scapigliati that were sore points, and he once declared that "the Scapigliati did not have my infancy, the war, the Predappio: many, like Dossi and Arrigo Boito and his brother, were well-off" (LPGC 86).[16]

The hostility was undoubtedly fueled by the accusations of stylistic affectedness and lack of motivation in Gadda's own early works which had generated the first comparisons to Dossi. In subsequent years those critics such as Gian Carlo Vigorelli (1955) or Gian Carlo Roscioni (1969b) who have downplayed or denied the affinity between Gadda and the Scapigliati have emphasized precisely the motivational factor which distinguishes Gadda's necessary style. Nevertheless, a consonance between Gadda and the Scapigliati, and in particular between Gadda and Dossi, is manifest in Gadda's earliest works. Only when Gadda would motivate his satiric deformation with a truly painful sense of tragic pathos and the complex perspective of his later grotesque and macaronic styles would the surface resemblance to the Scapigliati yield to Gadda's own organic and necessary form.

The resemblance is immediately visible in "Teatro," published in *Solaria* but apparently sketched as early as 1924 (RI 521) and later chosen to open *La Madonna dei Filosofi*. In "Teatro" the theater is a symbol of the conventionality and falsitude of bourgeois Milanese culture in much the same way that it had been for the Scapigliati. The characters in "Teatro" are little more than shallow caricatures, fodder for the ironic ruminations of a first-person narrator, who, like his Dossian counterpart in *La desinenza in A,* is never developed beyond his function as a bemused ironist of the Milanese bourgeoisie and its banal aspirations to sublimity.

What most interests Gadda in this comic satire is the shallow fictitiousness of conventional melodrama itself. In his presentation of "Teatro" to *Solaria* editor Alberto Carocci, Gadda described it as an ironic and negative piece on the theater and the Foscolian and Wagnerian "Marriage of the Arts" (LS 16). The melodramatic spectacle is decomposed into its basic elements of scenery, staging, and language. The narrator experiences a racing heart and confusion when he notices some rocks moving onstage; he discovers a telltale mark where the cloth sky has been repaired; he compares the dragging train of the leading lady's gown to a street sweeper and dissects her speech into its operatic archaism and artificiality.

This smug satire of theatrical conventionality, reminiscent of Tolstoy's curt dismissal of operatic art in *War and Peace* through the eyes of young Nastasha Rostov, seems sadly inadequate as a pretense for Gadda's insistence on the necessary motivation of his style. As a "negative" jab at the melodramatic theater, "Teatro" never moves beyond a relatively gratuitous satire. It is a limitation partially overcome in another short piece of the same period on the cinema. Gadda wrote to Carocci that "Cinema" (published in *Solaria* in 1928 and later included in *La Madonna dei Filosofi*) was the "positive" half of "Teatro"; he felt that it contained a continuation of his ideas on art, but now in relation to the experiences of

the individual who "lives with the most baroque appearances of the phenomenal world; his grief, his fantasy, his ingenuousness and his greed
mix with the most bizarre unforseen events of color, sound, names, memo-
ries" (LS 16, 61). In its still somewhat awkward amalgam of subjectivity
and phenomenality, "Cinema" is a more sophisticated and expressive work
than "Teatro," and it points the way to the more motivated expressionism of *L'Adalgisa*.

Among the Scapigliati, Gadda's early prose is most akin to the tendentious humor of Carlo Dossi. Both authors undermine the middle line
of postunification Italian detested by Pasolini through the use of personal neologisms, archaic forms, Latinisms, onomatopoeia, foreign terms,
rare or constructed Italian forms corresponding to Lombard dialectics (although the concordance of these dialectics in the two authors is limited
[Lucchini 1988, 57]). Both indulge in synesthesia and the superimposi-
tion of impressions such as "una cucchaiata di silenzio" [a spoonful of
silence] in Dossi or "un cucchiaino di coraggio" [a teaspoon of courage]
in Gadda (Marinetto 1973, 117). Both practice a certain graphic experimentation such as accenting the antepenultimate vowel in proparoxytone
words. Contini points to Gadda's accenting of the word "ribòboli" in *La
cognizione del dolore* as an unmistakably Dossian flourish (Contini 1989,
23), but Gadda never indulged in naively programmatic and excessive
innovations as did Dossi in his use of double commas or the Spanish
inverted question mark.

Dossi, like Gadda, tended to rework certain core motifs (Isella 1958,
5), and the satirization of bourgeois Milanese conventionality and bla-
tant misogynism in the two authors result in a surprisingly consanguineous family of satirical caricatures. Both authors also cultivate an ironic
tension in their prose that is released in clever and often obscene witticisms, in erotic and misogynistic conceits (the obscenity is more vulgar
in Dossi than in Gadda). Typically these comic climaxes do not lend pro-
fundity or reflection to the events which precede them. As in a stand-up
comic routine, the events function as a buildup for the final quip. In act 3
of Dossi's *Desinenza in A*, the reader is presented with a menagerie of
grotesque feminists who have come to listen to the tirades of the "celebrated Sofonisba Altamura of Connecticut." At the end of Altamura's
harangue, the narrator turns to his female companion Delia, "a most ignorant child who only knows how to love, a canary who keeps my cage
merry," and asks her if she too wishes to be "emancipated." Delia responds that as far as she is concerned she is happy to spend her entire life

under him: "m'accontento di starti tutta la vita sotto" (Dossi 1981, 220). Numerous other sketches in the work end in similar obscene witticisms, lending the volume the somewhat monotonous rhythm of a string of narrative jokes.

Analogous examples of gratuitous and obscene wit pervade Gadda's early prose. In "La Madonna dei filosofi," a long excursus on Sir Ishmael Digbens's philosophical opus concludes with a comic and vaguely obscene allusion in the crescendo of increasingly detailed tracts in Latin by his aged widow on how widows can find consolation for their grief (MF 92). In "Crociera mediterranea" a brief digression on pious modesty in response to the "pantaloncini bebé di seta verde pisello" [pea-green silk baby shorts] of the fetching Signorina Clorinda climaxes in a sexual pun concerning the Catholic mass: "Certo però, durante l'Elevazione, quei, diremo così, pantaloncini, anima mia!, non era il caso di insistere" [Certainly however, during the Elevation, those, let us say, little shorts, oh my soul!, it was not opportune to dwell upon them] (CU 191). Both authors engage in the four forms of Freud's tendency-wit: obscene, hostile, cynical, and skeptical; but their tendentious satire often does not rise above a shallow delight with prurient obscenity.

Any discussion of Gadda's relationship to the Lombard line and the Scapigliati must have as its endpoint the "Milanese sketches" of L'Adalgisa (1944). In L'Adalgisa Gadda becomes the portraitist of the turn-of-the-century "grand Milan, still traditional (and positivist) and already futurist (and industrial): hard-working and intensely Liberty, and tormented by a crisis of transition and growth, dramatically ambiguous" (Arbasino 1971, 188). Gadda had written to friend Ambrogio Gobbi in 1934 that he wanted to be the "Robespierre of the Milanese bourgeoisie" (LAM 46), but as the sketches of L'Adalgisa began to appear in various literary journals several years later, the Terror had been transmuted into a satiric but also nostalgic document of a fading Milanese milieu.

L'Adalgisa is a final, ironic tribute to the Milanese society of Gadda's formation, and in particular to the intertwined upper-middle-class clans of the Caviggioni, Trabattoni, Berlusconi, Gnecchi, Cavenaghi, and others, "[m]arried amongst themselves, related amongst themselves, business associates amongst themselves" ("Un 'concerto' di centoventi professori," A 468). This closed world of Milanese society with its aged patriarchs, philological societies, young engineers, and confused homonymy constitutes a veritable tribe or gens mediolanis. It is a people distinguished by a forma mentis sui generis which finds its expression, and can only find its expression, in its native dialect. The linguistic innovation in *L'Adalgisa* is the explosion of Milanese dialect as the necessary form for the expression of Milanese thought.

A connection between language, ethnicity, and ethos appears throughout Gadda's works from his early adherence to Fichte's thought on linguistic nationalism in *Racconto italiano* to his numerous references to the "Celtic" and "Germanic" constitution of himself and his Lombard folk. "Our dialect, in whose cordial and frank sounds are evidenced such a large part of our temperament, more sincere than persuasive, bears imprinted in itself the traces of our history" (VM 515). Thus begins the 1953 "Il terrore del dàttilo," Gadda's humorous treatise on the relationship between the Milanese spirit and the Milanese dialect, a linguistic theory anchored to a biological and ethnic concept of language: "Not infecund . . . are the Longobard blood and descent, the *mens germanica*, which emerges in the expressive attitude: because of which the lips seem to emit the utterance more from an innate logical emotion, carried originally in the blood, than from the paralogisms derived from the schools or the forum" (VM 515).

The positive Longobard component of the Lombard mind lies in the ethical pragmatism of the Milanese: "in the sense that he judges the action by its end, he measures against the action and adapts to it the value of the idea since the idea is only valid to the extent that it elaborates pragmatically a reality" (VM 515–16). For this reason, Gadda continues, it is difficult for the Milanese writer to detach storytelling from his own "judgment and sentiment," from "an ethical system in force in his lineage and his blood," from an "applicative end" (VM 516). The Lombard dialect bears in its very form the imprint of this ethnic mindset, beginning with its horror of the Latin/Italic dactylic word. The tendency of Milanese to reduce the Latin lexeme to the limits of the monosyllable is a rejection of the superfluous, an unconscious operation "of an economic nature: saving time, saving saliva" (VM 518). It is also the stubborn rejection of the Latin domination first encountered in the ubiquitous paroxytone accusatives of the Latin military machine—"*militem, consulem, ordinem, consulem*" (VM 521). The underside of this "Celtic inferiority complex" (VM 521) is the primitive narrow-mindedness, avarice, and egoism of the tribe. It is assailed without mercy in the hallucinatory rage of *La cognizione del dolore* ("with eyes hollowed in distrust, with the sphincter blocked by avarice and red within the shadow of his nits . . . a dark red . . . like a Celt who's taken to the woods in the mountains . . . who fears the pallor of Rome and is terrified by its dactyls . . .

militem, ordinem, cardinem, consulem . . . the I of the shadows, the animalesque I of the forests" [C 638; AWG 89]). It is whimsically mocked in *L'Adalgisa*. *L'Adalgisa* is the comic affirmation of the linguistic vis of the Lombard and Milanese spirit summed up at the conclusion of "Il terrore del dàttilo": "'Mì voeuri pensà con la mia testa.' 'Mì son vün che bisogna lassà büi in del sò broeud.' 'I mè danée me piasen a mì'" [I want to think with my head. I'm the type you have to let simmer in his stew. I like my money] (VM 521). The same narrow-minded ethnic and linguistic pragmatism is comically celebrated and ridiculed in *L'Adalgisa* via the syncopated vigor of Milanese speech, as when a group of concert goers assaults the number 24 tram:

> Elsa poté ricevere una prima dose di gomitate da parte della società musogònica: la quale, assalito il tram, lo aveva poi saturato in un attimo con grida di "Karlòta kì! Kì! Ven kì! setesgiò-kì! Vegnìi kì, kì! Gioàn! . . . Gioàn! Karlòta! . . . Karlòta! . . . Teresina! Occupato! Karlòta! Occupàaato! S-ciào, meno mal che semm reüssìi a tchapàll"; anzi ciapàll, in grafìa nostra. E ancora, e mentre quello scatolone già rotolava, ciapàll, e l'èmm ciapàa, e a momenti le ciapàvom no, poi però l'èmm ciapàa, e hô finìi per ciapàll: e s'el füdèss stàa de minga ciapàll, cioè fosse accaduto non arrivare a prenderlo, il tram: o non si sta parlando del 24? ("Un 'concerto,'" A 452–53)

> [Elsa was able to receive a first dose of elbowing by the snoutogonic society: which, having assaulted the tram, had then saturated it in an instant with cries of "Carlotta, here! Here! Come here! sit down here! Come here, here! John! . . . John! Carlotta! . . . Carlotta! . . . Theresa! This seat's taken! Carlotta! It's taaaken! Hi, thank goodness we managed to ketch it"; or rather, kech it, in our spelling. And still more, and while that big box was already rolling, kech it, and we kod it, and we almost didn't kech it, but then we kod it, and I ended up keching it; and if it happened that we didn't kech it, that is to say, if it had happened that we had not been able to catch it, the tram: we are talking about the 24, aren't we?]

The widespread appearance of dialect in the speech of the characters of *L'Adalgisa* does initiate a transformation of the authorial caricatural parody of *La meccanica* into the artistically more satisfying self-caricature of the characters who channel their spiritual vigor into a narrowly comic linguistic form. They still remain caricatures, however, imprisoned in that linguistic form. Only Adalgisa, a woman who comes from the popular class, can overcome narrow caricature with dialect. She remains comic but manages to express an array of true emotions and sentiments in dialect. Apostrophized as "la Tettón" ("L'Adalgisa," A 529), in memory of the voluptuous and crafty beloved of Carlo Porta's forelorn Marchionn di gamb avert, Adalgisa is the only character in *L'Adalgisa* who infuses dialect with the imprint of humanity and pathos of Porta's memorable characters. When she mockingly berates her lover Carlo, who has complained about the inferior quality of her ink, Adalgisa asserts her independence and worth as a person even if she comes from a less-cultured class than Carlo: "E poeu ten bée a ment che chí sèmm in cà mia, e minga in cà toa! . . . E in cà mia gh'è l'inciòster che me fa còmod a mì . . . cara el me bel ragionàtt!" [And you can just keep in mind that here we are in my house, not in your house! . . . And in my house you'll find the ink that I like . . . my dear Mr. Bookkeeper] ("L'Adalgisa," A 542).

With its twin poles of dialect and refined literary eclecticism, *L'Adalgisa* is the culmination of Gadda's early expressionism. The centrifugal plurilingualism works toward the eccentric poles of a stylized Tuscan Italian, and a stylized Lombard dialecticism is now fully exploited (see Lucchini 1988, 93–94). This is evident in the erudite and literary manipulation and reification of dialect, in the continual glosses of dialect words in lengthy and digressive notes, in the active engagement of Milanese dialect and dialecticism with the rest of the eclectic assortment of heterogeneous linguistic materials. Not merely a privileged linguistic instrument for the representation of a certain Milanese milieu, dialect becomes a central component of Gadda's foregrounded milieu of literary expressionism itself.

In *L'Adalgisa,* as will be the case in all of Gadda's mature macaronic works, dialect is one of many languages, and not always the dominant one. In *L'Adalgisa* it has not yet penetrated into the narrative discourse itself. It remains circumscribed in the speech of the characters, and not all the characters. It is not through the discursive language of dialect and mimetic discourse that subjectivity seeks its authentication in the Gaddian text, but, in a way analogous to the poetry of Eugenio Montale, in the momentary glimpses of another possibility beyond the thicket of reality and language. Language is a part of the chaotic cacophony that surrounds troubled subjectivity. Transcendence occurs in a moment of separation and dispersion into an ineffable other place. This is the journey of the young bride Elsa Caviggioni, whose sublime dispersion amid the "ribòbolo" of the symphony violins anticipates that of her Roman counterpart Liliana Balducci: "Così, fra ventriloqui e trilli, il ribòbolo e le piroette dei legni: la cavata diritta e languida d'un solitario violino. . . . Lei, lei sola, era stata strappata via dalla comune speranza, divelta dal credere: come stanca foglia il vento dalla chioma tempestosa del faggio" [So, among ventriloquies and trills, the witticism and pirouettes of the woods: the straight and languid air of a solitary violin. . . . She, she alone, had been torn away from the common hope, uprooted from the faith: as the wind rips a tired leaf from the stormy crown of the beech tree] ("Un 'concerto,'" A 460).

In *L'Adalgisa* Gadda does not refute his native temperament for the *ribòbolo*. His great polyphonic works are not the result of a conversion to mimetic and linguistic realism but of a maturation of his native literary expressionism. From the sterile witticisms of "Teatro," the *ribòbolo* in *L'Adalgisa* becomes part of a dense literary expressionism at the service of a complex and motivated ontological tension. One finds in its pages flashes of the universal struggle between subjectivity in search of authenticity and the prisonhouse of reality and language. Expressionism in Gadda is always at the service of an ultimately irrational or intuitive transcendence to the Kantian "Ding an sich." The more intricate the linguistic and phenomenal morass, the more compelling and necessary the linguistic short-circuiting which propels subjectivity beyond the circumscription of tribe, reality, and language to the realm of renewed possibility.

Absurd Analogies: Philosophy, Technology, and Literature

Il metodo è oscura prescienza, analogia—(si ricostruisce indovinando per analogia) (MM 1324).

[Method is an obscure prescience, an analogy—(one reconstructs guessing through analogy).]

Gadda's multiple interests in the fields of philosophy, technology, mathematics, science, and literature result in a promiscuous mingling of specialized languages in his search to capture the world's totality. It is not a consolatory amalgam but one which hinges on the contrast of discourses in a "spastic tension" between language, subjectivity, and referentiality.

"Spastic tension" is a term that has become associated with Gadda's literary method, especially with what the author declared to be his subjection of words to a "new utilization" which "torments" and "deforms" them like a "taut rubber-band" ("Come lavoro," VM 437). Gadda first used the expression in a note in the *Racconto italiano* in which he defended his native eccentricity and expressionism as a motivated epistemological exercise: "Besides the absurd for ironic (Leopardi, paradoxes) or comic reasons, besides the absurd 'ridendi causa' there exists an absurd 'ratiocinandi causa,' for greater emphasis, or 'docendi causa,' or even the *symbolic* absurd 'efficiendi causa,' the absurd in depiction (my examples: the 'white hermitages'). This is like a spastic tension between the intelligence of the author and of the reader and seems also to pertain to the '*ab exteriore* effect'" (RI 484). The absurd is linked here not only to humor but to a global encounter of reason, learning, and representation which transcends the text as story to engage author and reader actively in a constructive collaboration toward new syntheses.

The necessity of linguistic and intellectual spasticity for Gadda gains in motivation in light of his vision of knowledge articulated in the *Meditazione milanese*. Knowledge is elastic and erratic because, like the reality it is and seeks to know, it is subject to polarization, multiplicity, differentiation, deformation, and impermanence. It is this affirmation that compels Gadda to submit the speculative discourse of *Meditazione* to the same spastic function he advocates for literature. Gian Carlo Roscioni observes that the autobiographical digressions, witticisms, comic notes, and erratic and aberrant exemplification in Gadda's philosophical treatise "effect a very precise function in the general economy of the work, contributing to the realization at the level of language of the 'critical dissociation' which is one of the author's fundamental objectives" (Roscioni 1974, xxxiii).

The dispersive features of Gadda's literary style in *Meditazione milanese* exist in a state of polar tension with the rational synthesis of philosophical discourse. The validity and contours of the one are measured against those of the other (Risset 1975). Literature penetrates the rational harmony of philosophy as a subversive force, undermining clarificatory order and logical closure through the aggression of expressive eccentricity. Philosophy gives focus to the literary dispersiveness, motivates its function as dialectical critique. It has been argued that the relationship is not symmetrical. The harmonious constructs of philosophy arise from the primordial disorder that literature claims for itself. Philosophy is exposed to the erosive force of literature that nestles in the "point of impossibility" of every philosophical system (Risset 1972, 258).

The tension between philosophy and literature in *Meditazione milanese* is evident in Gadda's use of analogy. Analogy is a process of thought integral to both philosophy and literature, although it typically functions in a different manner in each. In philosophy analogy is pragmatic, a means toward semantic clarification and solidity. It translates the abstract into a concrete equivalent, empowering philosophical discourse in its role as "the vigilant watchman overseeing the ordered extensions of meaning" (Ricoeur 1977, 261). Literary discourse, on the other hand, can accentuate the centrifugal or anomalous function of analogy. The goal of analogy is not to order meaning but to foster its force of refraction through the cultivation of semantic ambiguity and dissonance. Against the background of philosophy "the unfettered extensions of meaning in poetic discourse spring free" (Ricoeur 1977, 261).

In *Meditazione milanese* literary method's unfettered extensions of meaning undermine the centripetal force of philosophical analogy. Philosophical analogy retains its movement from the elusive abstract to the categorizable concrete, but it is marked by a high degree of "difference" between these two referents. The result is an interference in the hermeneutic closure of philosophical analogy, the perception of an incongruity or comic dissonance in the clarificatory analogical function, a tendency toward "distraction" (MM 807). The wayward analogies in *Meditazione milanese* corroborate philosophical affirmation with concrete examples, while simultaneously short-circuiting semantic closure with a conceptual vision that grows in centrifugality. Despite the decline at times into what Gadda himself called his "cattive facezie" or "bad witticisms" (MM 850), the analogical operation seeks to be a motivated one. The intentional eccentricity of the analogies is meant to subject the closure of ideas to the spastic tension of intelligence of Gadda's category of the absurd.

Gadda accentuates the absurd difference in the analogical comparisons by turning to both the low (comic) strata of concrete, biological physicality and to the lofty (sublime) strata of poetic mythos. The first of the "fixed ideas" that Gadda proposes to dismantle in the critical philosophy of *Meditazione* is that of substance, "la grama sostanza" [wretched substance] (MM 868). The impermanence of substance as a phenomenon and concept is illustrated by eccentric lower-stratum analogies of putrescent chickens and steak-shoe soles in a dung pit and by high literary references such as Virgil's exhortation to Dante in canto 24 of the *Inferno* on the evanescent fame of the indolent ("qual fummo in aere od in acqua la spuma" [like smoke in air or in water foam]), by the mention of Leda's twins infants or the poetic image of the chameleon's changing rainbow of colors (MM 872). This expressionistic elaboration of the analogies and examples in *Meditazione milanese* is accompanied by their erratic accumulation in Gadda's technique of chaotic enumeration. Philosopher and critic refer in these pages on substance's impermanence to girls on a swing;

the sand which covered Cyrenaic cities; the dynamics of a chess match (the central repeated analogy in their conversation); the relationship between the individual and the nation; bricks and walls; conservatives and incendiaries; spheres; grains of rice; theater gods; Heliogabalus's missing arm; passive people; the vertebrae of aqueducts in the flourishing civilization of ancient Rome; a majolica pitcher; imperial bronze and tin coins; the becoming of stars and worlds; radioactive and electrochemical phenomena; Venus emerging from her bath; machines; lumps; plant stalks; the soul of man; distant mountain peaks disappearing in the mist; alternators with vertical and horizontal axes and Mitchell suspension; the Platonic struggle between *üle* and *morphé*; automated telephone exchanges; radio stations; modern theater stages with all the latest mechanical, photogenetic, and electrical arrangements; the sulfurous volcano; the dry bed of a torrent; the dung of four-footed and two-footed beasts; modern cheese factories and Polyphemus's cheese baskets; steam-powered autoclaves; centrifugal driers and Nausicaa's laundry; the superficial biological transformations encouraged by selective cultivation; the muscles of the arms of a blacksmith, violinist, athlete, and soccer player; the nerve centers that transform the stammering solfeggio into the execution of a piano sonata (MM 866–77).

Gadda's abundant and de-automatized analogies foreground what Umberto Eco has called the hidden metonymic chain which every metaphor carries in its wake (Eco 1979). Some, perhaps many, of the analogies in *Meditazione* would be judged as falling into Eco's category of "deceiving" or "baroque" metaphors in which the excessive distance between vehicle and tenor corresponds to an intellectually and aesthetically "weak necessity" (Eco 1979, 83). Nevertheless, the intent and result of the analogies remain constant. In the continual metonymic reconstruction required by both the "good" and "bad" analogies, metonymic digression and distraction enunciate *Meditazione*'s "extentional" (Lucchini 1988, 31–32) recasting of Leibniz's *mise-en-abyme*–like monadology and preestablished harmony into Gadda's philosophy of multiple relationships, differentiation, and impermanence.

This critical dissociation at the level of language and trope is furthered by the dispersiveness of literary language in *Meditazione milanese*, in particular the diachronic expansion of discourse through the use of archaic and rare forms and abundant Latinisms. All of the other philosophical constructs discussed or dismantled in the treatise undergo a similar process, as in the deformation of Leibnizian monads into ramshackle shanties or the comparison of the system to a malefic and prattling stairwell.

As Roscioni notes, given Gadda's native style, it is perhaps not the verbal pyrotechnics that are most surprising in *Meditazione* but the seriousness and ingenuity of the speculative setup that sustains them (Roscioni 1969b, xxxiii). Literary eccentricity is grounded to a motivated core of cognitive concerns that renders Gadda's odd philosophical treatise one of his most felicitous early literary efforts as well.

Even more than philosophy, it is in technology and its language of precision that Gadda sees a positive and productive tension for literary discourse. Technology, "a field of tedious and diligent actions" (AAF 44), is how Gadda marketed his special contribution to the genteel pages of *Solaria*. Many of Gadda's essays on language stress the contributions of technology to literature, in particular the 1929 "Le belle lettere e i contributi delle tecniche" (VM 475–88). The various technical fields, which may range from science to farming to petty thievery, are, Gadda wrote in that essay, the sites of elaboration for the expressive material of language "in corpore veritatis" (VM 479). Technology brings to language the precision of experts guided by an interested and motivated pragmatism. As in Primo Levi's *La chiave inglese* (*The Monkey Wrench*), there is a deep respect in Gadda for the exactitude and "instinctive praxis" of the skilled and experienced industrial worker ("Tecnica e poesia," GA 246). Each technician "maneuvers in his field ferociously and directly, in accordance with an idea, and he manages to write as the idea demands and not with the long-winded and aimless wanderings of the pseudo-writer" ("Le belle lettere," VM 481). The literary author can create an expressive tension with the language of technology only after he has mastered that language, but he cannot overlook the contribution of a given technology because of laziness or ignorance, "by saying: 'that's difficult, I don't feel like it'" (VM 486).

It is this faith in an intimate technical knowledge that fuels much of Gadda's polemic against Filippo Tommaso Marinetti and the futurists whom he accuses of much noise built upon a profound mechanical ignorance ("L'uomo e la macchina," GA 255–61). And yet Gadda's own reverence for the machine is itself an example of what a postmodern critic such as Gianni Vattimo has termed modern culture's faith in technology and science as the final outpost of metaphysical truth. In *Meditazione milanese* the Leibnizian monad-God verticality is replaced by the empirical system endowed with a consciousness, the system-battleship and the engineer who has designed and created it: "He [the engineer] can be compared to the determining Spirit which creates the ship-organism" (MM 729). Theistic allusions and mysteries of genesis are abundant in

Gadda's reverence of the machine. The construction of a nitrogen-fertil-
izer plant in the Belgium countryside becomes a cosmogonic tale of order emerging from chaos: "Then, little by little, from the countryside of
irrationality everything was gleaned as if by the hand of a mysterious
gatherer; by the command of an invisible master; everything was found,
computed, listed, put into its place. . . . That disorder first dissolved and
then congealed in more and more valid forms, according to the most valid
guidelines of crystalization. Chaos, after months and months, generated
the organism: A factory for the fixation of atmospheric azote in fertilizer
salts" (GA 248–49).[17]

Nor is the mystification of the industrial machine and human labor
constituting Gadda's "Italian work" motif without political overtones. The
closure of factories by socialist agitators in the years immediately following World War I was anathema for Gadda because of its revolutionary implications and its adverse effect on him as a neo-graduate with a
degree in engineering (see Cattaneo 1973, 94), but also because of what
he saw as the unconscionable disdain for the pragmatic cult of the machine and the technical job performed well and without complaint. In the
1934 "Un cantiere nelle solitudini," a sort of armchair ethnography on
industrial colonialism concerning Gadda's experience at the work site for
a cotton mill in the Argentine Chaco, Gadda wrote of being impressed at
the sight of alcoholic and distrustful local *indios* "intent and bent in a
European labor":

> The man from the outside, "the gringo," whom they despise and would
> like to hate, exercises on them the effective superiority of money, mind,
> and actions. He raised factories and walls where they had huts of reeds
> and rotten straw.
>
> I found confirmation, at the worksite, of an affirmation already made
> many times and popularized in the Hegelian world of histories: the
> unconscious of every man accepts the command of those similar or
> different provided it is motivated, even if it goes against the patterns of
> habit. He abandons himself, reluctant or docile, to the technology of
> the real event. A "religio" and an economy suggest to him the acts of
> submission. (MI 114)

The lesson of Italian technical construction in the South American
outback and the religious submission of the natives to a European labor
must have been pleasing to official ears on the eve of Italy's embarkment
on the Ethiopian campaign. It is difficult to gauge if there was a propa-
gandistic intent on Gadda's part or merely a coincidence of discourses

between his faith in industrial technology and the fascist rhetoric of colonial expansion. What is certain, as Robert Dombroski has demonstrated, is that Gadda wrote a series of technical articles throughout the 1930s and early 1940s indicative of his measured support for the fascist government's policy of autarchy, its mining policy in the newly conquered Ethiopia, its massive projects of drainage and land reclamation, its resettlement policies in Sicily (Dombroski 1984a, 94–102). And while these articles are usually distinguished by their sober emphasis on technical issues and their unpolitical tone, Gadda does occasionally yield to the hagiographic reverence for Mussolini typical of the official press: "The Mussolinian spirit, which has replaced the grumblings of the Anglomaniac or Francomaniac or whatever *laissez-faire* era, is the faith in the redeeming validity of action" ("Combustibile italiano," in *La gazzetta del popolo*, 27 July 1937; cited in Dombroski 1984a, 98).[18] Many of these articles were written during and even after the veiled but scathing satire of the regime in *La cognizione del dolore*. Only in the realm of technology could Gadda remain somewhat consonant with a regime that in every other way had betrayed his hopes of a new reality in Italy.

The relationship between technology and literature and philosophy and literature is different for Gadda. Technology, like science, enjoys a pragmatic advantage over philosophy in that it does not try to encompass a totality: "ciascuno dice nel suo campo" [each speaks in his own field] ("Le belle lettere," VM 480). Unlike literature and philosophy, technology is not doomed from the start to unravel in contradictions and impossible syntheses. And while philosophy, in its realm of abstraction, may do without the concrete color of the technical word, literature, in its encapsulation of the abstract in the concrete, cannot: "that color . . . which perhaps the philosopher does not need, but which the poet certainly does" ("Le belle lettere," VM 488).

Technology endows literature with precision, but literature (and philosophy) can endow technology with metaphysical vision and universality. This collaboration becomes manifest in Gadda's third published book, *Le meraviglie d'Italia* (1939). In it are gathered for a general public various articles on Gadda's travels and technological encounters (from the construction of factories to colorful pieces on the Milanese stock market or flea market). Technology and literature complement one another in an analogical relationship meant to enhance the cognitive functions of each. In the 1934 "Un romanzo giallo nella geologia" [A detective novel in geology], the "grief" of the 1915 earthquake in the Abruzzi and the "acquired knowledge of the deep" which it has made possible underscore the need to revise anachronistic literary models no longer capable of expressing the new vision of the land gained through the discipline of geology (MI 146–47).

In "Una mattinata ai macelli" it is literature that endows the efficient technology of the slaughterhouse with the fantasy of Shakespearian tragedy. The butcher's hand is "stained like Macbeth's, horribly armed, like Macbeth's," while the medicinal distillations of the organotherapists evoke the eerie image of Shakespeare's witches as they hover over their brew intoning sorcerous incantations (MI 22, 26). A frightened steer, whose "melancholic eye seems to ask the reason from things, from the world," becomes the bovine epiphany of the bludgeoned mother and butchered Liliana in Gadda's later novels (MI 20). Amidst the pathetic cries of the young pigs, "clamorous and stridulant, uselessly stridulant," the lengthy germination of life is snuffed out by the synesthetic contraction of a "red moment" (MI 22, 23).

Throughout these essays the reader encounters the repeated conjunction of literary fantasy and technical precision through the use of bold analogies. The importance of this analogical function is perhaps most evident in the 1940 "Anastomòsi," in which there is an extended comparison between a surgical anastomosis, in this case the connection of the small intestine to the stomach, and Gadda's vision of the literary act as the extirpation of fraud in the name of the word's cognitive re-creation:

> Il maestro senza parole ha stretto la sua penna tagliente, lucidissima. . . . Ecco gli atti necessari, le escogitazioni d'una premeditante prammatica. . . . l'operatore lo solleva d'una sua mano sopra le garze e la raggiera delle pinze, lo 'esteriorizza' nella chiarità dell'elettrico, frugandovi, frugandovi, come a volervi scoprire una qualche ostinata reticenza, una simulazione pervicace, antica. . . . Le dita ironiche sembravano palpare la frode. . . . Nel nefando pasticcio della vita 'esteriorizzata,' stanata fuori dalla sua caverna come preda nell'orrore, l'uomo bianco, adesso, insinua gli aghi. Insinua la punta del suo conoscere imperterrito in quell'ammucchio delle trippe flaccide. . . . La sua dialettica si manifesta nei silenti atti; è un rifacimento biologico, un ripensare coi ferri e con le agugliate la costruzione di natura, un rivolere, un ripristinare la forma. . . . Profanando il buio segreto e l'intrinseco della persona, ecco il risanatore ha evidenziato lo schema fisico: ha letto l'idea di natura nel mucchio delle viscide parvenze. (VC 332–38)

> [The master without words has grasped his sharp, shining pen. . . . Now the necessary actions, the excogitations of a premeditating prag-

matics. . . . the operating surgeon lifts it in his hand above the gauzes and the corona of tweezers, he "exteriorizes" it in the clarity of the electric lights, and searches, searches it as if he wants to discover an obstinate reticence, a stubborn, ancient simulation. . . . The ironic fingers appeared to be fondling the fraud. . . . Into the iniquitous mess of "externalized" life, routed out of its cavern like a prey in horror, the white man, now, insinuates his needles. He insinuates the tip of his unperturbed knowledge into that heap of flaccid tripes. . . . His dialectics is manifested in his silent acts; it is a biological remaking, a re-thinking of nature's construction with needle and thread, a rewilling, a restoration of form. . . . By profaning the secret darkness, the healer has made its physical scheme manifest: he has read the idea of nature in the heap of the viscid appearances.]

In "Anastomòsi," as Gian-Paolo Biasin argues, "Gadda's word almost imperceptibly transforms the surgical operation into a cognitive one, and the latter into a literary operation." Biasin goes on to add that Gadda, "master of the word," puts his word, his pen, into the hands of the silent surgeon, "the master without words" (Biasin 1975, 131). Here, however, the equation is not quite so straightforward, for Gadda knows that the poetic word can be based only on the precision and color of the technical word, and this other pragmatic word can come only from the technicians themselves—in this case, an assistant surgeon with the author in the observation booth who "can suggest to me the name of things or actions, the most perspicuous formalities of the process" (VC 329). The poetic word does not replace or speak for the technical word that is self-sufficient in its task. The poetic word is born from the technical word, but it has the power to transform it into the metaphysical and universal word.

Chapter 3

Grotesque Tragedy: *La cognizione del dolore*

La cognizione del dolore marks a turning point in Gadda's literary career. The early attempts to merge philosophy and literature, rage and reason, satire and lyricism come to fruition in a novel that is both tragic and hilariously comic. Set in a fictitious South American country very much like Gadda's native Lombardy, the novel is an anguished desecration of subjectivity and the world. At the core of this amalgam lies Gadda's pitiless exhibition of self in his malignant and maligned autobiographical protagonist, Gonzalo Pirobutirro d'Eltino, whose troubled relationship with his aged mother would seem to reflect Gadda's own and who is trapped in a pathology and a pathos of madness.[1]

THE PATHOS OF MADNESS

> Questa frase non aveva senso, ma la pronunziò realmente (C 737).

> These words had no meaning, but he really uttered them (AWG 214).

Cognizione's discourse on madness constitutes, in classical fashion, a discourse on truth and illusion. For the world, Gonzalo is mad because he is fixated on his delirious illusions of persecution by the world: "He abandoned himself again to his delirium. Coercive ideas girded that skull with their iron crown" (C 645; AWG 98). At the same time, Gonzalo's madness is a truth which reveals the deception of the world's false truth. His raving but cognizant delirium exposes the illusionary delirium of the world, a madness which lies precisely in the world's denial of its madness, in its pretensions to rationality and seriousness: "Yes, yes, they were highly considered, those tailcoats. Serious gentlemen, in the 'restaurants' of the station, and to be taken seriously, ordered of them in perfect seriousness an 'ossobuco with rice.' And they, with eager motions, agreed.

And this, in the full possession of their respective mental faculties. All were taken seriously: and each held the other in great esteem" (C 699; AWG 164–65).

Cognizione configures its discourse on madness as a satire of mores, but the pathology of Gonzalo's malady is, or should be, psychiatric. The good doctor Higueróa, who is not a psychiatrist, comes to examine the ailing hidalgo. He finds no trace of a Leibnizian *"mal physique,"* of a "visible sickness" (C 623; AWG 69). His diagnosis of Gonzalo's psychological malady, the stress of prolonged bachelorhood, seclusion, and reading, is sorely inadequate: "Living alone like that . . . barred into his room . . . reading . . . daydreaming" (C 612; AWG 57). His remedy, an automobile outing with his own marriageable daughter, is even more inadequate. The doctor maintains a positivistic faith in the healing force of civic philanthropy whereby the intervention of a strong and charitable "social fabric" will heal the mentally ill (C 623; AWG 70). It is a diagnosis which is rejected. "Only a psychiatrist," the novel declares in earnest, "and one who knew in detail the torment of that miserable biography, could have attached a tag to the illness" (C 645; AWG 98).

It is the novel itself which suggests a plausible psychiatric classification for Gonzalo's delirium: "Perhaps he suffered from what Sérieux, Capgras, and other contemporary psychiatrists have effectively called 'interpretative delirium,' distinguishing it from classical or hallucinatory delirium, as well as from delirium of imagination" (C 650; AWG 105). The names and classifications came from an essay by Benjamin Joseph Logre, "Le délire imaginatif de Don Quichotte," published in the April 13, 1939, issue of *Le Temps*, which Gadda had clipped and kept with his notes to the novel:

> On sait qu'il existe, en thèse générale, trois variétés du mécanisme intellectuel aboutissant à la formule des idées délirantes; on distingue, en effet: I^0 les délires *hallucinatoires*, très fréquents et très anciennement connus, où la certitude se fonde, avant tout, sur des perceptions fausses: on a, par exemple, des idées de persecution parce qu'on croit s'entendre injurier ou menacer; 2^0 les délires *interprétatifs*, décrits par les psychiatres français Sérieux et Capgras, où le sujet construit ses idées morbides à l'aide de raisonnements tendancieux portant sur des faits le plus souvent réels: il voit, par exemple, quelqu'un marcher derrière lui dans la rue et il en conclut qu'il est espionné; 3^0 les délires *imaginatifs*, isolés par notre maître Dupré et nous-même, où le malade conçoit son erreur par affirmation gratuite et immédiate, simple décret de sa

fantaisie: il raconte, par exemple, sans avoir rien perçu ni conclu, qu'on l'a proclamé roi de France. (cited in Manzotti 1987, 210–11)

[We know that there exist, generally speaking, three varieties of the mental mechanism resulting in the formulation of delirious thoughts. We can distinguish, in effect, 1) *hallucinatory* deliriums, quite frequent and known in quite remote times, in which the certainty is founded, first and foremost, on false perceptions: one has, for example, thoughts of persecution because one believes to understand oneself to be insulted or threatened; 2) *interpretative* deliriums, described by the French psychiatrists Sérieux and Capgras, in which the subject constructs his morbid ideas with the aid of tendentious reasoning applied to facts which are usually real: he sees, for example, somebody walking behind him in the street and concludes from this that he is being spied upon; 3) *imaginative* deliriums, identified by our teacher Dupré and ourselves, in which the patient conceives of his error through a gratuitous and immediate affirmation, a simple decree of his fantasy: he claims, for example, without having perceived anything nor concluded anything, that he has been proclaimed king of France.]

Logre's schema undoubtedly appealed to Gadda on several counts. From his earliest writings, Gadda had been attracted to Cervantes's Don Quixote as a possible model for his own notion of delirium. In *Racconto italiano* he had contemplated elaborating Grifonetto's autobiographical predicament of a great soul crushed by an insufficient environment as a modern instance of "Don Chisciottismo" (RI 469–70). The term recurs repeatedly in *Meditazione milanese,* in a Lukácsian sense, to describe the utopian dreamer who strives to apply his fixed idea to an inhospitably complex reality (MM 721, 744, 767, 769). The problem with the imaginary, quixotic classification, grounded, as Logre put it, on a "gratuitous affirmation," is its detachment of the delirium from reality, a detachment endemic to the hallucinatory paradigm as well, based on "false perceptions." Given this scenario, the "interpretative delirium" must have seemed particularly appealing to Gadda in its unique status as a madness based on real facts and their interpretation, which Logre associates with a form of paranoia. In his notes to *Cognizione* Gadda seeks to strengthen the "real" or "truth" basis for the delirium, emphasizing that Gonzalo's "persecution mania" is also a response to a true, "historical" intent of persecution (the pillaging of the family villa) on the part of others. Much of the novel's dramatic tension was to be based on the "uncertain" and "ambiguous" interplay between the two (C$_2$ 541).

Logre's "interpretative delirium" must also have appealed to Gadda as a possible model for explaining a malady rooted in neurosis but which rises above its immediate occasion to present a general epistemological problem on the interpretation of the world. Here too the classical struggle between truth vs. illusion in *Cognizione* cannot be resolved by a "psychiatric" or subjective dilemma. In Gadda's 1963 postscript to the novel, the thesis that Gonzalo's obsession derives from an inner "interpretative delirium of reality" is explicitly rejected in favor of an external cause, the madness of the world itself, "the folly and foolishness 'of others'" (C 764). Gonzalo's is "an ire which has exploded and so to speak gushed forth from the very fountain of reason" (C 762). The hall-of-mirrors assignment of blame between the pathology of the subject and the insanity of the world would seem to have no solution, and one eventually realizes that they are manifestations of a single, all-encompassing malady.

In this sense, the most accurate label for Gonzalo's obscure illness would seem to be the one applied by Piero Pucci, who has argued that Gonzalo's obsessive rage is symptomatic of what Jacques Lacan described as the modern madness of "méconnaissance," or "lack of recognition." In "Propos sur la causalité psychique" Lacan described the madness as follows:

> Cette méconnaissance se révèle dans la révolte, par où le fou veut imposer la loi de son coeur à ce qui lui apparaît comme le désordre du monde, entreprise "insensée,"—mais non pas en ce qu'elle est un défaut d'adaptation à la vie, formule qu'on entend couramment dans nos milieux, encore que la moindre réflexion sur notre expérience doive nous en démontrer la déshonorante inanité,—entreprise insensée, dis-je donc, en ceci plutôt que le sujet ne reconnaît pas dans ce désordre du monde la manifestation même de son être actuel, et que ce qu'il ressent comme loi de son coeur, n'est que l'image inversée, autant que virtuelle, de ce même être. Il le méconnaît donc doublement, et précisément pour en dédoubler l'actualité et la virtualité. Or il ne peut échapper à cette actualité que par cette virtualité. Son être est donc enfermé dans un cercle, sauf á ce qu'il le rompe par quelque violence où, portant son coup contre ce qui lui apparaît comme le désordre, il se frappe lui-même par voie de contre-coup social. (Lacan 1966, 171–72; cited in Pucci 1967, 44–45)

> [This lack of recognition is revealed in the rebellion, through which the madam wishes to impose the law of his heart on that which appears to him to be the disorder of the world, an "insane" enterprise,—but not in that it is a lack of adaptation to life, a formula which is currently

heard in our circles, even though the least bit of reflection on our experience should demonstrate to us the dishonorable inanity of it,—an
insane enterprise, I say then, in rather that the subject does not recognize in this disorder of the world the very manifestation of his actual
being, and that that which he feels to be the law of his heart, is nothing
but the mirror image, as well as the virtual image, of this same being.
He thereby fails to recognize it doubly, and precisely in order to double
its actuality and vituality. Now he cannot escape from the actuality
except by means of this virtuality. His being is thus enclosed in a circle,
unless he should break it through an act of violence whereby, bringing
his blow down on that which appears to him to be the disorder, he
strikes his very self by means of a social counterblow.]

Pucci notes the "surprising affinities" between Gadda/Gonzalo's mad
attempt to impose order on the world and Lacan's "méconnaissance du
fou." And he draws a further analogy with what Lacan calls the knowledge of Molière's Alceste that in his furious attacks against Oronte he is
attacking his own mirror image. Each sarcastic blow is also a blow against
his own self, blows which are received with delight, "avec délices" (Pucci
1967, 45). Gonzalo engages in a similar exchange of blows and counter-
blows in his diatribe against the blind narcissistic attachment of others to
their first-person pronoun "I/me," which concludes, surprisingly, in a
delirious defense of that same narcissism regarding his own house and
private property: "Inside, I, in my house, with my mother. . . . away,
away with them! Out! Out with them all! This is, and must be, my house
. . . in my silence . . . my poor house" (C 639; AWG 90–91; Pucci 1967,
46–47). The circle of madness in *Cognizione* is not only obsessive, it is
also sadomasochistic, and yet it is not posited as an illusion but as a reality with pretensions to the discourse of reason.

The circle of madness is also a subterfuge, a game of appearances in
which the pathology of madness is a cover for what is actually a pathos
of madness. *Cognizione*'s continual recurrence to reason and reality as
the source of Gonzalo's obsessive delirium merges with its attempt to
provide a rational psychiatric label for what is, nonetheless, a delirium.
Both are manifestations of the modern project outlined by Michel Foucault to subdue madness, or, rather, to silence madness, in the name of
logos. For all of *Cognizione*'s pitiless exposure of naked subjectivity and
its discourse of excess, madness never truly speaks in the novel. The pathological veneer is just that. The novel seems repeatedly to hint as much in
its insistence on an "obscure" and "invisible" (we could add "inaudible")

source of Gonzalo's malady and rancor that goes beyond war, childhood, and even Oedipus, to the "dying words of the Incas" according to whom "death comes for nothing, suffused in silence, like a tacit, final combination of thought" (C 607; AWG 50). The metaphors for the exclusion of madness and its discourse pile up. The discourse of madness belongs to an extinguished race. Its "tacit, final combination of thought" is the death of thought, the unraveling into disorder, into madness. It is a thought which cannot be articulated: it is beyond the pale of language. The text would end where it would begin.

Madness can only be approached from elsewhere. It can only be given language in a language that is not its own. The language of pathology is considered as a possibility, but when pathology is spoken of in the official discourse of clinical pathology it becomes the language of logos, the language most distant from madness. Ultimately the languages Gadda recurs to are from the more genuine archives of literature. Giving a discourse to madness becomes an archaeological operation. The pathos of madness explodes and is pacified in *Cognizione*'s archaic art of grotesque and macaronic realism: the mad obsession falls wonderfully to the minutiae of the world creating a laughter that is "liberating." But the novel is very much a chiaroscuro of literary discourses. When the madness sinks to its moments of deepest anguish and darkness, when it travels with the Romantics into Tasso's prison cell, then *Cognizione* appropriates for it yet another stylized and ancient language, that of tragedy, and Shakespearean tragedy in particular. In this other, tragic language madness becomes *dolore*, a metaphor of mourning, a knowledge of grief.

GROTESQUE TRAGEDY

> Lo scherno solo dei disegni e delle parvenze era salvo, quasi maschera tragica sulla metope del teatro (C 355–56).

> Only the contempt for designs and appearances was safe, that tragic mask on the metope of the theater (AWG 171).

Few critics have failed to note the centrality of the competing codes of grotesque and tragic discourse in *La cognizione del dolore*. Both codes have been seen as a narrative screen or mask which permitted Gadda to treat the traumatically autobiographical material in the novel: "with the protagonist Gonzalo, we have a transparent mask of autobiography, covered by the more concealing disguise of grotesque caricature that produces a tragic-comic deformation of the self, a form of baroque objectification meant to disclose only some traces of what is claimed to be the subject's extraordinary experience" (Dombroski 1984b, 129). The novel's grotesque and carnivalesque discourse has been proclaimed to be a liberating explosion of verbal invention, but it has also been criticized as an avoidance of critical responsibility.[2] The ambiguity is increased by Gadda's mélange of different historical stratifications of grotesque discourse.

Carnivalesque inversion dominates the narrative framework of *La cognizione del dolore* and contributes to its satire of Italian mores and official rhetoric. The novel's Southern Hemisphere locale, similar in many ways to Argentina (where Gadda worked with the Compañia General de Fósforos from December 1922 to February 1924), but which is, in reality, Italy, is a constant reminder of this topsy-turviness. So is the rest of its topographical palimpsest. The Néa Keltiké region with its "gutturaloid Calibans" is the Brianza region north of Milan; Lukones is Longone al Segrino, where Gadda's father had constructed the odious family villa in 1899; Pastrufazio is Milan; the ominous Serruchón mountain range which towers above is the Resegone of Manzonian memory. There is a similar sardonic overturning of the patriotic and cultural icons of Gadda's own formation: Gen. Juan Muceno Pastrufacio, Maradagalese national hero and liberator, "terror of the 'gringos' and scatterer of the Indios" (C 589; AWG 27), is Giuseppe Garibaldi; Carlos Caçoncellos, the Maradagalese national poet who has recently expired leaving behind a haunted villa filled with toothbrushes and combs, is Gabriele D'Annunzio. Even more significant are the political allusions. The devastating war recently concluded between Maradagàl and neighboring Parapagàl (World War I) has created a situation of displacement for many soldiers, who end up providing Mafia-like protection for villa owners with the local *Nistitúos proviniciales de vigilancia para la noche*. The latter are thinly disguised substitutes for the provincial cells or *fasci* of Mussolini's regime, and the dictator himself towers in the distance as the Inca volcano god Akatapulqui (Italian *accattapulci* or "flea gatherer"): "the god of sulphur and of flames . . . who looms up and shoots off, there, in the darkness . . . after the squalor of the Cordillera" (C 653; AWG 109).

The novel is also a comic and pitiless turning-on-its-head of the autobiographical self. Gonzalo's macaronic surname, Pirobutirro d'Eltino (butter pear of the wine vat), is a sardonic reference to father Francesco's (Francisco in the novel) mania for raising pear trees on the grounds of the family villa and for bottling his own wine (Manzotti 1987, 199). Both surnames also allude to traumatic childhood experiences of sadistic punishment for Gonzalo (and for Gadda as well): for having lost the cork stopper to the flask for his water and wine and, in an unpublished fragment, for having stolen some "marble-hard pears" from the orchard of a Signora Biffi (C₂ 535). In a typical example of the tangled knot of reality which constitutes Gonzalo's epistemological nightmare, pears and Pirobutirros become confused when the local librarian and head of the pear-growers association proposes in the association's journal, *La pera*, the curious philological thesis "one doesn't quite know whether in honor of the Pirobutirro or the Butter-Pear, and that is to say that 'hacer una pera,' to 'make a pear,' in the idiom of Castilla la Vieja, meant to carry out a great feat" (C 583; AWG 49). As one might expect, *fà on per (ona pera)*, in Milanese means instead "to fail miserably" (Manzotti 1987, 105), an apt description of what Gadda, in 1938, felt to have been the failure of his own life and chance for greatness.

Gonzalo's name and its carnivalesque etymology are representative of the obsessive presence of food, food consumption, food digestion, and food evacuation which constitutes the lion's share of the carnivalesque imagery in *Cognizione*. The vast Olympus of cheese mountains in Folengo's *Baldus* has its counterpart in the stinking cheeses of the Monte Viejo, most infamous of which is the fetid croconsuelo, Maradagalese equivalent of Lombard gorgonzola. "Fat, sharp, smelly enough to make an Aztec vomit" (C 583; AWG 19), croconsuelo is enjoyed best when transformed into a "foul mush" with some red wine and the ubiquitous butter pears for which the Néa Keltiké is so famous.

Beginning with its opening commentary on the recurrent failure of the local *banzavóis* crop due to adverse weather or pestilence, *Cognizione* embarks on a broad extension of its food motif to its core themes of illness and economic hardship.[3] The blighted landscape also functions as a comic contrast to the mock-epic introduction of Gonzalo as a gluttonous giant in the hearsay and speculation of the local peasants and townsfolk: "To be sure, around him the strangest opinions had been formed in Lukones and, for some time now, rumors of every sort had been circulating. His greed for food, for example, had become legendary" (C 600; AWG 40–41). Accused of engaging in "crapulous banquets" and "Dionysian celebration," "as if he, the voracious son, were banqueting with the shades of his Vikings" (C 598–600; AWG 39–41), Gonzalo's gargantuan feasts are raised to the status of carnivalesque "myth" and "folklore":

> Nel 1928 si era detto dalla gente, e i signori di Pastrufazio per primi, che egli fosse stato per morire, a Babylon, in seguito alla ingestione d'un riccio, altri sostenevano un granchio, una specie di scorpione marino ma di colore, anziché nero, scarlatto, e con quattro baffi, scarlatti pure

essi, e lunghissimi, come quattro spilloni da signora, due per parte, oltre alle mandibole, in forma di zanche, e assai pericolose loro pure; qualcuno favoleggiava addirittura di un pesce-spada o pesce-spilla; eh, già! piccolo, appena nato; ch'egli avrebbe deglutito intero (bollitolo appena quanto quanto, ma altri dicevano crudo), dalla parte della testa, ossia della spada: o spilla. Che la coda poi gli scodinzolò a lungo fuor dalla bocca, come una seconda lingua che non riuscisse piú a ritirare, che quasi quasi lo soffocava.

Le persone colte si rifiutarono di prestar fede a simili barocche fandonie: escluso senz'altro sia l'ittide che l'echinoderma, ritennero di dover identificare l'orroroso crostaceo in una aragosta del Fuerte del Rey, stazione atlantica assai nota in tutto il paese per l'allevamento appunto delle aragoste. Por suerte qualche notizia della sistematica d'Aristotele era loro arrivata ad orecchio. La quasi ferale aragosta raggiungeva le dimensioni di un neonato umano: ed egli, con lo schiaccianoci, ed appoggiando forte, piú forte!, i due gomiti in sulla tavola, ne aveva ferocemente stritolato le branche, color corallo com'erano, e toltone fuora il meglio, con occhi stralucidi dalla concupiscenza, e poi di piú in piú sempre piú strabici in dentro, inquantoché puntati sulla preda, a cui accostava, papillando bramosamente dalle narici, la ventosa oscena di quella bocca!, viscere immondo che aveva anticipatamente estroflesso a properare incontro l'agognata voluttà. Un animale compagno, a Babylon, stando alla leggenda, non lo avevano ancora veduto. E aveva anche avuto cuore, il sin vergüenza, d'intingerli in salsa tartara, uno a uno: cioè quei ghiotti e innocentissimi tréfoli, o lacèrtoli (d'un color bianco o madreperla rosato come d'aurora marina), ch'era venuto a mano a mano faticosamente eripiendo, e con le unghie, dalla vacuità interna delle due branche, infrante! . . . scheggiate! . . . E, usatosi financo delle mani, e dei diti, se li era condotti alle labbra unte e peccaminose con una avidità straordinaria. (C 600–601)

In 1928 people had said, the gentlemen and ladies of Pastrufazio among the first, that he had been on the point of death in Babylon after having swallowed a sea urchin; others said it was a crab, a kind of sea scorpion colored a scarlet color rather than black, with four moustaches—also scarlet, and very long, like four ladies hatpins, two on either side—in addition to the mandibles, in the form of steering oars, and also highly dangerous; some mythologized also about a swordfish or a brooch fish— oh yes! tiny, barely born—which he must have swallowed whole (having boiled it the bare minimum, but others said raw), head first, or rather sword, or brooch. They said the tail then flapped for a long time outside his mouth, like a second tongue he could no longer retract, and came close to suffocating him.

Cultivated people refused to credit such baroque tales: having dismissed unquestionably both the ichthyoid and the echinoderm, they believed they could identify the horrendous crustacean as a lobster of Fuerte del Rey, an Atlantic resort well known throughout the country precisely for its lobster beds. Por suerte some inkling of the Aristotelian system had reached their ears. The almost fatal lobster assumed the proportions of a human infant: and he, with a nutcracker, and pressing hard—harder!—both elbows on the table, had fiercely crushed its claws, coral-colored as they were, and had removed from them the best part, his eyes supergleaming with concupiscence and then squinting more and more inwardly, since aimed on the prey to which he neared, his nostrils flaring desirously, the obscene sucker of that mouth!—foul entrail which he had in anticipation extruded to approach the longed-for voluptuousness. Such an animal, in Babylon, according to the legend, they hadn't seen before or since. And he had had the nerve, the sin vergüenza, to dip them in tartar sauce, one by one—that is, those appetizing and quite innocent strands or shreds (of a white or pink mother-of-pearl color like a marine dawn) which he had been gradually extracting, also with his fingernails, from the inner void of the two claws, crushed! shattered! And, having also used his hands, and his fingers, he brought them to his greasy and sinful lips with an extraordinary greed. (AWG 41–43)

Grotesque hyperbole, amazement, anecdotal imprecision, and mock horror dominate this popular epos of gigantesque gluttony.[4] Carnivalesque themes of dismemberment, anthropophagy, and confusion of food and the body which ingests it are accompanied by a parodic pastiche of culinary, scientific, scholastic, moralistic, declamatory, and erotic registers along with a macaronic sprinkling of Hispanic creolism. Gonzalo's consumption of the unidentified sea creature–newborn baby builds to a crescendo of sexual frenzy and voluptuous agony in the disintegration of the confines separating the bodily functions of consumption, procreation, and death typical of the Rabelaisian grotesque. In a subsequent description of Gonzalo's wanton disembowelment of roasted pigeons stuffed to overflowing with soft, mushy potatoes, the erotic function yields to the excretory one as Gonzalo ravenously gorges himself on the mealy paste of the "evacuated and restuffed animal" in a gluttonous exhibition of his oral-anal eroticism.

Despite the similarities between the saga of Gonzalo's gigantesque feast and the Renaissance carnivalesque, *Cognizione*'s grotesque realism is not an unqualified celebration of the Rabelaisian universal body. A more precise historical model is what Bakhtin calls the early bourgeois appropriation of popular-festive banquet imagery to the realm of individual and class gluttony and cupidity (Bakhtin 1984b, 301–2). In *Cognizione*'s hall-of-mirrors environment of satiric ridicule and ridiculousness, Gonzalo's "vice of the palate" is execrated as a sin and a crime by both the undernourished local peasants and the abstemious villa owners. In a parody of Giuseppe Parini's civic neoclassicism, Gonzalo, comparable to the indolent young master of Parini's *Il giorno,* has coffee brought to him, "stretched out in bed like a cow . . . whereas as the peasants have been sweating for three hours, and have to stop and sharpen their scythes" (C 599; AWG 37). Gonzalo's private gluttony is ironically removed from "the process of labor and struggle" that marks the popular-festive forms of banquet imagery (Bakhtin 1984b, 302).

Gonzalo's gormandizing is not legitimate celebration but sinful transgression, and like the other forms of transgressive rebellion in the novel, it sets into motion the punitive mechanism of the repressive deities, "[T]he vindictive Powers of Heaven chose that here should follow, for him, thanks to their rightful intervention, a long and very costly disease . . . [which] forced him to eternal fastings, and reduced him to powdering the mucus membrane of the gastric system with powdered kaolin, or discipline of bismuth" (C 603; AWG 45). The epos of Gonzalo's colossal gluttony stands in stark contrast to the protagonist's true situation of melancholic illness. The universal body's brief affirmation of excess is replaced and repressed by the malfunctioning mechanism of the neurotic individual. Gastronomical celebration becomes obligatory fasting, and food is transformed into medicine, powdered kaolin, or discipline of bismuth. The costly illness inflicted on Gonzalo corresponds to Gadda's own gastrointestinal disturbances, ubiquitous in the pages of his war diary and anticipatory of the gastric ulcer which plagued him for many years.

The seat of oscillation in *Cognizione* between the archaic universal body and the modern individual body is the belly/stomach. In its role as the metaphorical locus of the hidalgo's voracious vices, Gonzalo's belly is larger than life: "José, the peon, insisted that he had in him, all seven, in his belly, the seven deadly sins—locked in his belly like seven serpents; that they bit and devoured him from within, from morning to evening—and even at night, in his sleep" (C 597; AWG 36–37). The hyperbolic ability of the grotesque belly to consume is reversed and is itself devoured by the guilty neuroses and nightmares of Gonzalo's psychological and existential angst. The insatiable belly of the Renaissance grotesque with its symbolism of man's triumph over the world has become the stomach of the modern neurotic and hypochondriac, continually plagued by incurable ailments. The curative powers of laughter itself have been inverted. No longer physician Rabelais's therapeutic remedy for the elimination of trapped and corrupt internal airs of illness through a cathartic expurgation via the body's orifices, laughter becomes a ridiculing repression, forcing eccentricity inward to be channeled and controlled by will and conscience. Gonzalo's "invisible illness" of melancholic madness and impotent rage is forced into the villa, into the stomach, where gather the nihilistic bile and foul humors of the modern satirist: "when righteous wrath becomes heavy in a belly . . . in mine, for example" (C 637; AWG 89).

Gonzalo's grotesque satire is expressed within the context of his interpretative delirium. He is the raging madman and the melancholic clown who exposes the absurd underbelly of reality. His patrimony having been squandered by his parent's public munificence and cultivation of the inane symbols of bourgeois status, most prominent of which is the country villa itself, Gonzalo sits down to a meager meal of watery soup and drifts into an oneiric tirade against the wretched hordes who descend "ass-backwards, down, down from the green croconsuelo of Monte Viejo to the swelling tide of the avenida" (C 695; AWG 160). Carnivalesque imagery is called to the service of a rancorous class discourse against the cretinous morons, who are endowed, for that very reason, with the vulgar vital force which will permit them to replace the dispossessed and withered caste of the "last hidalgo." As Gonzalo's ascetic delirium continues, these morons are transformed into "manichini ossibuchivori" "ossobucovore dummies" (C 701; AWG 168), pompous and asinine nouveaux riches who flaunt their affluence by surrounding themselves with "flowerbeds of rosbiffe" and "unexpected windspouts of risotto" (C 695–701; AWG 160–68).

Carnivalesque abundance has become a pathological attraction/repulsion complex for the hallucinating Gonzalo in which the symbolism of popular ritual is mapped onto a bourgeois fear of the low. As the etiology of the pathology is plumbed, we eventually arrive, in true psychoneurotic fashion, at Gonzalo's childhood trauma at the Pastrufazian-Milanese carnival:

> And the roundabouts and the threadbare magic of the Spanish bastions, at carnival, were discomfort and shame amid the insults of the crowd, in the vulgar cloud of confetti. A discomfort, an anguish, reduced the frightened child to nervous collapse. . . .
>
> Stupefied horses circled, swaying, in a ring, horns grasped by women riders with legs spread, with torn drawers, he couldn't tell whether they were rents or lace, pieces of skin surely. . . . A faint nasal music came forth from the pivot of the great machine . . . it seemed to him the music of raggedness, of runny nose, of revolt, of nougat, of jostling and fritters, of roast peanuts which precipitate the bellyache into shit.
>
> The hoped-for poem with a pink maiden aloft on the trapeze, who blows kisses, also to the child, to him, to him, was wrecked in the smell of rotting almond paste in the gluey whites of egg . . . ah! how disgusting. The spun sugar, in the brute's huge hands, terrified him. The rogue had hung the pitchy skein of his sugar from a hook the color of colophony, and he shouted: he shouted from his swollen neck: everyone stopped, to hear curses in dialect: and he pulled it, that sticky sugar, and spun it and twisted it, and then he kneaded it into a braid and shaped it into a figure-eight, the sugar, with his hands: and even that skein, subject to constant metamorphosis and stress, to the child seemed guilty, lying: an accomplice of the obscenity: and the man spat on his hands one after the other, to grease them, so that they would slip more easily in that task, the pig. . . .
>
> But nothing could be salvaged from the stink, from the horrible dialect, from the braggadocio . . . from the confetti, from the peanut shells and roast chestnut hulls, from the naranja rinds, called also skins. Pink almond sweets, chewy, and girls became foul, in the child's eyes, in the disappearance of all gentility. . . .
>
> What the child suffered was not the festival of a people, but the screeching of a horde of devils, crazed, filthy, in a futile, bestial, devilishness. . . . His was surely, the son now thought, a sick childhood. (C 734–35; AWG 210–12)

The carnivalesque has its origins for Gonzalo in a terrifying, satanic, and monstrous world of estrangement. Its archaic gay abundance of food has been transformed into a sticky nausea, its popular speech and celebration of community into obscene dialect and bestial devilry, its amorphous open-endedness into the deceitful grotesqueries of the cotton-candy skein, symbol of the disorder and mess that fray the neurotic nerves of the hidalgo. Gonzalo's reaction to the carnival is not dissimilar from that of Freud's hysterics. The public festivity has been internalized and inverted into "the morbid symptoms of a private terror": *Cognizione* offers a pathological version of a general tendency in early-twentieth-century bourgeois culture to demonize carnival into an alienating "festival of the Other" (see Stallybrass and White 1986, 171–90). The hidalgo's fear of the carnivalesque is a fear of the low. It is a class fear, the fear of the peons who penetrate into the Pirobutirro villa with "dung pancakes" clinging to their clogs and their guttural dialect, and it is a sexual fear, the sublime lady in pink on the trapeze who has become the foul and sexually threatening bareback-riding fair girls, with their spread legs, torn lace, and lack of gentility. Class and sexual Others, masses and women come together to haunt the hidalgo in a single tide of the low.

It is this alienating carnival of the Other that ultimately wins the battle between the competing historical codes of the grotesque in *Cognizione*. The novel ends tragically. Gonzalo's mother is brutally bludgeoned at night, in bed, as the ancestral villa is invaded by the grotesque pandemonium of the amazed townsfolk and peasants who warn one another in the "agilulfo-Celtic uproar" of their primitive dialect not to pierce their bellies when climbing over the sharp spikes of the gate: "e allora appunto i nomi tripa, büsekka, plurale tripp, büsekk" [and then in fact the word tripe, "büsekka," plural: "büsekk"] (C 751; AWG 232). *La cognizione del dolore* ends with a sardonic ridicule of the popular festival of grotesque realism, the lower bodily stratum of the universal paunch and the vitalism of popular dialect, but also with the triumph of the hordes of stupidity and vulgarity.

"Poor fellow, he seemed to be reciting an 'aside' in the aristocratic theatricals" (C 631; AWG 80). Faced with the obsessive paroxysms of the son Gonzalo, the good doctor Higueróa strives to bring their conversation back to the world of normalcy and reasoned discourse. It is an exercise in futility, however, and the doctor seems to sense his own estrangement in the novel's circumvention of narrative conventionality for a theatricality of tragic excess.

In its rejection of a discourse of reason, justice, and the commonsense acceptance of reality, the tragic is antithetical to the measured realism of traditional novelistic discourse. Gadda, a troubled novelist, gravitates to the antinarrative of the tragic. He is one of a few modern writers who "tries to invent literary metaphors adequate to the objective violence of the world" (Bàrberi Squarotti 1978, 96). *La cognizione del dolore* does not organize its narrative tension along the contingent axis of plot. The novel's plot is willfully inconclusive and digressive. Grounded instead in Gonzalo's nihilistic rejection of reality, the novel's "story" is an idée fixe reiterated and exasperated in the language of tragic metaphoricity. *Cognizione* is inundated, in a highly conscious and estranged manner, with the ostensible signs of dramatic tragedy. The title itself points to the economy of tragedy. Its *dolore* and its *cognizione* correspond to the tragic mechanisms of peripeteia and recognition.

Cognizione's tragic imagery, especially dominant in the novel's second half, revolves around the isolated figures of Gonzalo and his mother, both of whom are besieged in a desperate agon against the severe law of a malevolent destiny. Frequently referred to in archetypal antonomasia as *Figlio* and *Madre*, Mother and Son, their tragic stature is thrown into relief by the sea of indistinct Josés, Giuseppes, Giuseppinas, and Pinas who compose *Cognizione's* malodorous chorus of minor characters, "like the chorus in Euripides," the novel glosses sarcastically. Marked by their "magniloquent gestures" and "solipsisms," Gonzalo and his mother undergo a "stylistic dignification" in their tragic theatricality reinforced by references to celebrated personages of antiquity and the Shakespearean stage (Roscioni 1969b, 108; Sereni 1972, 368; Baldi 1972, 104).

At the core of the tragic mother-son dyad lies a pathological, repressed, and evasive Oedipus-Orestes complex alluded to in Gonzalo's syncopated outbursts and the stupefied witness of the doctor Higueróa and the chorus of guttural Calibans. The complex assumes the figural dimensions of dramatic tragedy in Gonzalo's narration to the patient Higueróa of a frightful dream, "un sogno spaventoso":

> "A figure of shadow . . . black, silent, very tall: as if she had come back from the cemetery. . . . Veturia, perhaps, the motionless mother of Coriolanus, veiled. But she wasn't the mother of Coriolanus! Oh! the veil didn't dispel my obscure certainty: it didn't mask her from my grief.
>
> I knew her, I knew who it was. It could be no other—tall, motionless, veiled, black." (C 633; AWG 83)

The highly stylized account with its repetition, ellipses, and Livian (and Shakespearean) evocation of Coriolanus's mother is part of *Cognizione's* complex signifying game of subjective revelation through literary allusion-elusion.[5] The reference to Veturia and Coriolanus is a screen, a *locus tragicus* which momentarily lifts Gonzalo's vision beyond its personal and psychoanalytic specificity, casting into larger-than-life roles both mother and son (like Gonzalo, Coriolanus is infamous for his aristocratic disdain of the plebeians). That the allusion is a veil is acknowledged immediately by Gonzalo, but the tragic self-fashioning has succeeded. The son's admission that he knows who the figure truly is instills the tragic iconography of the characters with the horrific pathos of the personal revelation. But revelation is never a finished process in *Cognizione;* it always maintains the tragic metaphoricity of incomplete allusion; it is an "obscure certainty." In a manuscript note Gadda had written that the dream figure is a synthesis between Coriolanus's mother and Gonzalo's mother, "because the mother had taught these stories to the child, and in his unconscious the two figures had merged" (cited in Manzotti 1987, 170). The figure is an oneiric amalgam of literature and reality. It is a construct, not just a vision but a thought, "a thought," the son offers, "in the dark catalogue of eternity" (C 633; AWG 83). As thought it is not Gonzalo's mother but his matricidal projection of his mother. The figure, which arises from Gonzalo's tormented psyche, is also his homicidal urge toward his mother and the image of death itself: "And this black, ineluctable force . . . heavier than a tombstone . . . fell upon her! As the outrage falls, beyond all reparation. And it had risen in me, from me!" (C 633; AWG 83–84).

The dream is a complex construction of literature, reality, and thought. It is also a metaphorical premonition for the crushing blow to the head that leaves the mother moribund at the novel's end, itself an alluding and elusive vision. Gonzalo dreams a guilty stance for himself at dream's end with receipts for the villa in his hand, just as a similar guilty stance had been projected for him in the novel's unwritten final chapter. Like so many of the numerous revelatory allusions in *Cognizione*, the dream is not contingent plot but a metaphor for the ubiquitous but elusive final catastrophe of murder and guilt. The novel is an obsession, a need to articulate its horror at every turn while simultaneously postponing its realization through the constant deferral of metaphoricity. The elusiveness lifts the story beyond Gonzalo to Gadda. It points the finger of revelation outside the text, to its author, who also has an empty villa, a dead mother, receipts from a prospective sale initiated almost immediately after the mother's death, who writes, in 1938, for a small coterie of friends who know all of this.[6] It is the dream of the author himself, a manuscript note reveals: "the vision of death on the terrace (my dream)" (C₂ 564). We are continually reminded that the author's situation is so similar, so metaphorical, to Gonzalo's own. *Cognizione*'s meticulously crafted allusions and elusions become uncomfortably revelatory because they continually point to an authorial presence of complicity and guilt. The tragic screen becomes all the more imperative from this perspective. By becoming literary tragedy the metaphoricity of Gonzalo's dream is forced back into the text. Part of the metaphorical web of tragic discourse within the text, the dream becomes a vaticinal premonition, a visitation from the deities, a *textual* "obscure certainty" of the ineluctable final catastrophe.

The tragic metaphoricity in *Cognizione* is most evident in the dark overture to the novel's second part: the mother's descent into the cellar at the onset of a violent autumn storm. The scene, like Gonzalo's dream, is another metaphor for the mother's tragic fate. "It was the blow, it was the mockery of unknown powers, or beings, unknown yet inexorable in their persecution" (C 674; AWG 135). Without the protection of her sons, the mother is pursued by the ferocious forces of evil, emblematized by a black scorpion on the cellar floor and the "repentine lame" [sudden blades] of the blasts of wind (C 677; AWG 137). The latter evoke the bladelike eyes of the Nsititúo guard Mahagones, the mother's eventual assassin: "I due piccoli occhi scintillarono, da parere una lama" [The two tiny eyes flashed, like a blade] (C 656; AWG 112).[7] The wind is an accomplice to the evil. It ripped from life the mother's aviator offspring, and it now comes for her too, like an assassin: "The wind, which had carried off her son toward oblivion-making cypresses, at every window seemed to be seeking her, too, her, in the house. From the little window over the stairs, a gust, bursting in, had gripped her by the hair" (C 675; AWG 135).

The mother and her fate continue to receive the ennobling force of dramatic allusion, this time to Shakespeare's *King Lear*. "With one hand, then, wearily, she rearranged her hair, whitened by the years, spread from her forehead without caresses like the hair of King Lear" (C 684; AWG 146). This gesture, which appears at the chapter's end, reverberates on everything that has preceded, locking her tragic descent into the archetypal horror of Lear's battered senility at the onset of the storm in act 3. Shakespeare's verses had once been a source of knowledge for Gonzalo's mother, who would read them by a little lamp. Now she recites them as dark metaphors of her life: "she still spoke some verses, as from a broken tombstone forgotten syllables are scattered, and in the past they were the light of knowledge, and now the horror of the night" (C 684; AWG 146).

The mother as victim is perhaps the more consistently noble and tragic figure in *Cognizione*. She, it has been argued, and not Gonzalo, is the bearer of the novel's tragic aporia (Pucci 1967, 53). Nonetheless, Gonzalo is the tragic protagonist in *Cognizione*, and like his mother, he too undergoes an impressive dramatic investment. To begin with, Gonzalo's physiognomy, character, and motivations are elaborated via a barrage of allusions to famous and infamous figures from literature and history. If the mother's association with Veturia, Lear, and, later, Caesar casts Gonzalo in the corresponding roles of Coriolanus, Lear's ungrateful daughters, and Brutus, he is also associated more or less explicitly with a host of other figures: Don Quixote, Molière's Misanthrope and Avare, Manzoni's Don Gonzalo Fernandez de Cordoba, *The Tempest*'s old councillor Gonzalo, and Francisco and Rodrigo Borgia. The association of Gonzalo with so many literary personages makes him a rich condensation of psychological and dialectical connotations, but at the expense of lacerating contradictions (Roscioni 1969a, 92). The swings in personality border on the schizophrenic; the masks bear the marks of estrangement. In Pirandellian fashion, Gonzalo seeks liberation from the assigned identities, through his awkward and impetuous demonstrations of affection for his mother or his search for assistance from the doctor Higueróa: "he looked at the doctor, staring, as if he were asking of him, 'What did I say?'—as if imploring, 'Tell me what I said! I was ill! Couldn't you see?'" (C 631–32; AWG 81). Often the neurotic and impotent last hidalgo cannot sustain the weight of the literary allusions he has been called upon to bear; the discrepancy and resulting estrangement leave him looking pathetic, even ridiculous.

The tragic figure upon whom Gonzalo's estranged rebellion against the world is modeled most is Shakespeare's Hamlet. Both characters are engulfed by a furor against the world with Orestean/Oedipal overtones, both are visited by specters, both anguish between an imaginary and a real matricide, both speculate on the liberation and prison house of dreaming, and both are plagued with the excess of thought: "I think; già: but I'm ill of thinking," Gonzalo utters in English to the doctor Higueróa (C 636), mixing the Cartesian affirmation of self-consciousness with Hamlet's lament that "the native hue of resolution / is sicklied o'er with the pale cast of thought" (*Hamlet* 3.1.92–93).[8] Gadda's interest in Hamlet can be traced to his notes to *Racconto italiano* in which he praises the character's richness as both dramatic agent-manager and philosophical consciousness-commentator. In 1925 he made a notebook entry for a possible university thesis on Shakespeare's play. He was most taken by the notion of Hamlet's revenge as the restitution of order to a disordered reality: "A noteworthy item, in the play the idea 'revenge' is explained with the idea (which assumes a truly finalistic character) of 'the restoration of the disturbed natural order.' 'Such disorder' (sic), says Hamlet; 'and I had to be born, to set it all right!'" (cited in Roscioni 1974, 353). "The time is out of joint. O cursed spite / That ever I was born to set it right!" (*Hamlet* 1.5.215–16). As with other literary sources dear to his heart, Gadda effects an idiosyncratic appropriation of *Hamlet,* in which he superimposes on Shakespeare's character his personal ethos and poetics of a revenge against disorder. One is reminded of T. S. Eliot's claim that the creative critical mind tends to find in Shakespeare's protagonist "a vicarious existence for [its] own artistic realization" (Eliot 1934, 95). In the 1952 review "*Amleto* al Teatro Valle," and with echoes of comments made in the 1927 "I viaggi la morte," Gadda returns to Shakespeare's play to project onto the Prince of Denmark the same "heroic operation" against the disorder of the world that is the ideal core of Gonzalo's tragic rebellion. Hamlet's enigmatic discourse, Gadda writes, springs from a "derisory ferocity," not of a madman but of a character who is "lucid," "resolute," and "conscious" in his actions and reactions (VM 543–46). For Gadda, Hamlet's mission of vengeance is similar to that of the matricidal Orestes: it is necessarily negative and self-destructive. His reconstitution of the moral order of the world can only be achieved at the cost of his own life: "Hamlet senses the annihilatory character of his action, he knows that he himself must fall, in the act of performing the extreme cautery of the disease, shame and guilt" (VM 541).

Gonzalo is not able to carry out his tragic mission in this heroic fashion. His neuroses get the best of him, diverting lucid ferocity into delirium and transforming reconstitutive cauterization into impotent rage. The difference between the two heroic missions of negativity comes to the fore in Gonzalo's "soliloquy" on appearances and negation:

Cogliere il bacio bugiardo della Parvenza, coricarsi con lei sullo strame, respirare il suo fiato, bevere giú dentro l'anima il suo rutto e il suo lezzo di meretrice. O invece attuffarla nella rancura e nello spregio come in una pozza di scrementi, negare, negare: chi sia Signore e Principe nel giardino della propria anima. Chiuse torri si levano contro il vento. Ma l'andare nella rancura è sterile passo, negare vane immagini, le piú volte, significa negare se medesimo. Rivendicare la facoltà santa del giudizio, a certi momenti, è lacerare la possibilità: come si lacera un foglio inturpato leggendovi scrittura di bugíe.

Lo hidalgo, forse, era a negare se stesso: rivendicando a sé le ragioni del dolore, la conoscenza e la verità del dolore, nulla rimaneva alla possibilità. Tutto andava esaurito dalla rapina del dolore. Lo scherno solo dei disegni e delle parvenze era salvo, quasi maschera tragica sulla metope del teatro. (C 703–4)

To seize the lying kiss of Appearances, to lie with her on the straw, to breathe her breath, to drink in, down into the soul, her belch and strumpet's stench. Or instead to plunge them into rancor and into contempt as into a well of excrement, to deny, deny: to be Lord and Prince in the garden of one's own soul. Closed towers rise up against the wind. But the progress of rancor is a sterile footstep; to deny vain images, most of the time, means denying oneself. To assert the holy faculty of judgment, at certain moments, is to tear possibility: as one tears an indecent paper, reading lies written in it.

The hidalgo, perhaps, meant to negate himself: claiming for himself the motives of grief, the acquaintance with grief and the truth of it, nothing was left to possibility. Everything was exhausted by the theft of grief. Only the contempt for designs and appearances was safe, that tragic mask on the metope of the theater. (AWG 171)

Gonzalo mixes Hamlet's celebrated quandary on "to be or not to be" with Dantean echoes of the fetid siren of earthly pleasures and adapts it to his own dilemma on whether to acquiesce to the world of false appearances or to negate and deny the world and, therefore, his own self (since no one is an independent and self-contained monad). In *"Amleto al teatro Valle"* Gadda provides a similar interpretation of Hamlet's "famous monologue": *"not to be* is to adapt oneself to life and to the shameful contingency of the world, *to be,* is to act, to carry out one's charge (one's mission) even if it means facing death" (VM 542). The difference, as Manzotti indicates, between Gonzalo's dilemma and Hamlet's is that Hamlet's negative mission is, in the end, one of action (Manzotti 1987, xxxiv). Hamlet's charge is carried out. The cautery, albeit tardy and messy (in Elizabethan fashion), is performed, and a new day dawns in Denmark. For Gonzalo there can be no such active heroism, not even in literature, which in its mimetic relation to life is an indecent paper of lies. Gonzalo never moves beyond his impotent nihilism of rancor, denial, and negation. The new day announced by the cock at novel's end shines not on the cauterization of evil and reconstitution of the moral order, but on the unavenged horror of the mother's offended person: "that outraged face . . . debased by a wicked cause operating in the absurdity of the night" (C 754; AWG 237). Hamlet is a modern tragic hero, but a tragic hero nevertheless. Gadda's Gonzalo is not a tragic hero but a modern antihero, an embittered testimony of the failed dreams of heroic praxis and affirmation.

A final explanation for Gadda's attraction to Hamlet has to do with T. S. Eliot's claim that Shakespeare's tragedy is imperfect because of an inexplicable discrepancy between Hamlet's intense feeling of disgust for his mother and Gertrude herself as the "objective correlative" of that feeling.

> Hamlet (the man) is dominated by an emotion which is inexpressible, because it is in *excess* of the facts as they appear. . . . Hamlet is up against the difficulty that his disgust is occasioned by his mother, but that his mother is not an adequate equivalent for it; his disgust envelops and exceeds her. It is thus a feeling which he cannot understand; he cannot objectify it, and it therefore remains to poison life and obstruct action. . . . The intense feeling, ecstatic or terrible, without an object or exceeding its object, is something which every person of sensibility has known; it is doubtless a study to pathologists. It often occurs in adolescence: the ordinary person puts these feelings to sleep, or trims down his feeling to fit the business world; the artist keeps it alive by his ability to intensify the world to his emotions. (Eliot 1934, 100–102)

Eliot's confused and pathological Hamlet seems much closer to the "real" Gonzalo than Gadda's heroic Hamlet. Gonzalo's reaction of excess against his mother, his shamefully childish displacement of his parricidal and fratricidal urges onto anyone who approaches the radius of his mother's affection, his confused need for help and love—all are manifestations of the intensification of the world to Gonzalo's emotions. The novel itself is cognizant of the excess, and the observation is made that Gonzalo's "irreparable" rancor toward his mother comes from "a grimmer remoteness" than his "incinerated youth" or the loss of his brother in the war (C 692; AWG 157). It is this enigmatic, mystified "obscure sickness," beyond Oedipus but which the novel refuses or is incapable of defining, that envelops and exceeds Gonzalo's mother as the object of Gonzalo's intense feeling.

"Under what compulsion of experience [Shakespeare] attempted to express the inexpressibly horrible," Eliot concludes, "we cannot ever know" (Eliot 1934, 102). The same is true for Gadda, perhaps, even though his obscure sickness, at least from the biographical material available, appears linked to his pathological desire for a heroic affirmation and plenitude which was repeatedly denied. It was an illness of lack and negativity which Gadda, the Romantic kicked in the pants by destiny and reality, and his creature, Gonzalo, sorely felt. In a 1965 review of Giuseppe Berto's *Il male oscuro*, Gadda offered an explanation of the illness as the result of just such a life of hard knocks: "The obscure sickness is as obscure as the grief that tears us apart as soon as we feel ourselves to be the object of reiterated blows or wounds, of insistent outrages. It is the strain we are subjected to, day in day out, hour by hour, by our 'Erlebnis,' the experience of living, the endured pain and fatigue, the 'hard necessity'" (SD 1202–3).

The excessive objective correlative that the novel posits for this sickness, the same one Gadda had indicated in his war diary, in *Meditazione milanese*, and in his comments on *Hamlet*, is the pernicious disorder of the world. The ferocious derision of disorder and a pathological rancor toward the mother: these are the axes on which *Cognizione*'s literary screens of the tragic and the grotesque converge.

As the novel builds to its tragic climax, derision of disorder and rancor toward the mother come ever closer in a series of emotionally intense and intimate encounters between son and mother. Immediately after his monologue on whether to accept the lies of reality or to negate all, Gonzalo makes a desperate attempt to at least salvage the love between a son and his mother from the destructive force of rancorous negation. In a compromise with the contingency of the world, Gonzalo gives to his mother some newspapers he has brought to the villa. Her eyes well over with tears of recognition, and she lifts her face in anticipation of a greeting or a kiss, as if until that moment she had been prevented from being "la mamma":

> The son then clasped her to him, desperately; he kissed her at length. An old silver brooch, with a garnet, flower of the maternal years, adorned (and slipped from) the poor trappings of old age.
>   Meanwhile there came in, clogging, the poverty and fetor of a peon.
> (C 704; AWG 172)

The sublime moment of union and plenitude is destroyed as the world of contingency comes flooding back. As if sensing the first sign of a pernicious and rapid contagion, the hypersensitive narrative gaze, which undoubtedly follows the trajectory of Gonzalo's own, quickly moves from the embrace and kiss to the minutiae of the mother's brooch. Despite its lyrical description in the key of a weathered still life, the brooch silently alludes to the topos of Gonzalo's ferocious anger at the sight of his mother's jewelry. It is the visible sign for him of her inane attachment to bourgeois conventionality, her shameful exposure of his rightful patrimony to the possibility of theft, her denial of affection to him to the benefit of the others (in an unincorporated note Gonzalo suspects his mother of having given one of her jewels to the peon [C₂ 555]). Inevitably, this first intrusion of the world's contingency is followed by the intolerable entrance of the malodorous peasant, sign of the fetid disorder of the world and object of Gonzalo's jealousy. The embrace between son and mother gives way to Gonzalo's delirium against the ostentatious filthiness and poverty of the peasant, whom, in an outburst of rage, he fires, thereby removing the only obstacle to the nocturnal assault on the mother.

Later, Gonzalo himself will physically and verbally assault his mother after she has received a throng of equally malodorous peasants bearing gifts. He violently grabs her arm, outstretched in a gesture of defense. The mother recoils from her son, like Suetonius's Caesar from his assailants: "So Suetonius reports of Caesar, who raised his toga to his head, before the sudden gleam of the blades" (C 737; AWG 214). The Caesarian allusion (the imagery of the blades recuperates the mother's Learian stance before the storm and the sinister eyes of Mahagones, her actual assailant) is another tragic intertext, and its obsessive web of imagery appears at various points in the novel's concluding chapters.[9] The encounter, the last between Gonzalo and his mother in the novel, is also Gonzalo's final chance at overcoming the cycle of rancorous negation and denial, but to no avail as he utters his senseless matricidal threat: "He would have liked to kneel and say: 'Forgive me, forgive me! Mama, it's I!' He said: 'If I find you again in that pack of pigs, I'll cut your throat and theirs too.' These words had no meaning, but he really uttered them" (C 737; AWG 214).[10]

The tragic is an absolute protest, a refutation of the world of history and phenomena. In his soliloquy of negation, Gadda's Gonzalo aspires to this tragic pose, but he is plagued by his own pathological focus on phenomenal reality. His rage in the end seems inactive and aimless because it is enveloped and exceeded by its chosen objective correlative, the minutiae of the world's contingency itself. The novel's tragic drama of a son's wayward emotions for his mother is continually undermined by the perception of grotesque reality and by Gonzalo's delirium that to set the world straight is to annihilate it.

Chapter 4

Macaronic Pastiche: *Quer pasticciaccio brutto de via Merulana*

If *Quer pasticciaccio brutto de via Merulana* had not been published as a novel in 1957, Gadda might have remained an author appreciated only by Contini's "happy few" (Contini 1989, 75). Unlike the limited copies of Gadda's earlier published works, many of which remained unpurchased, his detective novel was swept up in the publishing boom in Italy in the late 1950s that saw tens of thousands of copies printed and sold (Cattaneo 1987, 246). With typical paradox, the prolific and fiercely Milanese Gadda was launched into the spotlight of public notoriety for the first time through the Roman *Pasticciaccio,* his last novel. It was a newfound fame, and at such a late point in the writer's active career it was received with a mix of reservation and fatigue: "My health is not that great: my book has put me in a sea of nuisances, flashes, wastes of time of every type" (LAM 60).[1]

As with so many of Gadda's works, *Pasticciaccio* underwent a lengthy and tangled publishing history. Based on an actual crime, the novel had its genesis in late 1945 as part of a proposed series of six crime stories or *gialli* to be published by Alessandro Bonsanti in *Letteratura* and later in book form. Five chapters of *Pasticciaccio* appeared in *Letteratura* in 1946, but by the end of 1947 Gadda had not met his contractual obligations, and the publisher Vallecchi canceled his monthly advances. Refused by Mondadori in 1948, Gadda passed over to Longanesi and in the interim wrote a screenplay version of the novel, *Il palazzo degli ori,* for Lux-film.[2] A position at the RAI in 1950 curtailed further work on the novel. In 1953 Garzanti convinced Gadda to take up work once again, but only four years later and after much prodding by Garzanti—"with pointed rifle" as Gadda put it (LPGC 91)—did it appear in July 1957.[3]

It has been said that Gadda's main purpose in *Pasticciaccio* is not narrative. The novel's giallo plot is confusing and without resolution. It concerns two crimes which occur in the same building on via Merulana in Rome within a few days of one another. The first crime is a jewel robbery of the Venetian Countess Menegazzi. The second is the horrific murder and robbery of Liliana Balducci, an acquaintance of investigator Francesco Ingravallo, the novel's primary protagonist. The subsequent dual investigations lead the police and carabinieri to the Alban hills with its underclass of poor and voluptuous girls in the tavern-brothel-sewing shop of the disreputable hag Zamira Pácori. Eventually Menegazzi's jewels are discovered in a chamber pot, but the actual criminals are never apprehended. The events take place in early 1927, during the period of consolidation of Mussolini's dictatorship, and the regime and its leader are never far from the stinging barbs of the novel's satire. *Pasticciaccio* treats many of the obsessive themes Gadda had explored in *Cognizione* and throughout his earlier fiction: the messy interrelatedness of reality with its concausality and impossible closure; the cognitive process as grotesque deformation and tragic awareness; the problems of evil, dissipation, and death; the attraction/repulsion to the popular classes, popular epos, and the carnivalesque; and the Oedipal/matricidal urge and autobiographical neuroses. These interests lift the novel beyond its crime-story format to a metaphysical speculation on humankind, history, and the universe.

The similar themes in *Cognizione* and *Pasticciaccio* are embedded in substantially different narrative universes. *Cognizione*'s confessional and pathological autobiography make it a unique experience in Gadda's works, a novel that had to be written but could be written only once. It is the culmination of a personal mythos and trauma of denied greatness and nihilistic negation. *Pasticciaccio* diffuses autobiographical pathos across a broad spectrum of characters including but not limited to the novel's philosophizing protagonist Detective Ingravallo or the persecuted "prosciuttophile" Filippo Angeloni. *Pasticciaccio* is also a post–World War II novel, which for Gadda meant a shift from the failed dreams of youth to a vituperous focus on the dictator Mussolini as responsible for so many years of personal suffering and embittered silence.[4] Just as important is the move from Gadda's detested Lombard Brianza in *Cognizione* to the Roman world of *Pasticciaccio*. *Pasticciaccio*'s Rome is a linguistic crossroads marked by a continual flux of language confusion, macaronic interference, and multiplicity of perspective. The result is a rich pastiche of different linguistic registers and languages which subjects each discourse in the novel to an erosive irony.

MACARONIC PASTICHE

> La risciacquatura de' miei cenci è stata una fatica da non dire
> ("Il Pasticciaccio," VM 511).

> [The rinsing of my rags has been an incredible effort.]

"Baroque" and "grotesque" were labels applied to Gadda's works, labels for which he was in part responsible. They date back to his early fashioning of a baroque Manzonian heritage in the 1924 "Apologia manzoniana." "Pastiche" and "macaronic" were labels Gadda inherited. Their genesis can be located in friend Gianfranco Contini's seminal 1934 essay "Carlo Emilio Gadda, o del pastiche," in which Contini first traced an ideal literary lineage for Gadda with its origins in the Renaissance *"pasticheurs"* and "macaronics." It was a definition Gadda did not accept wholeheartedly. In a letter of July 20, 1934, Gadda wrote to Contini thanking him for his essay—"you have been a most attentive and acute reader"—but politely took issue with Contini's emphasis on the element of "pastiche" in his work over that of native spontaneity (LGC 13–15). An even more dogged circumspection concerning the label "macaronic" can be found in the 1947 essay "Fatto personale . . . o quasi" (A personal matter . . . or almost), in which Gadda laments that "that measure of *macaronic*" which Contini had written of had since germinated into "the index-card with which I find myself by now labeled in the filing cabinet of people's opinion, in a way that is too coarsely collocative" (VM 495). One wonders just how much Contini, whose well-read erudition and "arduous" style generated envy and intimidation in his friend, influenced Gadda's movement toward the ideas of pastiche and the macaronic as conscious coordinates of his prose. Gian Carlo Roscioni, who worked at length with Gadda in his later years, doubts that in 1934 Gadda knew the literary significance of the term *pastiche* and speculates that Contini contributed, in a decisive way perhaps, to alerting the author to the sort of writing he was engaged in and its implications (Roscioni 1988). There are indications that Gadda turned to Contini for information on such matters. He wrote of wanting to "desfrutar el amigo" for his omniscience concerning Rabelais (LGC 25). Perhaps the most telling testimony of Contini's influence appears in a letter of September 25, 1957, at the height of Gadda's newfound fame with *Pasticciaccio,* in which the author confesses that he writes for Gianfranco more than for anyone else (LGC 97). As Roscioni notes, Contini, perhaps in deference to Gadda's objections to the term *pastiche,* had changed the title of his 1934 essay from "Carlo Emilio Gadda, o del pastiche" to "Primo approccio al *Castello di Udine*" when it was republished in 1939 in *Esercizi di lettura*. Even more significantly, Gadda exhumed the same censured term, now in more plebeian garb, in the title of *Quer pasticciaccio* itself, perhaps in tribute to the acumen and foresight of his younger friend.

The *pasticciaccio* [awful mess] in the title is also indicative of Gadda's adaptation of the literary notions of "pastiche" and "macaronic" to his ontological and epistemological vision of the manifold and often horrific messiness of reality. As if to underscore this ontological, even biological, interpretation, a wicked allusion to the poetics of macaronic pastiche appears when one might least expect it, in the description of the savagely severed neck of Liliana Balducci:

> Un profondo, un terribile taglio rosso le apriva la gola, ferocemente. Aveva preso metà il collo, dal davanti verso destra, cioè verso sinistra, per lei, destra per loro che guardavano: sfrangiato ai due margini come da un reiterarsi dei colpi, lama o punta: un orrore! da nun potesse vede. Palesava come delle filacce rosse, all'interno, tra quella spumiccia nera der sangue, già raggrumato, a momenti; un *pasticcio!* con delle bollicine rimaste a mezzo. Curiose forme, agli agenti: parevano buchi, al novizio, come dei *maccheroncini* color rosso, o rosa. "La trachea," mormorò Ingravallo chinandosi, "la carotide! la iugulare . . . Dio!" (P 59; my emphasis)

> A deep, a terrible red cut opened her throat, fiercely. It had taken half the neck, from the front towards the right, that is, towards her left, the right for those who were looking down: jagged at its two edges, as if by a series of blows, of the blade or point: a horror! You couldn't stand to look at it. From it hung red strands, like thongs, from the black foam of the blood, almost clotted already; a *mess!* with some little bubbles still in the midst. Curious forms, to the policemen: they seemed holes, to the novice, like red-colored little *maccheroni*, or pink. "The trachea," murmured Ingravallo, bending down, "the carotid, the jugular! . . . God!" (TAM 69; my emphasis)

As we gaze into Liliana's biological organism we see the horror of death which disintegrates the complex system of the individual life to its material foundations. Liliana's severed arteries become a pasticcio of what appear to the stunned agents to be red or pink "maccheroncini." This is the concrete, physical reality of the pasticcio as mess for Gadda. In its nega-

tive sense, this physiological pasticcio is synonymous with the dissipation of reality's manifold relationships into the less real evil, the criminal
act, the regression from the heuristic becoming of n + 1 to the dissipation of n - 1. The macaronic is a symbol of both reality's disordered messiness and man's confused attempt to understand it. The references to macaroni and immediately afterward to a *sanguinaccio* [blood pudding] in describing Liliana's bloody wound are not, or not only, brazen analogies
chosen to "épater la bourgeois" (RI 396). They faithfully transcribe the
cognitive attempt of the police agents to comprehend the horror. The
agents grasp for an analogy that is part of an understandable epistemological paradigm, even if for the gormandizing Pompeo it entails a leap to
the hearty victuals of Peppì, "er Maccheronaro" [the macaroni provider],
famous for his "rosbiffe ar sangue" [blood-rare roast beef] (P 43; TAM
44).[5] The entire description is embedded in a macaronic conflux of interpretative codes, registers, and perspectives: emotional empathy and
horror from the opening description of the terrible wound to Ingravallo's
final invocation of God; an ironic professional precision in the description of the direction of the blows and the speculation concerning the cause
of the jaggedness of the wound's edges; the descent into dialect and
strained analogies in conveying the mental language and viewpoint of
the onlooking policemen; the anatomical taxonomy of Ingravallo's cata-
log of the severed trachea, carotid, and jugular.

Macaronic pastiche, however, is not just the reflection of reality's disorder in *Pasticciaccio*; it also encompasses an aggressive, useful dimension. The macaronic, Gadda wrote in "Fatto personale," can pulverize and
dissolve every abuse that reason and language commit through the words
of fraud (VM 496). That is why Ingravallo, philosophical detective and
enunciator of Gadda's own "theoretical ideas" on the plurality of causes
responsible for the pasticcio of reality, is presented from the opening pages
of the novel as an authorial stand-in for whom macaronic pastiche is part
and parcel of his speculative-investigative technique:

> Sosteneva, fra l'altro, che le inopinate catastrofi non sono mai la con-
> seguenza o l'effetto che dir si voglia d'un unico motivo, d'una causa al
> singolare: ma sono come un vortice, un punto di depressione ciclonica
> nella coscienza del mondo, verso cui hanno cospirato tutta una
> molteplicità di causali convergenti. Diceva anche nodo o groviglio, o
> garbuglio, o gnommero, che alla romana vuol dire gomitolo. Ma il
> termine giuridico "le causali, la causale" gli sfuggiva preferentemente
> di bocca: quasi contro sua voglia. L'opinione che bisognasse "riformare

in noi il senso della categoria di causa" quale avevamo dai filosofi, da Aristotele o da Emmanuele Kant, e sostituire alla causa le cause era in lui una opinione centrale e persistente: una fissazione, quasi . . . Così, proprio così, avveniva dei "suoi" delitti. "Quanno me chiammeno! . . . Già. Si me chiammeno a me . . . può stà ssicure ch'è nu guaio: quacche gliuommero . . . de sberretà . . ." diceva, contaminando napolitano, molisano, e italiano. (P 16–17)

He sustained, among other things, that unforeseen catastrophes are never the consequence or the effect, if you prefer, of a single motive, of *a* cause singular; but they are rather like a whirlpool, a cyclonic point of depression in the consciousness of the world, towards which a whole multitude of converging causes have contributed. He also used words like knot or tangle, or muddle, or *gnommero*, which in Roman dialect means skein. But the legal term, "the motive, the motives," escaped his lips by preference, though as if against his will. The opinion that we must "reform within ourselves the meaning of the category of cause," as handed down by the philosophers from Aristotle to Immanuel Kant, and replace cause with causes was for him a central, persistent opinion, almost a fixation. . . . This was how, exactly how he defined "his" crimes. "When they call me . . . Sure. If they call *me*, you can be sure that there's trouble: some mess, some *gliuommero* to untangle," he would say, garbling his Italian with the dialects of Naples and the Molise. (TAM 5)

Ingravallo, with two perennial little stains of olive oil on his lapel and his "Molisan poverty," is of humble origins, but his philosophical ideas, we are told, are not to be taken lightly: "on first hearing, they seemed banalities. They weren't banalities" (P 16; TAM 4).[6] Coming at the very beginning of the novel, these ideas acquire the quality of a programmatic declaration of *Pasticciaccio*'s epistemological and metanarrative method (see Fratnik 1990, 153–58). The detective's task and the text's task are the same: to retrace and unravel the manifold threads that constitute the mess or evil of reality gone awry. The metanarrativity is underscored by the inseparability of Ingravallo's method from its articulation in a language of multidirectional multiplicity. Ingravallo's pastiche of juridical, philo-sophical, and popular codes and his macaronic mixture of Italian with the dialects of Rome, Naples, and the Molise are the declaration of a textual modus operandi in which the word will be as complex and changeable as its referent.

Gadda was conscious of the positive-negative duality of the macaronic. In "Fatto personale" he notes that the macaronic can be a "useful jest" but also "useless, foolish and tedious" (VM 496). What is useful, and novel, in *Pasticciaccio* is the positive and inclusive sense of popular vitality and triumph occasioned by the macaronic. "To tell via the macaronic," Gadda declares in "Fatto personale," is "to immerse oneself in the living community of souls, to anticipate or second on the written page its inherent impulse to describe, its will to define reality, through merry signs" (VM 498). The macaronic defers to the sentiments of the many; it has its origins in the vitalistic "people's voice" pitted against the "dead muddle" of official discourse (VM 499–501).

Pasticciaccio approaches popular language and its carnivalesque backdrop in a substantially different fashion than is the case in *La cognizione del dolore*. Despite the virtuosity of its grotesque realism, *Cognizione*'s view of the carnivalesque is vitiated by the neurotic hypersensitivity and class consciousness of Gonzalo Pirobutirro. The carnivalesque and popular speech are seen as grotesque vulgarities concomitant with the disappearance of all gentility. In *Pasticciaccio* the autobiographical pathology of the carnivalesque is mitigated, in part through the refraction of authorial viewpoint across a myriad of characters and narrative voices, in part through a philological and sympathetic recuperation of popular speech and dialect. Contrary to Gonzalo's agoraphobic obsession with silence and solitude, *Pasticciaccio* gravitates merrily toward common meeting places: the street and courtyard of via Merulana 219, the police station, Zamira Pácori's den of voluptuous seamstresses, the Roman marketplace. The Roman crowd that gathers in front of Merulana 219, "sto porto de mare der palazzo" [this port of call of a building] (P 40; TAM 40), is described with a comic levity that is devoid of the traumatized disgust and rage of *Cognizione:*

Donne, sporte, e sedani: qualche esercente d'un negozio di là, col grembiule bianco: un "uomo di fatica" e questo col grembiule rigato, e col naso in veste e in colore d'un meraviglioso peperone: portinaie, domestiche, ragazzine delle portinaie che strillavano "a Peppì!," maschietti col cerchio, un attendente saturo d'arance, prese in una sua gran rete, con in cima i ciuffetti di due finocchi, e di pacchi: due o tre funzionari grossi, che in quell'ora matura agli altri gradi avevano appena discolto le vele: diretti, ciascuno, al suo ministero: e un dodici o quindici tra perdigiorno e vagabondi vari, diretti in nessun luogo. Un portalettere in istato di estrema gravidanza, più curioso di tutti, dava, della sua borsa

colma, in culo a tutti: che borbottavano mannaggia, e poi ancora mannaggia, mannaggia, uno dopo l'altro, man mano che la borsona perveniva
ad urtarli nel didietro. Un monello, con serietà tiburtina, disse: "Sto
palazzo, drento c'è più oro che monnezza." (P 28)

Women, shopping bags, and celery stalks: a shopkeeper or two from
across the street, in his white apron: an "odd job" man, also in an apron,
striped, his nose the shape and color of a wondrous pepper: concierges,
maids, the little daughters of the concierges shouting "Peppiiino!," boys
with hoops, an attendant saturated with oranges, trapped in his great
net bag, and crowned by the ferns of two big fennels, and packages: two
or three important officials, who in the hour ripe for the higher ranks
seemed to have unfurled their sails: bound, each of them, for his personal Ministry: and a dozen or even fifteen idlers, headed in no direction at all. A letter carrier in a state of advanced pregnancy, more curious than all, with his brimming bag which smacked everyone in the
ass: some muttered goddamnit, and then goddamn, goddamn, one after the other, as the bag struck them, in turn, on the behind. A gamin,
with Tiberine seriousness, said: "This building here, inside it, there's
more gold than there is garbage." (TAM 22–23)

In the novel's final chapter we enter the marketplace, ideal incubator
of popular speech and culture. As the narrative eye follows the police
agent Biondone through the bustling stalls of the open market in Rome's
Piazza Vittorio Emanuele II, past the *porchétta*, greens, and fresh sea-
food, there is none of the pathological desecration of *Cognizione*, but
rather a truly celebratory feast of abundance. Not a locus for the sarcastic
indictment of popular grotesqueness, as is the Milanese carnival in
Cognizione, *Pasticciaccio*'s market is "the place of a cosmic and popular
harmony" (Biasin 1993, 94), with its origins in Gadda's colorful journal-
istic pieces on markets and fairs: "Mercato di frutta e verdura" (1935–
36), "Alla fiera di Milano" (1936), "Carabattole a Porta Ludovica" (1940),
and, in particular, "La festa dell'uva a Marino" (1932).[7]
    The celebration of carnivalesque abundance is extended in Gadda's
Roman novel to popular language as well. In *Cognizione* marketplace
language is rarely heard as the "people's voice" but is reported from
Gonzalo's traumatic viewpoint, as in the case of the disgusting cotton-
candy vendor who yells out "curses in dialect." In *Pasticciaccio* there is
instead an exuberant vitalism of dialect, as in young Ascanio Lanciani's
boisterous invitation to the housewives to buy his porchétta: "'Carne fina

e dilicata, pe li signori propio! Assaggiatela e proverete, v' 'o dico io, sore spose: carne fina e saporita! Chi prova ciariprova, er guadambio è tutto vostro. La bella porca de li Castelli!'" (P 254–55) [Nice, tender meat, meat for ladies and gentlemen all right. Taste it and you'll see what I mean: tender and tasty meat! If you try it once you'll come back for more, I promise you. You're the ones who make off of this deal. The lovely pork from the Castelli!] (TAM 356–57). Popular speech in *Pasticciaccio* is free of the "gutturaloid," "epigastric," and "monosyllabic" negativity of Milanese dialect. It is marked by the "vivid accents" and "deductive sonority" of Inspector Fumi's persuasive Neapolitan voice, "pleasing, pleasing to our ears," as the narrator glosses (P 103; TAM 135).

Gadda's attraction to Roman and Neapolitan speech predates *Pasticciaccio*. The Neapolitan Fumi has a predecessor in the medical colonel Di Pascuale, whose eruptions in Neapolitan in the closing pages of the first part of *La cognizione del dolore* constitute the most exuberant treatment of dialect in the novel. As early as the *Giornale di guerra e di prigionia* Gadda evidenced his appreciation of the witty "Roman spirit" and "sweet Neapolitan tongue" (GGP 495, 506), while a letter of January 21, 1916, to friend Ambrogio Gobbi contains his first extended Italian-Roman pastiche (LAM 16–17). But the evocation of Roman expressivity in *Pasticciaccio* was especially influenced by the Roman sonnets of Giuseppe Gioachino Belli (1791–1863). Gadda's encounter with Belli occurred much later than those with Manzoni or D'Annunzio, precisely in the gestational period of the original 1946 *Pasticciaccio*. In a 1945 essay entitled "Arte del Belli," Gadda provides an intellectual and literary biography of Belli, declaring that Belli's poetry "draws on the equally painful and equally fecund limits of an attempt at a gnoseological vindication and a dissolution of inanity in the macaronic. The orchestrator of this epos is the people: the servant, the whore, the coachman, the mistress and the 'berzitello' or shop boy, the women from their windows" (VM 555–56).

The linkage of Belli's use of the macaronic to a gnoseological vindication casts the Roman poet as a strong literary precursor. This appropriation is underscored by Gadda's emphasis on the commonality between Belli and the Milanese dialect poet Carlo Porta, but even more so through his coupling of Belli with Manzoni. Both Manzoni and Belli seek resolutions to the dilemma of expression which share with Gadda's own "approaching as nearly as possible what one's own consciousness certifies to be true, in eventual opposition to the slothful recourse of all verbal conformity" (VM 554).

The Bellian inheritance in *Pasticciaccio* distinguishes the novel's positive popular epos from the ridiculous and ridiculed "bitumous epos" of *Cognizione*'s filthy calibans and inane villa dwellers. In *Pasticciaccio* ridicule and expressionism are fused in an ironic but sympathetic participation with popular perspective and narration, akin to what Gadda admired in Belli: "Belli's truth, his dialectics, includes or involves the plebeian myth of the city and of its ways and people. He incorporates this into his poem, and not only as an antithesis, that is to say, making it the target of a possible or actual satire. In fact, he embellishes it and promotes it to epic material" (VM 559). Language too, Gadda adds, is raised by Belli to the same epic status.

Pasticciaccio bears tribute to the Roman master poet in its recurrence to Bellian vocabulary, popular imagery, neologisms, and amphibologies.[8] A particularly strong Bellian presence can be found in the novel's colorful and antiquated popular analogies and hyperboles:

> E il palazzo poi, la gente der popolo lo chiamaveno er palazzo dell'oro. Perché tutto er casamento insino ar tetto era come imbottito de quer metallo. (P 19)[9]
>
>   ... senz'addarsene acciaccò un piede ar barboncino, che sbottò in un diavolío di caí caí da doverlo udire il Papa a palazzo. (P 36)
>
>   ... un sottanone de pezza forte che pareva la bandiera der Giudizzio. (P 98)
>
>   ... du quarti de luna d'oro che ciaveva agli orecchi: che ar primo rigirà la testa pareva le dovesser fare cin cin. Come a un'odalisca der Sultano. (P 110–11)
>
>   ... e gente in anticamera! Madonna! più che ai piedi de la gran torre de Babele. (P 124)

> And in the neighborhood the building itself was called by the poor people the palace of gold. Because it was as if the whole place right up to the roof were crammed with that precious metal. (TAM 9)
>
>   ... without noticing, he stepped on the poodle's paw, and the beast unleashed a yelping that the Pope must have heard over in the Vatican. (TAM 35)
>
>   ... a skirt of strong cloth that looked like the Banner of Judgment. (TAM 128)
>
>   ... two golden crescents she wore in her ears: which, at the first turn of her head, seemed about to go ding-ding. Like an odalisque of the Sultan. (TAM 146)

... and people in the waiting room! Madonna! more than at the foot
of the great tower of Babel. (TAM 166)

The Bellian reminiscences endow *Pasticciaccio's* 1927 Rome with the
flavor of Papal Rome a century earlier (see Papponetti 1985, 59). This
Bellian anachronism bears a crucial influence on the form of Gadda's political satire in the novel and his treatment of the humble classes.

In the grand tradition of the Roman pasquinades, Belli's sonnets are a
vehicle for the satirization of the figures of authority in papal Rome
through the chorality of the people. In "Arte del Belli" Gadda underscores the technique, in particular the satirization of "Papa Grigorio"
(Gregory XVI) from Belluno, in which Belli captures "all of the caprice
and envy of the Romans for a 'foreign' pope" (VM 558). *Pasticciaccio's*
Roman choral voice pokes fun in a similar manner at their own 1927
"foreign" pope, the industrious and mountain-climbing "gran papa
alpinista" Pius XI (Achille Ratti). Gadda was no stranger to Pope Pius's
Vatican. From 1931 to 1934 he had worked for the Vatican Technical Ser-
vices, "presiding over the toilets, sewers, electricity, water and gas" (LAM
43) and on the construction of the Vatican power plant commissioned by
Pius (a job Gadda had perhaps obtained via the friendship between the
Gadda and Ratti families and which he detested from the beginning [see
Gadda Conti 1974, 34]). Gadda was never a fan of priests, and there are
various malicious references to the Church and sacrilegious interjections
in the 1946 *Pasticciaccio.* These were attenuated in the 1957 version, very
possibly in a act of anticipatory revision provoked by the entrenchment
of a Christian Democratic regime which was not averse to practicing a
"moral" censureship when necessary (see Dombroski 1971, 65; Fiorillo
1983, 29–31).

In any case, the principal target of popular satire in *Pasticciaccio* is not
the Church but Mussolini and his fascist *gerarchi.* With the enlarged
portrait of "Quer Tale" [That One] hanging on the government and school
walls of Rome, "un grugno, perch'era nato scemo, de volé vendicasse de
tutti" [a mug, because he was born stupid, that seemed to want to take
his revenge on everyone] (P 265; TAM 371), Mussolini is the invasive
foreign presence in Gadda's Bellian Rome. He and his regime are the
continual butt of the people's sarcasm and irony, not only at the hands of
the novel's plebeian Roman narrator but from the perspective of the
novel's various characters as well, as when Liliana's aunts vent their
rage at having lost Liliana's gold coins on the ridiculous dictator: "Queli

marenghini gialli gialli tonni tonni de quanno nun c'era ancora sto Pupazzo a Palazzo Chiggi, a strillà dar balcone come uno stracciarolo" [Those nicely round, bright yellow pieces of the days before that Puppet in Palazzo Chigi, yelling from his balcony like an old-clothes man] (P 90; TAM 116).

In *La cognizione del dolore* and in *Eros e Priapo* the satire pits the autobiographical railer against both the inane dictator and the masses who subscribe to his folly. *Pasticciaccio's* anti-Mussolinian satire fuses authorial sarcasm with that of the novel's characters in a bond of communality as fellow disparagers of the ridiculous Duce.

The aura of a Bellian nineteenth-century Rome also contributes to the positive recasting of the humble classes that are derided and demonized in *La cognizione del dolore*. Although *Pasticciaccio's* plot hinges around the greed of the popular folk for the gold and jewels of via Merulana 219, they are depicted in an archaic and romanticized preindustrial garb. They are not the threatening plebs of the Socialist propagandists or the "trade-unionist" peons who enrage Grifonetto Lampugnani and Gonzalo Pirobutirro.[10] Class characteristics are eclipsed in *Pasticciaccio's* young thieves and prostitutes by a focus on the vitalistic sexuality that thrives on their "healthy" indigence. A case in point is the voluptuous "poor creature" Ines Cionini. Sick, the narrator states, only with hunger, beauty, puberty, filth, impudence, and abandon, Ines's tattered rags struggle to contain her voluptuous forms and pungent odor of the haystack from the aroused gaze and olfactory sense of the investigators: "'Mm! che robba!'" si dissero tutti, mentalmente" [Mmm! Get a load of that!' all of them said to themselves, mentally] (P 145; TAM 197). Ines's "animal warmth" and "gemlike eyes of a child" convey the possibility of happiness and a transcendental truth to the hardened officers, and the narration indulges at length in a pastoral depiction of her destitution. In *Il palazzo degli ori*, Gadda's screenplay of the novel, the author stresses that the indigent young characters should be stunning exemplars of the "bloom and beauty of the people of the Lazio region," and that the young lovers Lavinia Mattonari and Enea Retalli should engage the sympathy of the viewer in their "serious" farewell scene, to be shot "with a slight romantic-heroic emphasis, in the manner of the poor, for whom sometimes crime is an act of holy rebellion etc., and the carabinieri on their trail are the persecution of destiny, etc" (PO 969). Gadda's sympathizing attitude toward the poor in the screenplay is perhaps a concession to the triumphant wave (1946–48) of neorealist sensibility (Andreini 1988, 143), but a vein of compassion for the destitute and humble (those unsullied by worker trade-unionism) can be found in Gadda's works dat-

ing from the honorable Stefano in the 1918 "La passeggiata autunnale."
In the 1970 "L'umanità degli umili," one of Gadda's final essays, published in the very Milanese *Il corriere della sera*, the author reiterates his
long-standing admiration for the humble workers and tradesmen of Rome,
from the dusty brick masons to the deliverymen and female wine mer-
chants who continue their traditional professions in the modern capital
(SD 1224–26).[11]

Pasticciaccio's Rome is tinged with the popular archaism of its Bellian
intertext. It is also the unique incubator for the linguistic confusion and
interference that is the historical core of macaronic discourse. Rome has
always occupied a singular position in Italy's linguistic panorama. Aside
from Tuscany, it was in Rome that dialect differed least from the normative Italian laid down by the grammarians of the Renaissance. The presence of the Vatican court and later of the Italian central government fos-
tered the development of an official koine that gradually became more
southernized in the postunification waves of immigration into the city.
The contrast between the official languages of the courts and public pal-
aces and the inventive popular argot of the Roman underclass resulted in
a fertile ambience for linguistic instability and confusion between competing codes, a confusion which Belli, who felt that Roman speech was
more a "corruption" and "distortion" of Italian than an autonomous dialect, had exploited in his Roman sonnets (Belli 1961, 441–42; De Mauro
1979, 312).

Pasticciaccio organizes its digressive and nonconclusive detective-novel
plot around destabilizing confusion. At the core of the befuddlement lies
a fundamental linguistic confusion that affects referentiality and communication at all socio-economic levels. A case in point is the ongoing
uncertainty concerning the pronunciation and orthography of the lengthy
or unfamiliar words that penetrate into the offices of the Santo Stefano
del Cacco police station. Proper names in particular are subjected to a
relentless mangling. Name confusion is not unique to *Pasticciaccio*, being one of Gadda's obsessive cauchemars. Only in *Pasticciaccio*, though,
does name confusion regularly result from a general state of linguistic
instability characterized by phonetic transpositions and hypercorrections.
The comic emblem of this instability and ignorance is the concierge
Manuela Pettacchioni's misspelling of her own name into "Manuella
Petachoni," via the typically Roman transposition of double and single
consonants and elimination of diphthongs (P 43; TAM 44–45).

Name distortion in the novel also points to a comic confusion between
linguistic signifier and semantic referent in which the spirit of popular

epos distorts the name to match what is seen to be the bearer's distinguishing characteristic. The zealous brigadier Pestalozzi becomes the bone-crushing Pestalossi (P 140; TAM 189); the voluptuous Tina Crocchiapani or "bread cruncher" becomes Crocchiapàini, "dandy crusher" (P 103; TAM 134); the young gigolo Diomede Lanciani is apostrophized by Fumi as "'o Lanci-ere" or "the lancer" (P 172; TAM 237); Giuliano Valdarena becomes Valdassena, echoing suspicions that he may be Liliana's assassin (P 57; TAM 66); the northern ski resort Cortina d'Ampezzo becomes, for Fumi, Ccortina d'Ampiezzo, in which the typical Neapolitan diphthongization is evocative of Italian "amplesso" [embrace, coitus], an association suggested by the fact that Fumi is naming places to which nubile American tourists abscond with Italian gigolos (P 174; TAM 240). Ingravallo himself, whose name in its allusion to "ingravidare" [to impregnate] and "cavallo" [horse] echoes the novel's obsession with the themes of impregnation and sexual prowess (somewhat lacking in the not very handsome Don Ciccio), is momentarily associated with the confusion he is charged with solving when he is referred to as "er dottor Ingarballo" with its Roman echo of "ingarbugliare" [to muddle] (P 92; TAM 118). The crowning example of semantically charged name distortion concerns the surname of the floozy Venetian countess Menegazzi. On the "stupendous lips" of the envious young Roman brides, the Venetian name totters on the brink of obscenity throughout the novel, slowly making its way, "with the perforating vigor of an eel" (P 51; TAM 56), against the historical current of its etymology ("Menegaccio," "Menecacci") until it succumbs in an official police document to its obscene evocation: "Menecazzi [loosely prick thrasher], who returned, this time, to the definitive possession and full enjoyment, by right and by might, of her own z's: her Venetian g, for the rest, joyfully commuted into a central-Italian c" (P 185; TAM 257).

The novel's name distortions are reflective of the idiosyncratic playfulness (at times triteness) that characterizes Gadda's macaronic pastiche. But they also typify the assault on language ossification brought on by the macaronic's sociohistorical genesis in linguistic confusion and instability. Name distortion highlights the tenuous and fluid connection between words and reality; it is a means of dismantlement of the myth of self-contained self and an attack on language's lazy fall into complacent automatism. It is also part of a broader condition of macaronic interference in *Pasticciaccio*'s Rome, emblematized in a garbled telephone communication midway in the novel:

Da quanto le diligenze auricolari del Di Pietrantonio pervennero infine a racimolare dal naufragio del testo (il crepitio del microfono e l'induttanza della linea sonorizzavano il testo: interferenze varie, da contatto urbano, intercicalavano, straziavano la recezione), apparve a un dipresso che l'incauto Enea Retalli o Ritalli, *sive* Luiginio (ma evidentemente Luigino) aveva dato a tinger la sciarpa . . . trentasei quintali di parmigiano! brondi ghi barla? spediti ieri da Reggio Emilia . . . Parla il tenente di vascello Racace. Brondi, brondi! Tenenza carabinieri Marino! Di parmigiano stagionato brondi . . . gasa del signor ammiraglio Mondegùggoli! Società Bavatelli di Parma, sì, a mezzo camion. . . . Tenenza carabinieri di Marino, precedenza di servizio. Trentasei quintali, sì, tre camion, partiti ieri alle dieci. No, la signora gondessa è in gliniga. . . . In gliniga dal signor ammiraglio . . . a via Orà-zio: Orà-zio! Sì, signorsì. No, signor no. Mo domando. Precedenza servizio polizia, questura di Roma. Trentasei quintali da Reggio Emilia, tipo Parma, di prima assoluta! Il signor ammiraglio ha fatto l'oberazzione lunedì: l'oberazzione della vescica: della vescì-ca. Sì, signorsì. . . . No, signor no. (P 139–40)

[From what Di Pietrantonio's auricular diligence managed at last to salvage from the shipwrecked text (the receiver's crackling and the line's inductance sonorized the message: various interferences, an urban crossed line, laced it with chatter, tormenting reception), it seemed more or less that the uncautious Enea Retalli or Ritalli, *sive* Luiginio (but obviously Luigino) had taken the scarf to be dyed . . . thirty-six quintals of Parmesan! Heddo, who's sbeaking? shipped yesterday from Reggio Emilia . . . Lieutenant-commander Racace here. Heddo? Heddo? . . . Abmiradal Mondeguggoli's house! The Bavatelli Shipping Company from Parma, yes, by truck . . . carabinieri headquarters, Marino, we have precedence. Thirty-six quintals, yes, three trucks, left at ten o'clock yesterday. No, the condessa's in the hospiddle . . . in the hordpiddle, visidding the admiradal . . . via Ora-zio! Yes, sir. No, sir. I'll ask. Police here, we have precedence, Rome Police Headquarters. Get off the line. Thirty-six quintals from Reggio Emilia, Parma-type cheese, absolutely first class! The admirabdal was obberadated on Monday: gallbladder: *bladder.* Yes, yes, sir . . . no, sir, no.] (TAM 188–89)

Telephone lines are crossed and three distinct conversations and realities are confused: the official world of a police communication (with its characteristic name distortion) from Marino to Rome; the commercial (northern) and gastronomical world of a transpeninsular shipment of Parmesan cheese; the physiological lower stratum of an admiral's bladder operation (in caricatured southern speech). True to the corrosive quality of the macaronic, the muddle involves not just the mixing of two or more languages but their mutual interference as well ("various interferences, from an urban crossed line"). Despite the efforts of the police to reestablish the "precedence" of official discourse, the hierarchy between high and low is scrambled as each "text" asserts the centrality of its own concerns.

The communicative muddle is a metaphor for the linguistic confusion and interference that characterize *Pasticciaccio*'s Rome in its entirety. As a consequence of its unique situation as the historical, social, political, bureaucratic, and linguistic hub of the peninsula, Rome *urbs* becomes a modern bazaar in *Pasticciaccio*, where all roads lead and where all lines cross. At the core of this interaction is the police station in Santo Stefano del Cacco where more people congregate than at the foot of the great Tower of Babel. The police station is the place where linguistic confusion is at its greatest. It is the modern institution where the "low" elements of society come together with officialdom, where the social and linguistic clash between high, official discourses and low, transgressive discourses is most manifest. *Pasticciaccio*'s Rome is a uniquely modern site of Bakhtin's "polyglossia" and language "hybridization," the interaction and interference of competing languages which constitutes the foundation of novelistic discourse. Not just another example of the postwar Italian boom of the *romanzo dialettale* (novel in dialect), *Pasticciaccio*, with its archaic Bellian atmosphere and its ironic excavation of a millennial-old civilization, is also an archaeology of the macaronic heritage of the novel as genre.[12]

The macaronic interference in *Pasticciaccio* is horizontal, bringing together various dialects, but it is also vertical, juxtaposing dialect, the bureaucratic koine of the middle classes and fascist hierarchy, and the cultured Italian of the aulic-literary tradition.[13] The resulting upheaval in the traditional stratification between high or sublime language codes and low or comic codes occurs not so much through autobiographical invective but through an ambiguous and ironic subversion that underscores in the official codes of discourse their "contingencies, incongruities and relativities" (Furst 1984, 12). Macaronic interference can dismantle an entire cultural discourse through the opposition of a single word in Italian and dialect. This is what happens when Ingravallo's investigation subjects him to a marketing director's panegyric of his company's industrial transformer oil:

"Il nostro gran segreto, vede, è quello che ci piace di raccontare a tutti: *la costanza dei requisiti per ogni determinato tipo di olio.* Prenda, per fare un esempio, il nostro imbattibile Transformer Oil B marca undici Extra. . . . Anidricità assoluta: è il requisito essenziale: va bene: condizione sine qua non: temperatura di congelamento . . . bassissima: viscosità. . . . 2,4 Wayne, a far tanto: grado di acidità, trascurabile: potere dielettrico, stupefacente: punto di infiammabilità . . . il più elevato di tutti gli oli industriali americani." (P 84)

["Our great secret, you see, is the secret we like to tell everybody: *the constancy of the specifications for each different kind of oil.* Now, for example, take our unbeatable Transformer Oil B, Grade 11-Extra. . . . Absolutely anhydrous: this is the most basic essential; yes, the *sine qua non:* freezing point . . . extremely low: viscosity. . . . 2.4 Wayne, at the outside: acid value, negligible: dielectric strength, amazing: flash point . . . the highest of all American industrial oils."] (TAM 106)

The executive's pitch is a finely crafted pastiche of technological jargon, salesman's enthusiasm, and seductive rhetoric (including the offer of a cigarette at its end). It is lost, though, on the somnolent Ingravallo, who, with his oil-stained lapel and gifts of bottles of oil to Liliana Balducci, is himself a connoisseur of oil but of the more archaic and Italic variety: "Olio! Ne avivene, d'uoglie, la gente, in terra di Apulia. E lui, di quest'altro . . . non sapeva davvero dove attaccarselo" [Oil! The people back in Apulia, they live on oil. But this other oil . . . he really didn't know where to stick it] (P 85; TAM 108). The ironic contrast hinges on the juxtaposition of the Italian and dialect versions of a single lexeme, *olio/uoglie,* and the diametrically different referential worlds they signify. The technique is similar to that of *ingénu* irony in which the subversion of the high or official perspective is accomplished through its contrast with an "inferior" perspective (Muecke 1969, 91–92). It is a technique used repeatedly in *Pasticciaccio:* in the young carabiniere Fara Filiorum Petri Cocullo's macaronic distortion of roadside Latin inscriptions or in Zamira Pacori's association of the nineteenth-century poets Giovanni Prati and Giovanni Pascoli with "posti da facce er fieno" [places where they make hay], a pun, as translator William Weaver points out, on the words *prati* [meadows] and *pascoli* [pastures] (P 204; TAM 283).

Macaronic pastiche is central to the narrative refraction of perspective in *Pasticciaccio*. The macaronic affords a remedy to the dilemma in Gadda's early fiction concerning his intrusive authorial lyricism and the narration of character sentiment *ab interiore* or *ab exteriore*. These problems are resolved through a fusion of popular epos and narrative satire in a macaronic free indirect discourse.

Pasticciaccio is a novel with many narrative voices and tonalities, from Manzonian to classicist, from baroque mock-epic (especially in the novel's second half) to tragic oration (see Citati 1963, 32–33). Opposite these manifestations of a high, literary narrative pole there exists a crude and rude Roman narrator, with Bellian overtones, who is particularly adept in providing scurrilous or lewd analogies and denigrating the dictator Mussolini. This Roman narrative alter ego is not Gadda, nor a character, but is instead the author's deformation into a stylized and vulgarized narrative embodiment, an incorrigible Manuela Pettacchioni of himself (Citati 1963, 29).

Furthermore, all aspects of inner life become public domain in *Pasticciaccio*. Characters are called upon to testify and contribute to the novel's narration from their own viewpoints and in their own languages. This presence of character voice extends to the narration of their thoughts as well, via the novel's extensive use of free indirect discourse, the third-person narration of a character's thoughts in the language of the character.

Gadda had recurred to free indirect discourse frequently in his early fiction, often with limited success, as a method alternatively to establish an ironic distancing from a character's thoughts or to infuse those thoughts with the sublime lyricism of the Gaddian narrator. In *Pasticciaccio* this interpenetration of discourses is rendered more complex and ironic by the novel's "linguistic promiscuity" grounded in its macaronic mixing of dialect and Italian (see Cane 1969, 100–102). An example of a dissonant irony effected by macaronic free indirect discourse can be found in the narration of the inner thoughts of Liliana's aunts:

E poi avevano il pensiero a Giuliano. Quel fermo lo sentivano come un oltraggio: un torto fatto a loro, alla casata bellissima dei Valdarena, "na famija che in tutto er generone nun ce n'è un'antra": delle più floride, delle più piantate in terra: ommini, donne, pupi. L'idea che una figliola come quella fusse precipitata in braccio ar diavolo co li mejo regali der matrimonio, co tutto l'oro e le gioie, senza lassà un ricordo, senza una parola d'addio! Un'idea così, povere zie! stava pe diventà un tormento, un male ar core. (P 89–90)

[And besides they had Giuliano on their minds. That arrest, they felt, was an outrage: an offense against them, the splendid house of Valdarena, "a high-class family whose like you can't find in the whole of Rome"; a family of the most florid, the most solidly rooted: men, women, kids. The thought of a girl like that, plunged into the devil's arms, with all her finest wedding presents, all her gold and jewels, leaving nothing to remember her by, not even a word of farewell! The idea, for the poor aunts!, was about to become a torment, heartache.] (TAM 114)

After the opening sentence in a neutral Italian narrative voice, the presence of the inner perspective of the aunts is first revealed in the superlative "bellissima," an affective, subjective judgment that establishes an initial hint of ironic dissonance between narrator and characters. The successive plunge into quoted speech in dialect, "na famija . . ." exposes the egoistic family pride of the aunts in their own voice. The hyperbolic absolute superlative, with its Bellian overtones—"in tutto er generone," is typical of the novel's use of popular speech in the service of a "caricatural mimesis" (Cane 1969, 104). As the emotional fervor of the aunts increases, the narration of their thoughts is penetrated by their own narrated dialect, a juxtaposition of languages which unmasks the hypocrisy of their grief. What truly is a "male ar core" to the "povere zie" (the supposedly sympathetic qualifier "povere" is replete with ironic dissonance) is not that Liliana has been taken from them without having had the opportunity to leave a final sentimental "ricordo" or "parola di addio" (expressed in Italian), but that "li mejo regali der matrimonio, co tutto l'oro e le gioie" have gone to Balducci, "in braccio ar diavolo" (penetration of dialect). Mimetically, dialect accurately reproduces the verbal intonation and emotional immediacy of these characters in the narration of their thoughts. Moreover, the macaronic back and forth between Italian and dialect heightens the ability of free indirect discourse to "throw into ironic relief all false notes struck by a figural mind" (Cohn 1978, 117). As Gadda put it, the macaronic pulverizes the abuses of fraudulent speech or reasoning.[14]

Very often in the novel macaronic pastiche blurs beyond reconstruction the demarcation between narrative voices and perspectives and character voices and perspectives. In this sense, it can be argued that *Pasticciaccio*'s true narrator is linguistic confusion and promiscuity itself. The novel's protean macaronic pastiche unhinges language from any privileged subjectivity. This is apparent, for instance, when the narration appropriates a character's voice in the description of that same character, as in the following examples concerning the Neapolitan Inspector Fumi:

> Poi, rivolto agli astanti, sul cerchio dei quali rigirò gli occhi, e con il tono pacificato *'e chillo* che disserta de moribus, de temporibus. (P 172; my emphasis)
> . . . il tono s'indurì, s'enfatizzò severo nel crescendo, ruga verticale *'n miezz'a* fronte. (P 174; my emphasis)

> [Then, turned to the others present, over the circle of whom he moved his eyes, and with the pacified tone of who is speechifying *de moribus, de temporibus.* (TAM 236)
> . . . his tone hardened, with stern emphasis in its crescendo, a vertical wrinkle in the middle of his brow.] (TAM 240)

The brief infiltrations of Neapolitan dialect ("'e chillo" and "'n miezz'a") in the description of Fumi cannot be justified "mimetically" in terms of free indirect discourse; Fumi does not "think" his own description. Nor can they be attributed to the intervention of the popular Roman chorus or the novel's sardonic Roman narrator, since they are in Neapolitan. What they do attest to is the disembodiment of the "linguistic" self from the "empirical" self in *Pasticciaccio*, not as a condition of subjective alienation but of ironic transcendence. Individual angst yields to the universal spirit of the linguistic community. Gadda's Roman novel is, in this sense, the most harmonious and serene moment in the author's dismantlement of the myth of subjective wholeness. In *Cognizione* the dismantlement of the myth is carried out in the guise of Gonzalo's pitiless and impotent negation of self and the world. In *Pasticciaccio* the inclusive technique of macaronic pastiche subordinates subjective sarcasm to the linguistic triumph of community over nihilism.

Eros and Death

> Femmine tutte, a *sensibbilità diffusa* (P 127).

> All of them women with a *widespread sensitivity* (TAM 171).

Erotic themes and imagery occupy a central position in Gadda's works, from the love-triangle plot of the early "La passeggiata autunnale" to the caustic sexual satire of *Eros e Priapo*. *Pasticciaccio* is a summa of Gadda's narrative treatment of Eros, in its appropriation of erotic archetypes from the author's early works or its use of sexual satire to criticize the fascist regime. *Pasticciaccio* also recuperates the incestual/matricidal motif of *La cognizione del dolore*, but whereas the immensity of the autobiographical transgression in *Cognizione* makes it unique in Gadda's major works for its lack of sexually connotated characters and overt erotic intrigue, the diffusion of autobiography in *Pasticciaccio* opens up the motif to an explicitly erotic treatment of sexuality, procreation, and voyeuristic sadism.

In "Fatto personale" Gadda argues that the macaronic is also the triumph of a "biological urgency" (VM 501). The vindication of Eros's biological rights is present on the "stupendous lips" of each of the novel's stunning young servants and prostitutes, who imbue the Roman dialect with an erotic resonance that is a defiant rebellion against official discourse. Even the ethereal Liliana Balducci, who is, despite her spirituality, "a desirable woman," can truncate the attentions of a particularly persistent suitor with a glance that merges the delicacy of her melancholic soul with a streetwise Roman sensuality: "d'una occhiata fra sdegnosa e misericorde, fra gratitudine e sdegno pareva chiedergli: 'Mbè?'" [with a glance, half-disdainful, half-pitying, between gratitude and scorn, she seemed to ask him: "Well?"] (P 26; TAM 20). The sonorous labials of Liliana's glance-retort evoke the steamy referentiality of Roman eroticism that would be exported worldwide by the seductive comedies of the postwar Italian film industry.

Eros is also used in the novel to deflate the fascist myth of virility and fecundity. Ingravallo's opening assertion that a "quantum of eros" is involved in all crimes, even those that appear most removed from the tempests of love, occasions suspicious reactions in the novel's ironic "so-called 'Latin' world" (P 15; TAM 3). In the climate of a 1927 fascist neo-idealism hostile to any such erotic psychopathology, colleagues, priests, and superiors speculate that Don Ciccio has been reading "strange books" from which he has gleaned his "terminology for doctors in looneybins" designed only to dazzle the naive and the ignorant (P 17; TAM 6).[15] Ironically, the suspicions of subversion are well-taken since Ingravallo's statements echo, in a different context, Gadda's diagnosis of Mussolinian fascism in *Eros e Priapo* as a "crime" whose origins lie in "a mainly 'erotic' motive" (EP 40). Much of *Pasticciaccio*'s satire against the Duce and his regime has its origins in a similar misogynistic critique in *Eros and Priapo*: "already, once they were confirmed, all the Maria Barbisas of Italy were beginning to fall in love with him, already they began to invulvulate him, Italy's Magdas, Milenas, Filomenas, as soon as they stepped down from the altar: in white veils, crowned with orange blossoms, photographed coming out of the narthex, dreaming of the orgies and the educatory exploits of the swinging *manganello*" (P 56; TAM 64).

Liliana Balducci's obsessive yearning for a child, "er pupo," is itself a satire of the regime's desperate campaign to increase births (begun precisely in 1926–27), as is the abundance of nubile Alban virgins, "demographic hopes . . . for the eternal Spring of the Fatherland" (P 152; TAM 207). *Pasticciaccio*'s so-called Latin world is abundantly fecund in potentiality. No longer is it necessary to take the Sabines by force, since "the Alban women, nowadays, came down to the riverbanks on their own" (P 24; TAM 17). The land itself is overflowing with fertility, a "great fertile womb," "swollen Fallopian tubes," a "great Ovary" furnishing a constant supply of nubile nieces to the Balducci apartment in search of the "spermatic aura" of the "male afflatus" (P 24; TAM 16–17).

This ubiquitous female fertility has its male counterparts: the handsome Giuliano Valdarena, who descends on his willing prey "like the hawk on the most resistant of the whole chicken coop" (P 66; TAM 79); the blond gigolo Diomede-Ganimede Lanciani, a fitting proof, the novel glosses, for the regime's later assertion of the splendid Aryanism of the Latin and Sabellian people (P 167; TAM 230). Nevertheless, the promise of future Roman progeny is hindered by the lack of an inseminating force able to match the ferocity of the female sexuality, a slap in the face of the myth of the Roman patriarchate (Tench 1985, 211–12). The sexually stunning men in the novel are segregated from its stupendous women (Diomede Lanciani and Enea Retalli are fugitives while Giuliano Valdarena is detained). Those men who remain, including Ingravallo, are comically inadequate to the challenge, voracious in their stares but sexually inactive, even bumbling. Unable to impregnate, the unvirile man is degraded to "[a] puppet: an infertile animal, with a big, fake carnivalesque head. An implement that is of no use: a gimlet with its threads worn out" (P 106; TAM 140). There is a pervasive male inferiority complex in *Pasticciaccio*, an obsessive rage on Ingravallo's part that his native Molise has been excluded from the fabled geodetic triangle of male potentiality postulated by the "minch . . . iòlogo" [prick-ologist] D. H. Lawrence or Norman Douglas (P 174–75; TAM 241). As a result, Eros becomes an essentially voyeuristic enterprise. It is engaged in through a desirous, male gaze, a "male delirium," that is alternatively stunned or repulsed but always obsessively fixated on the female sexual object (P 147; TAM 199).

Sexuality, eroticism, and love are typically dysfunctional in the Gaddian narrative universe. The result is a misogynistic estrangement of the female object of desire. Women are continually objectified and categorized in *Pasticciaccio*, discussed in the collective singular, seen as a "phenomenon" (Andreini 1988, 106). A corroborative case in point is Ingravallo's musing on the female "personality":

> La personalità femminile—brontolò mentalmente Ingravallo quasi predicando a se stesso—che vulive dì? . . . 'a personalità femminile, tipicamente centrogravitata sugli ovarii, in tanto si distingue dalla maschile, in quanto l'attività stessa della corteccia, int' 'o cervello d' 'a femmena, si manifesta in un apprendimento, e in un rifacimento, d' 'o ragionamento dell'elemento maschile. . . . La qualità eminentemente ecolalica della di lei anima (il concilio di Magonza, nel 589, le concesse un'anima: a un voto di maggioranza) la induce a soavemente farfallare d'attorno al perno del coniugio: plastile cera, chiede dal sigillo l'impronta: al marito il verbo e l'affetto, l'ethos e il pathos. (P 106)

> [The female personality—Ingravallo grumbled mentally, as if preaching to himself—what did it all mean? . . . the female personality, typically gravity-centered on the ovaries, is distinguished from the male insofar as the very activity of the cortex, in the brain of the female, is manifested in an acquisition, and in a reconstruction, of the reasoning of the male element. . . . The eminently echolalic quality of her soul (The Council of Mainz, in 589, granted her a soul: by a majority of one vote) induces her to flutter gently around the axis of matrimony: impressionable wax, she asks the seal of his imprint: for the husband, word and affection, ethos and pathos.] (TAM 139–40)

The misogynistic discourse is ironized through a macaronic mixing of psycho-medical terminology with low discourse in dialect and later via an absurd ecclesiastic scholasticism. The detective's archaic misogynism corresponds, however, to Gadda's own idée fixe (it appears in *Cognizione* in the Mother's attachment to her husband's Matrix Idea of the villa, in *Eros e Priapo* in the hysterical women-crowds impregnated by the phallic pronouncements of the dictator). Gadda consistently expounds his misogyny in a tone of ironic excess, as if in recognition of its absurdity, but the fixation remains very real and irremovable.

Elio Gioanola, who has examined at length the erotic dysfunctionalism in Gadda's works and personality, argues that the absence of a successful integration of affection and sexuality results in an obligatory idealization or denigratory deformation of his female characters (Gioanola 1987, 62–88). Female characters are polarized into "high" and "low" archetypes: woman as (threatening) sexual physicality and woman as idealized and untouchable sublimity. The biographical traces of this tendency can be seen in Gadda's war diary and wartime letters where there is a distinct division between maids and seamstresses who satisfy his physical needs ("I was also able to obtain the indulgence of a Hotel maid for another 'service' that I hadn't satisfied for months" [GGP 642]) and his timid aspiration to a love story with young women of the upper bourgeoisie, rendered impossible by his lack of money, will, and good looks (GGP 629; Sergiacomo 1988, 21–22).

At the lower end of the dichotomy, female physicality is represented either as repulsive grotesqueness or enticing sexuality. Repulsive female sexuality in *Pasticciaccio* is embodied in the hysterical, kimono-clad Menegazzi, who lives in fear and desire of domestic assault; in the garrulous and porky concierge Manuela Pettacchioni, "like an old sow on her trotters" (P 43; TAM 45); in the toothless sorceress Zamira Pácori, whose black hole of a mouth becomes the ubiquitous sign of her grotesque obscenity. This repulsive side of female physicality is juxtaposed with a bevy of stunning and sexually enticing servants, adopted nieces, and prostitutes. The overflowing abundance of these young women mesmerizes and excites sexual desire in Ingravallo and his cohorts at Santo Stefano, but the haughty disdain of the stupendous Tina Crocchiapani or Lavinia Mattonari, or the lesbian-associated disrespect of Virginia Troddu, are continual reminders of the sexual impotence of the desirous male gaze in the novel. Whether incarnated in grotesque hags or stupendous servants, the lower sphere of female sexuality is both transgressive and threatening.

Low, physical womanhood is contrasted by an equally exaggerated sublimation of femininity, embodied in *Pasticciaccio* by the noble and melancholic Liliana Balducci. Liliana continues two recurrent archetypes of sublime femininity in Gadda. On the one hand, she is the Roman representative of what Gioanola has called Gadda's ethereal and unreachable "beautiful châtelaines" (Gioanola 1987, 224–25). Incarnations of feminine gentility and benevolence (reflected also in their class status), these female characters are the potential soul mates for Gadda's semi-autobiographical male protagonists, as is Liliana for Detective Ingravallo.

Any union of erotic affection between them is inevitably hindered, however, by insuperable obstacles such as family objections or marriage to another.

The other sublimated female archetype she embodies is that of the mother, a figure wrought with ambiguity. She exerts a dominant hold over the affections of the autobiographical protagonist, but because that affection can only become erotic through a horrible transgression, she becomes the locus of all sexual repression and the resultant sadistic backlash. Liliana Balducci, despite her youth and childlessness (the latter of which underscores her maternal association), is Gadda's final incarnation of the mother figure. She is both the true object of desire in *Pasticciaccio* and the site of all sexual prohibitions and transgressiveness (Gioanola 1987, 224).

Although she is quite attractive, and all the more transgressive because of it, Liliana is idealized by Ingravallo as other-worldly spirituality. She is for the detective the sublimated icon of the repression of here-and-now physical sexuality. This is evident from the outset of the novel in the juxtaposition of Liliana's "noble melancholy" and Assunta Crocchiapani's "stupendous" physical charms. The disturbed Ingravallo instinctively looks to Liliana to assist him in repressing the sexual arousal stimulated by Assunta: "He tried to repress the admiration that Assunta aroused in him. . . . He had to repress, repress. Assisted in this harsh necessity by the noble melancholy of Signora Liliana: whose gaze seemed to dismiss mysteriously every improper phantom, establishing for their souls a harmonious discipline, like music, that is: a texture of imagined architectures over the ambiguous derogations of the senses" (P 20; TAM 11).

Liliana Balducci is the novel's eternal feminine, and Detective Ingravallo looks to her to lift him from the sins of passion. A sublimated, de-eroticized, and consolatory image, she promises the harmonic music and imagined architectures typical of the transcendental sublime of Gadda's early works, but only at the price of the repression of the sexual instinct through melancholic withdrawal. It is precisely her melancholic other-worldliness that draws Liliana toward the realm of death and dissipation in *Pasticciaccio*, but it is her association with the repression of desire that targets her for the holocaust of a horrific sadism.

Repression is inevitably linked with transgression and punishment in the Gaddian text, and Liliana pays the price in *Pasticciaccio* much as Gonzalo's mother does in *Cognizione*. In his dinner visit with the Balduccis at the beginning of the novel, Ingravallo, always acute in his observations of "the immediate psychic and physiognomical reactions" in others, notices Liliana's "subcutaneous flush" when her young and attractive cousin Giuliano Valdarena arrives: "Chiste è ll'amico" [this is her man friend]. Don Ciccio feels the disappointment of this realization with the ferocious "tan tan" of a splitting headache (P 25–27; TAM 19–22). Liliana's transgressions, brought on by her desperate delirium for a child, are many, as the jealous Ingravallo's painful investigation of her murder slowly brings to light: her incestual fantasies concerning Giuliano as a possible sexual partner and father of her baby (a fantasy consummated symbolically through her gift to him of the sexual substitutes of money and jewels), her "sublimated homoeroticism" and sense of "metaphysical paternity" of the barren woman who "caresses and kisses in her dreams the fertile womb of her sisters" (P 107; TAM 140), her fearful submission to the hard kisses and ear-biting aggression of the demonic "niece" Virginia Troddu, her inability to nurture a child, and her dissipation of the family wealth to others (similar to that of the mother in *Cognizione*).

Like Gonzalo-Gadda's other autobiographical pathologies, the double transgression of repressed love for the mother and a sadistic matricidal urge are displaced and diffused in *Pasticciaccio*. If Liliana is the displaced maternal figure, her coetaneous admirer Ingravallo is the displaced son. Ingravallo suffers from a seething jealousy over Liliana's attraction to her cousin Giuliano, whom he suspects of having ignobly seduced Liliana for money. His interrogation of Giuliano is punctuated by a pained and sinister (but also comic) jealousy when the young man tells him that the tormented Liliana had entertained the wild fantasy of trying to have a baby with him: "Ingravallo was biting back his fury, black as a thunderstorm. . . . A horrible grimace, his face like tar" (P 112; TAM 147). Ingravallo's jealousy links him to Gonzalo, but the displacement of the incestuous mother-son relationship with indirect substitutes weakens the tragic force of the Oedipus motif. Don Ciccio is jealous of all young, handsome men, jealous of almost any man and potential father figure, including Liliana's boorish husband Remo and even her massive confessor Don Lorenzo Corpi. The jealousy is often more comical than pathological.

Nevertheless, the displaced Oedipal/matricidal motif in *Pasticciaccio* generates the same textual mechanism of sadistic punishment evidenced in *La cognizione del dolore*. Gioanola's clinical reading of Gadda's works traces Gaddian eros to a substantially sadistic-anal obsession. An oneiric manifestation of this anal sadism in *Pasticciaccio* is brigadier Pestalozzi's erotic fantasy of Menegazzi's stolen topaz. Metamorphosed into a filthy mouse-topaz, "topazio-topo"-"topaccio," the "wild rat" caroms like "black lightning" through a shameless pack of naked and cavorting Nereids until it spots its final destination, the plastered privates of the vulgar and inebriated Countess Circea: "The wild rat had taken that path, which was the path of duty, for him and for his scenting scariness, climbing up her thighs now like ivy, fat and trembling in his terror, making her laugh and laugh in silly cascades, raving at his tickling: there: they were made of cardboard and plaster, her underpants, that time. Because once, in life, they had put a plaster cast on the trap" (P 194; TAM 269).

Jewels are a sexual metaphor in Gadda's works; Liliana is a "splendid girl" with a "little box" of jewels (P 90; TAM 115). Jewels are also, in the Gaddian sadistic-anal obsession, a substitute for the prohibited feces. Menegazzi's jewels are eventually found in a chamber pot, and their presence inevitably evokes the mandatory sadistic punishment. Gioanola's analysis of Pestalozzi's dream—the sadistic impulse is also diffused across various characters in *Pasticciaccio*—stresses the similarities with Freud's Rat Man's sadistic obsession of rats boring their way into the anus of his father and of a lady he admired (Gioanola 1987, 146–48). Certainly the phonic slippage from jewel, "topazio," to mouse, "topo" (creature of the dirty and excremental realm: "nera acuminata polpetta" [black, pointed meatball] [P 193; TAM 268]), is typical of the money-feces exchange in Gadda's grotesque imagery (a loose equivalent of *ratten/raten* exchange in Freud's analysis). The association of the crazed topaz with black lightning, "nera fólgore," and yellow substance, "il giallazio," evokes the similar imagery of the sadistic assault of the thunderbolt, or "giallone," on the female villas in *La cognizione del dolore.*

The sadistic assault of both the frenzied mouse and the errant thunderbolt are violent and failed enactments of a sexual encounter: the thunderbolt ends up in the dry tub of a maidservant; the mouse finds Circea's "trap" obstructed by underpants. For that matter, the entire Menegazzi case in *Pasticciaccio*, with its confusion of jewels and sex, thieves and assassins, is a grotesque inversion of the other, horrific case still to be resolved: "another list, more grimly horrid and splendid: of those other jewels, kept in a little iron coffer, in the first dresser drawer, by Signora Liliana" (P 186; TAM 257).

Eros and death come together in the most disturbing way in Liliana Balducci's murder. For Ingravallo, "the slaughter 'had all the aspects of a crime of passion'" (P 71; TAM 86). Liliana, the sublime sign of erotic repression for Ingravallo, who had covered his eyes at the mere thought of her in a bathtub, gains in death a sexual physicality that is both exposed and obscene. With its skirt and slip shamelessly tossed back and its

legs spread, Liliana's corpse, "that body of a woman which no longer pos-
sessed modesty or memory" (P 69; TAM 84), seems to beckon the mes-
merized detectives "to a horrible invitation" (P 59; TAM 69). The butchered Liliana's sex becomes a fetish of *Pasticciaccio*'s troubled and sadistic
gaze of male desire. The novel's fetishistic voyeurism, which lingers on
the scantily clad voluptuousness of Ines Cionini or the repulsive black
hole of Zamira Pàcori, is also a sadistic assault, a visual violence. The
obsession with women's undergarments is indulged at length in the quasi-
cinematic focus on Liliana's exposed sexuality. Narrative gaze, Ingravallo,
and police agents are drawn to Liliana's finely knitted white panties (with
sadistic-anal reference to the cleanliness of her bottom), to her elegant
stockings, to her lilac garters. The delicate shaping of the undergarments
represents the oxymoronic status of eros in the novel, both fascinating
invitation and prohibition, the presence of death and sex, barely exhaled
shudder, in the same mysterious carnal mark of mystery: "The precise
work of the knitting, to the eyes of those men used to frequenting maid-
servants, shaped uselessly the weary proposals of a voluptuousness whose
ardor, whose shudder, seemed to have barely been exhaled from the gentle
softness of that hill, from that central line, the carnal mark of the mystery . . . the one that Michelangelo (Don Ciccio mentally saw again his
great work, at San Lorenzo) had thought it wisest to omit. Details! Skip
it!" (P 58–59; TAM 67–68).

Liliana's dead sex is the ultimate erotic fetish in *Pasticciaccio*. It is a
sign that the novel, unlike Michelangelo, does not omit. If Ingravallo
reacts in the only way he knows, through the inappropriate and repressive reminiscence of the sublime Medicean Dawn in Florence's San
Lorenzo (Gadda was living in Florence in 1946), others cannot so easily
repress the arousal of "the swell and furrow of voluptuousness to in-
flame the weak" (P 69; TAM 84). And the nasty comic analogy provided
by the novel's crude Roman narrator is indicative of the hidden blame
ascribed to Liliana herself: "La solcatura del sesso . . . pareva d'esse a
Ostia d'estate, o ar Forte de marmo de Viareggio, quanno so' sdraiate su
la rena a cocese, che te fanno vede tutto quello che vonno" [The furrow
of the sex . . . it was like being at Ostia in the summer, or at Forte dei
Marmi or Viareggio, when they are lying on the sand baking themselves
and they let you glimpse whatever they want] (P 60; TAM 70). The enticing sexual furrow of desire must compete for the detectives' attention
with the other cut on Liliana's body, the "terribile taglio rosso" of her
severed neck, the "terrible red cut" of death. This second horrific cut elicits the same morbid fascination as its sexual counterpart, both in the scru-

pulous description of Liliana's severed arteries and in Ingravallo's visual reconstruction of the brutal assault: "The unexpected flash, the cutting edge, the brief sharpness of a blade. In her: alarm. He, certainly, had first struck all of a sudden, then worked on the throat, insisting, and on the trachea, with ferocious confidence" (P 67; TAM 81).

The symbolic and sadistic exchange between sex and violence reaches its apex in this scene of a voyeuristic double mutilation. Every act of violence in Gadda's narrative universe is an unfulfilled sexual act (Gioanola 1987, 73–74). Liliana's slaughter is also a rape, a defloration, which is truly completed only after her actual murder, by the desirous gaze that roves between her sex and her fatal wound.

The sadism is necessary for the sublime transcendence of the text. As is the case in *Cognizione*, the narrative universe of *Pasticciaccio* requires a sacrificial victim to achieve its fusion of suffering and knowledge. Death, like Eros, transits between the realms of the lower body and the ethereal spheres of the sublime. Liliana's death is not just an exercise in erotic sadism; it is the necessary occasion for the ritualistic Gaddian pietas of horror and commiseration at the brutality of the world. Liliana is the knowledge of death for Ingravallo. His vision of her mutilated body is a vision of death itself: "death seemed to Don Ciccio an extreme decompounding of possibles, an unfocusing of interdependent ideas, formerly harmonized in one person. Like the dissolving of a unity which cannot hold out any longer, the sudden collapse of relationships, of all ties with organizing reality" (P 70; TAM 84). The struggle to understand death is one of the obsessive themes of Gadda's works, linked to his exploration of evil in *Racconto italiano* and *Meditazione milanese* as an unraveling of reality, to the "invisible evil" and "tacit, final combination of thought" of *La cognizione del dolore*. In that earlier novel of denial, the mother's death is a horror, dissipation, and return to substance (n - 1), almost a verification of her son's ruthless ethos of negation. Liliana's "psychosis" of unrequited motherhood leads her to a similar dissipation into chaos, but as her only hope for a rebirth: "a dissociation of a panic nature, a tendency to chaos: that is, a longing to begin all over again from the beginning: from the first Possible" (P 105; TAM 138). Liliana unwittingly bequeaths to Ingravallo a glimmer into the power of the life force, of the "biological urgency" over sublimated repression, infertility, and death.

This biological triumph of eros is affirmed at the novel's conclusion when Ingravallo confronts the Balduccis' stupendous servant Assunta Crocchiapani in his quest for Liliana's assassin. Ingravallo cannot contain his anger at the thought of Assunta's lack of pietas toward her generous benefactress: "'How was it that the girl didn't rush to Rome? Didn't she feel it was her duty?': this was a compulsory idea, now, in his atrociously wounded spirit" (P 272; TAM 382). But Assunta is engaged in a different act of pietas, the care of her dying father, an outstretched little body, shriveled, sexless, already gripped by the greedy gaze of Eternity. The triumph of eros is underscored in this final juxtaposition of Assunta and her moribund genitor: "A splendid vitality, in her, beside the moribund author of her days, which should have been splendid: an undaunted faith in the expressions of her flesh, which she seemed to hurl boldly to the offensive, in a prompt frown, with a scowl: 'No, it wasn't me!' 'No, nun so' stata io!'" (P 276; TAM 388). The stupendous creature that is Assunta appeals precisely to her biological vitalism as proof that it is not she, cannot be she, who is guilty. Ingravallo is left paralyzed, we read, prompted to reflect, almost to repent.

Chapter 5

Satura tota nostra est: *Eros e Priapo*

Il mi' rospo, tre giorni avanti di tirar le cuoia, devo pur principiare a buttarlo fuora: il rospaccio che m'ha oppilato lo stomaco trent'anni: quanto una vita! (EP 236).

[Three days before I kick the bucket, I have got to start spitting it out: that filthy toad's bile that has stopped up my stomach for thirty years: a lifetime!]

The "acrid manner" Gadda had repressed in *La meccanica* because of political considerations issues forth with a vengeance at the end of the Second War World in the raging invective of the anti-Mussolinian *Eros e Priapo*. All dikes of reticence have been broken. Curse, diatribe, and derogation spew forth with little sense of restraint, not only in Gadda's pamphlet but in his personal correspondence as well, where the venom will gradually harden into melancholic paranoia and misanthropy. Satire is whittled down to its core in invective, blasphemy, verbal abuse. In other later works and correspondence there is a similar frenzy of cursing diatribe applied to diverse histrionic personages: Napoleon, D'Annunzio, and especially poet Ugo Foscolo in the 1958 satire *Il guerriero, l'amazzone, lo spirito della poesia nel verso immortale del Foscolo*.

The 1946 version of *Pasticciaccio* runs the risk of capitulating to the profusion of epithets and vulgar analogies. Much of the crudest imagery and language was expunged in the 1957 publication of the novel. The entire fourth chapter was obliterated, ostensibly, as Gadda reported, because it gave away too many clues and lessened the suspense ("Il pasticciaccio," VM 506). But the chapter is also the sudden darkening of a bilious cloud over Gadda's Bellian Rome, the invasion of the toad's venom. Remo Balducci, Liliana's husband, is interrogated by Fumi and Ingravallo, and the dirty secrets begin to flow: his infidelity to Liliana, his affair with the demonic "niece" Virginia. There is indignation in Fumi, and Ingravallo gnaws ferociously on a black pen. Balducci is the crude, skirt-chasing fascist archetype in this chapter, not far removed from Moravia's Leo Merumeci in *Gli indifferenti*. He is hairy and vulgar, but especially red and swollen, "un faccione de pomodoro" [a big fat tomato face] (PL 408). And then he explodes. Balducci, swollen with bile, becomes the satiric railer. It is he who has had to keep quiet because of Virginia's extortion, his house which has been invaded by the blackmailing plebs, he who is Gonzalo-Gadda. From the walls of the police bureau the persecuting mug of the "Pateterno" [Eternal Father] fascist demagogue looks down, "na faccia de maccherone" [a face like a macaroni]. Throughout the dictator is apostrophized as "il Merda" [the Shit], and the bureaucratic police state of fascist Italy finds its analogy in the maelstrom of a clogged and feces-filled toilet bowl (PL 412).

Satire floods into the pages of the 1946 *Pasticciaccio* without concern for character consistency or narrative balance. The angry flow, freed from all narrative concerns, is intensified and funneled with even more force into *Eros e Priapo*. Although it was published in 1967, the pamphlet's origins predate those of *Pasticciaccio*.[1] They can be traced to the summer and autumn of 1944 in Rome, where Gadda, at his request, had been transported by the English High Command with other refugees from war-torn Florence (Pinotti 1992, 994). Offered to Mondadori, its completion plagued by Gadda's proverbial slowness in "extruding" his manuscripts, the project dragged on throughout the fifties. By then, Gadda wrote to Vittorio Sereni, *Eros e Priapo* was "no longer publishable.... It would have to be rewritten, edulcorated from top to bottom: and even so it would procure hatred and nuisances, court proceedings and threats" (cited in Pinotti 1992, 1001). Some of the less vehement pages on narcissism and pedagogy had been published in the neo-experimentalist *Officina* in 1955–56 as *Il libro delle Furie* while the book manuscript passed from editor Alberto Mondadori to Livio Garzanti, who published it in 1967 despite its disorganized and incomplete form.

There is a great, millennial-old tradition of satire on the Italian peninsula, dating back to Quintilian's adage that the genre belonged wholly to the Romans, but the boisterous pamphlet has never enjoyed the popularity in Italy that it has, for instance, in France. Céline's anticommunist and anti-Semitic tracts, published in the bombastic era of the thirties, excited and continue to excite outraged reprobation, yet they belonged to an established genre (McCarthy 1975, 140–43). Gadda's pamphlet, published over two decades after the fall of the regime in a nation poised on the threshold of the struggles of 1968, was judged to be trivial and anachronistic: a "museum" of all the embryonic "errors" in Gadda's native satirical impetus (Pedullà 1968, 367–72). Gadda himself added to the abuse, calling the pamphlet "a crude and disagreeable old scrap" (LPGC 140). Notwithstanding subsequent reevaluations (Seroni 1969, Biasin 1975, Dombroski 1984a), *Eros e Priapo* continues to be the most neglected and unappreciated of Gadda's major works of maturity, so much so that Guido Lucchini, the best and most exacting of the new generation of Gaddian critics, degrades it to "the most minor of Gadda's minor works" (Lucchini 1988, 111).

MACARONIC SATIRE AND THE PSYCHOANALYSIS OF FASCISM

> Tutti i periti, e d'ogni sorta medici, hanno e aranno discettare sulla maialata (EP 223).

> [All the experts, and doctors of every sort, must and will have to comment at length on the swinishness.]

To a modern sensibility which has lost the taste for the hypertrophy and bombast of satirical prose, *Eros e Priapo* seems anomalous, rambling, disjointed, unpermissibly offensive. In matter of fact, it is very much in the mainstream of traditional Western satire. This is true as regards its bipartite structure of enraged diatribe (against the dictator and his sycophants) followed by corrective analysis and alternative (fascism was grounded in a dangerous, infantile narcissism; there must be a pedagogical sublimation of primal libidinal urges). It is also true as concerns its obsessive scapegoating, not only of the dictator Mussolini but of his frenzied female followers as well.

The pamphlet's misogyny is the most distasteful of its many distasteful features, from its "Machiavellian" declarations that "la politica non è fatta per la vagina" [politics is not made for the vagina] and that women's duty to the country is "di lasciarsi fottere" [to let themselves be fucked] (EP 245–46), to its base and racist accusations that northern Italian women looked forward to packing their menfolk off to war in order that they might enjoy fleeting orgiastic encounters with the dark and curly-haired southern soldiers passing through to the fronts, "almost an antipasto of our Mao-Mao and Bantu condisciples and equals (1963) now engaged to our sisters" (EP 290).[2] Originally the pamphlet was conceived as a satire on the Duce's female followers entitled *Le patriottesse* (MS 1393). There is a scene in *Eros e Priapo* in which Gadda's alter ego De Madrigal is accused of cowardice by a Florentine maenad for not fighting in the Second World War (315–17). It is here perhaps that we can locate the traumatic autobiographical origin of the misogynistic diatribe. In any case, the episode excites from the lips of De Madrigal the only true instance of a Latin macaronic in Gadda's works as De Madrigal fantasizes on dragging his companion to the rigors of the Alpine precipices of World War I where he and not Mussolini fought the true patriotic war: "Hic Patria, hic salta. . . . Sitisne? Exurisne? Pedesne? Valde gaudeo, sus. Nam jam jam Adamillum montem inter omnes Alpium montes nivalis comitissa non insiluit, neque pater patriae qui Faba Magna in volgus appellatur quique Faba Optima Maxima Unica a Sophonismis Ricciolonibus jactatur" [Here is the Fatherland, here is the leap. . . . Are you thirsty? Are you burning up? How about your feet? I am so very delighted, you pig. For indeed my countess did not leap about on Mount Adamello in the midst of all the snow-laden peaks of the Alps, nor did the father of the fatherland, proclaimed by the masses to be the Mighty Bean-prick and boastfully called by the curly-haired Sophonismas the Best, the Greatest and the Only Bean] (EP 317).[3]

The "patriotic" misogyny is dishonest. Gadda's own early admiration for Mussolini is now attributed to the irrational female hordes, as is his early Anglophobia. After the First World War Gadda had asserted that England was Italy's new natural enemy, that it had aggressively occupied Italy's "mare nostrum" (the Mediterranean Sea). He had depicted the English with vague anti-Semitic tones and a caricature of the ugly, barren English woman. These early outbursts of Anglophobia are in syntony with the rhetoric of the regime. Yet in *Eros e Priapo* it is Mussolini's frenzied female hordes who repeat mindlessly the dictator's pronouncement that England must pay for its crimes while hysterical and sadistic Florentine maenads cheer the bombing carnage in London ("l'incicciata" [the fleshing]) on their way to Mass (EP 301).

As far back as the *Racconto italiano,* and with reference to Otto Weininger and Aristotle's *Nicomachean Ethics,* Gadda had speculated on the female potentiality in the male's deep psyche (RI 463). His archetypal division of female characters into the bearers of a morbid melancholy or a frenzied hysteria were projections of his own soul and temperament. The fascist horror was viewed as an extension of the troubled family romance. The sadism with which Italian mothers gleefully sent the "living smile" of their sons to be slaughtered for the approval of the Duce (EP 260) bears painful echoes of Gadda's feelings of a maternal denial of love. In letters of October 28, 1946, and September 6, 1947, to Contini, he lamented that his sister, Clara, his hysterical alter ego as he referred to her, blamed him for the disastrous war which her "flag-waving Maria Luisa brain" and accompanying "marital organ" had desired.

He is abused by her "German and anti-English hysterics" (LGC 47, 53). But *Eros e Priapo*'s wildly obscene and exaggerated misogyny is also a traditional feature of the satirical genre, the exorcism through debasement of the threatening Other. Satire explodes the binary obsession of the Western symbolic imagination, its declaration of values through sexual difference. It releases a quaking fury against the feminine when desire and fear of the Other tread too heavily across its landscape. The frightening and guilty sorceress-hysteric identified by Catherine Clément (1986) is satirically exposed and denigrated throughout Gadda's works. *Eros e Priapo* marks her ritual immolation with the fornicating dictator-father.

Subjectivity also undergoes a final masquerade in *Eros e Priapo,* in the form of the autobiographical philosopher Alì Oco De Madrigal, a perfect anagram, as Gian-Paolo Biasin has pointed out, for Carlo Emilio Gadda (Biasin 1975, 150). Alì Oco's maxims are spoken through another autobiographical narrator who tends to slip into the archaic Florentine speech of yet a third narrator in Gadda's characteristic multiplication of autobiographical masks. The essay's misanthropic railer is an archetypal satirical persona with his origins in Homer's Thersites, and like Thersites, De Madrigal is thrust into the role of a victim by his sardonic truths, a convenient scapegoat for a society which, in Leopardian terms, never hates he who does evil, nor evil itself, as much as he who names it (EP 235–36).

In this and other ways, *Eros e Priapo* bears the dubious distinction of being the Italian work closest in spirit to Louis-Ferdinand Céline's obscene and outrageous political pamphlets. Céline also suffered from Anglophobia and disgust for the hysterical crowd, in his case the Aryan crowd manipulated by the Jewish-controlled media and movie industry. Renato Barilli pointed out shortly after the publication of *Eros e Priapo* that in their pamphlets Céline and Gadda finally feel they have located the concrete source of the universal evil they have been combating all of their lives, the machinating Jews for Céline, the priapic Duce for Gadda (Barilli 1968). It is an absurd reductionism that acts to discredit the pamphlets from the start and initiates their slippery game of truth or parody. The confusion is continued in the play of subjectivity in both authors. The Gaddian railer bears more than a passing resemblance to his Célinian counterpart. The Cerebus-headed De Madrigal is no longer subjected to the critical exegesis of subjectivity practiced on Gonzalo. He is no longer a fictional mask uncannily similar but kept at arm's length from the author through the devices of fiction. Instead, as with the railer of Céline's or rather Destouche's pamphlets (the maternal nom de plume is abandoned for a patrilineal identification with the Jew-hating father), the

Gaddian fictional persona assumes the dimensions of a hypertrophied and exaggerated "second nature." This hyperbolic, autobiographical I is accompanied in both Céline and Gadda by an equally hypertrophied exacerbation of the authors' respective stylized languages—the verbal abuse of the Célinian popular or spoken voice, the linguistic fragmentation and pastiche of the more eclectic Gadda (Barilli 1968). The grafting onto self of the swollen and bug-eyed carnival head of the railer makes it even more difficult to pin down either of the two psycho-neurotic discourses. André Gide wrote in 1938 about *Bagatelles pour un massacre* that Céline was obviously joking; Jewishness was only a pretext, the most trivial pretext for different concerns, and if he were not joking, he would be completely loony (Gide 1938, 195–96). Remove the explicit anti-Semitic and xenophobic references from *Bagatelles,* it has been argued by Céline's apologists, and one finds an impassioned tract for pacifism, an attack against the selfish materialism of the consumer society and the corruption of the media. Remove the misogynism and psychoanalytic demonization from *Eros e Priapo* and one finds a profound piety for the young men sacrificed in a senseless war and the intolerable burdens placed upon the disenfranchised poor.

Céline had framed the invective of *Bagatelles* in an allegory of ballets. Gadda embeds the invective of *Eros e Priapo* within a matrix of psychoanalytic discourse. Gadda had appropriated the Freudian theories of narcissistic delusion and the Oedipus complex in the thirties to cast his traumatic autobiographical fiction in the guise of a semianalytical exegesis. After the war he engages in an explicit recourse to psychoanalytic theory in a series of essays devoted in particular to the problem of narcissism: "Psicanalisi e letteratura" (1949), "Emilio e Narcisso" (1950), "L'Egoista" (1954). In *Eros e Priapo* unsublimated narcissism is posited as the cause of the fascist tragedy, a tragedy that was played out in the libidinal frenzy between the obscenely gesticulating Duce on the balcony of Palazzo Venezia and the acritical oceanic crowds below.

The "immediate" source for this depiction of the fascist phenomenon is Freud's *Group Psychology and the Analysis of the Ego.* Gadda had read Freud's work in French in the 1927 Gallimard collection of *Essais de psychanalyse.* From his underlinings and notes, he appears to have dedicated particular attention to Freud's chapters on "Suggestion and Libido," "Two Artificial Groups: the Church and the Army," and "Being in Love and Hypnosis," all of which concern the erotic bonds between group and the charismatic leader (Lucchini 1988, 110). Psychoanalytical analyses of fascism and its association with erotic abnormality or sexual deviation are standard fare. Italian cinema, beginning with the demonized homosexuality and lesbianism of the Nazis in Rossellini's *Open City*, has been particularly attuned to the erotic connection, as attested in the films of directors such as Bernardo Bertolucci, Lina Wertmüller, or Liliana Cavani. In Gadda's case, all the evils of society he had set about to denounce in his attempts at an "Italian tale" are channeled into the broad funnel of unsublimated fascist narcissism: the rhetoric of falsehood and exaggeration (narcissists are incurable liars); the incompetency of the Italian military machine (due to narcissistic vainglory that prevented Mussolini from seeing through the lies of his adulators); the unchecked libidinal drives of greedy industrialists at the expense of the nation; the malfunctioning institutions of family, education, and religion, all perverted by narcissistic self-interest; the disastrous cult of narcissistic youth. The Freudian matrix reformulates the national crisis of unrestrained egoism that had so enraged the author in his World War I diary.

Grafted onto the psychoanalytic matrix are the Gaddian polarities of the irrational and the rational, disorder and order, the grotesque and the sublime. Human activity is mapped onto a three-way psychic grid: Logos, Eros, Priapus. Eros, or the subjective and instinctual libidinal force, can either be sublimated into Logos or remain trapped in an exhibitionist and self-indulgent narcissism, Priapus. This is where Gadda and Céline part ways. In Gadda there is no celebration of the primordial emotion that Céline accused the Jews and materialism of extinguishing in the French soul, no sexual antics with long-legged dancers. Gadda does not embrace the id and the erotic; he despises them. Throughout his pamphlet Eros collapses into Priapus. It is not Priapus who is the enemy of Logos, but Eros itself: "Ora tutto ciò è Eros, non Logos" [Now all of this is Eros, not Logos] (EP 245; Gioanola 1987, 213–14). Eros is the irrational while Logos is the rational. Eros is disorderly energy; it knows no purposiveness beyond the satisfaction of immediate psycho-physiological urges. Logos operates in the service of a heuristic teleology. In normal development Eros is submitted to Logos, which directs its energy toward a series of sublimations. When sublimation does not occur, the adult or the collective remains trapped at an inferior level of development and the rational sublime is replaced by a foolish and narcissistic exhibitionism of the physiological self: "The narcissistic madman remains blocked at the first imbecilities of his youth; lacking in sublimating abilities, he is still waving his sexual organ at fifty in the public's face—coram populo—like a little boy who spews out rivers of pee right under the nose of his wet nurse" (EP 367).

Just under the surface of the essay's Freudian patina of libidinal sublimation is Gadda's pre-Freudian metaphysics of heuristic evolution. To
sublimate from Eros to Logos is to move from n to n + 1. To remain
blocked at the level of physiological Eros or degenerate narcissism is to
regress to n - 1. Logos is goodness; Eros, like fascism, is evil. The Gaddian
mythos of the "heroic" and "sublime" discipline of the philosopher, soldier, author, or leader to create a new and better reality of becoming at
the cost of sacrificing the personal self comes to the fore:

> In the normal man the normal emotional charge or erotic charge—
> that is to say, the love and desire directed toward women—is suscep-
> tible . . . to "sublimation" in states of mind which tend to lift the male
> from lowness of being to the shore or the dangerous slope of becom-
> ing. . . . And this impetus-discipline is extended and I would say dif-
> fused throughout your entire life and pervades it with the sublimity of
> actions, singularly premeditated, disciplined and carefully constructed,
> and for some, with the sublimity of works, and sometimes with the
> sublimity of renunciations and the holocaust of one's self. This is the
> heroic spirit . . . and it is emitted not only from the slaughter and ash of
> the battlefield, but also by daily discipline and obvious mortification:
> in labor, in thought and in works. A mortification that is true life, be-
> cause it is illuminated by the lamp and liquor of Athena. (EP 273–74)

Underlying Freudian sublimation is Gadda's own moral ethos and personal mythos of repression and individual mortification, the triumph of
the repressive superego. As a result, Logos is also dark Eros in Gadda.
The superego is at the service of sublimation, but it is also the instrument for the release of the sadistic forces of repression and punishment
(evidenced in the author's ubiquitous matricidal motif). The psychoanalytical machinations of *Eros e Priapo* are often little more than a flimsy
excuse for the pamphlet's gleeful sadism. In their application to the gesticulating theatrics of the Duce, the psychoanalytical matrices of crowd
psychology, libidinal drives and unsublimated narcissism undergo a parodic dislocation from their original analytical context to the grotesque
imagery of a bombastic and beastly fornication between the leader and
the hysterical female collectivity:

> Mr. Derby Hat alone had the vigor, as he mimed it, to fill to the brim
> (in proportion to that false frenzy) the vaginal funnel of the Bacchante.
> A filthy lie, up from the shadow of those souls. From their mouths, an
> uncontained slobber. Kù-cè, Kù-cè, Kù-cè, Kù-cè.[4] (EP 225)

Erect in his spasm on triple hoofs . . . the jackass with his x-like legs had hurled his bray to the Apennines and the Alps. And the Alps and Apennines echoed him, hee-haw, hee-haw, they echoed back ad infinitum hey-ya, hey-ya, through the infinite course of the valleys (and the Foscolian dales): so that all, all of them!, the whole cursed forty-four million of them, might each stick it into the tympanic chamber of their ears, each one satisfied and gratified in every itchy urge, edulcorated, soothed, buttered, bechameled and beatified.[5] (EP 243)

The phallic dogma or rather the dogmatic phallus managed to deposit into the uterus of certain poor creatures its wagging zoo, its seed of canonical certainty. (EP 258)

The complex social, political, and historical phenomenon of Italian fascism is reduced to a grotesque pantomime. The Duce is a carnival freak show, half ass and half man. Fascist indoctrination becomes fodder for a blasphemous bestiary. At the core of this debasing imagery is the identification of unsublimated, narcissistic Eros with the dictator's phallus: "The Bean-prick did not know, in his life, nor confer to his actions any sublimation" (EP 276). This is classical satire in its fullest ritualism. Satire renders the abstract physical and turns it into a demonic talisman, a demonic fetish. The object is pursued at close range, hypertrophied through grotesque distortion, dislocated from its bedrock of accepted conventionality and received ideas. It is buffeted on the wing in a vortex of displacement and dismemberment.

In *Eros e Priapo* the phallus becomes the evil signifier par excellence. The entire distorted universe of the fascist enterprise originates from it and refers back to it. The ubiquitous Duce is transformed incessantly and blasphemously into "il Fava" [the Bean], "l'indomita verga" [the indomitable rod], "il Priapo-Imagine" [the Priapus-Image]. His body and person are dissected and reassembled into an aggregate of phallic extensions, from his bulging belly, eyes, mouth, lips, and erect chin to his ornamental feathers and steely dagger ("l'inargentato pene" [the silvered penis]). The denunciation of narcissistic exhibitionism issues forth in a metaphoric parade of phallic and vaginal substitutes, from the female's "ficoborsa" [pussypurse], with its large and small "labbia" [labia] and "interiore nottolino-clitoride" [interior clitoris-latch], to the male's "canna da pesca" [fishing pole], to the obsessive "idea-cetriolo" [pickle-idea] that we all carry around in our "cervello-utero o cervello-minchia" [uterusbrain or prick-brain].

The satirist's mission lies not in the repression of the obscene phallic signifier but in its uncensored and hyperbolized exhibition. He is the frenzied pig, as Gadda puts it, who snorts and digs until he has fully exposed the erect mushroom (EP 238). Exposition of the obscene signifier constitutes the linkage between psychoanalytical and satirical practice. The "elective affinity" between the two methods has been duly noted (see Domenichelli, 1985). Both seek to engage in a therapeutic "hallucination" of the repressed obscene or "off-stage" hidden behind the curtain of false rhetoric. Both involve a specular relationship between the exposer and the exposed, the analyst and the patient. Every analysis is also a self-analysis; every satire is also a self-satire.

Gadda seeks to outdo the dictator at his own histrionic game. Mussolini and his narcissistic regalia continually occupy center stage in *Eros e Priapo*. The Duce's exhibitionism, the self-manufactured cult of "ducismo," is taken to its absurd extreme. Made fully visible, the phallic signifier is tumefied to the point of inscribing the entire fascist enterprise. *Eros e Priapo*'s satiric method is the exaggeration of narcissistic exhibitionism itself. It is here that Gadda's amalgam of satire and psychoanalysis is most revealing. It highlights the narcissistic tendency of satire as a genre, its inclination to excel in the depiction of the very vice it combats. And this, of course, is what compels the satirist's critics to accuse him of attributing to others what are his own repressed desires.

In explaining to cousin Piero the reasons for his tardy and vulgar anti-fascist pamphlet, Gadda referred to his trauma and lack of courage during the years of the regime: "as my tenuous and perhaps insufficient excuse, let it be said that I had been overwhelmed by terrible times (like everyone); that I did not have the force of spirit to face them with the *necessary* heroism; that, all told, I had failed in everything, all along the line" (LPGC 140). Gadda voiced open dissent with the regime only in the late thirties and early forties. After the war he tended to backdate the rupture to earlier times, to 1934 and the war on Ethiopia or even to a period before the infamous murder of Socialist senator Giacomo Matteotti by Mussolini's henchmen in 1924 (an event which precipitated Mussolini's full assumption of dictatorial powers the following year). Gadda even claimed he had written *Eros e Priapo* in a distant 1928, a claim for which no evidence whatsoever exists (IDM 17; Cattaneo 1973, 93). The dates do correspond, however, to evidence of early breaches in Gadda's relationship with fascism. There is a note of September 7, 1924, in the *Racconto italiano,* three months after Matteotti's murder, in which Gadda writes that Grifonetto will discover "the vile motives" that had determined a punitive fascist raid (RI 469); 1928 is the year in which Gadda complains in his notes to *Dejanira Classis* of the travesty of fascist grandstanding in the Renzo Pettine murder trial and, in his notes to *La meccanica*, of the political pressure which keeps him from expressing his true thoughts; in 1934 he undergoes a "humiliating" bout with the fascist censors over *Il castello di Udine*. Perhaps it was, as he claimed, a question of an early awareness without the individual fortitude sufficient for a heroism of open dissent.

The bitterness was compounded by the regime's terrible betrayal of Gadda's early idealization of fascism as the organ of social order and political pragmatism. Fascism was to have been the repressive, sublimating Logos, the political Superego that would have cured Italy's chronic narcissism, would have put a stop to the egoistic affirmation of its 44 million individual parts to the detriment of the national whole. This was Gadda's "rational" excuse for fascism. It was from the beginning, however, a rationalism based on an irrational fear of the low. There is the red tide, the Bolshevik flood, the marauding masses, the traumatic remembrance of the child Gadda, still vivid at the end of his life, of little plebeian hooligans who sullied him and his sister and their bicycles: "Imagine being on your bicycle and a boy gathers up a handful of mud and throws it on your white dress. It was the only decent white dress my sister had. I said had, because now she no longer does" (IDM 18). There is a child's nightmare of rape, the end of innocence, the fall of the dispossessed.

Gadda's political conservatism did not dissipate after the war. Unlike fascists turned neorealists such as Elio Vittorini or Vasco Pratolini, Gadda did not come to fascism from the Left and did not turn to the Left at war's end. A sardonic, self-confessed reader of "ultra-reactionary newspapers alone," as he mockingly described himself to cousin Piero in 1947 (LPGC 67), Gadda had voted for the monarchy and was ill at ease with the leftist clique that dominated the Italian cultural scene after the war (Alberto Moravia was a particular target for barbs, sometimes peppered with anti-Semitic overtones). The Resistance was denigrated into the frolicking of hairy-legged partisans in shorts and with red rags around their necks, a narcissistic homosexuality, "buchesimo," as Gadda described it with Florentine obscenity. Third-world liberation movements were later dismissed with the caustic comment that England and France should band together to keep their colonies—in any event, better a monarchy in those countries than a "repubblica di descamisados" (Cattaneo 1973, 28, 91). In old age Gadda wore with rebellious irony the sardonic mask of the political reactionary, but he had inherited from his earliest youth a cult of the

Caesarian strongman and a fear and hatred of the anarchic hordes (he confessed to having shed uncontrollable tears as a boy of seven at the news of King Umberto I's assassination by an anarchist's bullet in 1900).

In a lengthy excursus in *Meditazione milanese,* Gadda wrote that the primitive lawlessness he had seen in Sardinia and the Argentine Chaco necessitated the rise of a strongman to impose order, just as a dictator is necessary whenever civil society is plunged into anarchy: "An analogous situation arises unfortunately wherever the anarchy is so ingrained as to decompose the social reality. . . . Then the mangled social body generates its extreme defense and a voice yells 'I am the law.' Thus Caius Caesar commands, *dictatur,* to the disorderly and frenetic Roman society of that Republic that was so very public and so little *res*" (MM 699). The year is 1928, four years after the Matteotti affair. There is no reference to the fascist regime, but the threat of the lawless periphery or the anarchic society justifies rule by the strongman, be it in the disarray of Republican Rome or, one can only assume, that of post–World War I Italy. When the faith in fascism and its strongman crumbles, the imagery of the anarchic and peripheral hordes raises its head and fuses with the now-demonized vision of the regime. This is the situation in *La cognizione del dolore,* with its unionized guttural Calibans and the miscegenating hordes that descend from the Monte Viejo. The "hallucination" of the social evil is also a grotesque hallucination of the fascist rhetoric that would supposedly cure it. The fascists had demonized the anarchic and socialist hordes. The fascist press had demonized the inferior races and the evil of miscegenation during and after the conquest of Ethiopia in 1936 as a prelude to the anti-Semitic racism later aped from the Nazis.

The same demonization of the hordes occurs in *Eros e Priapo.* The pamphlet's vulgar imagery is a grotesque amalgam of the phobias that had originally led Gadda to fascism with the regime's own rhetoric. It has been asserted that Gadda had perhaps gleaned the notion of the feminine characteristics of the manipulated masses from Gustave Le Bon's *La Psychologie des foules* via Freud's *Group Psychology* (Lucchini 1988, 110). This would not seem to be the case, since crowd psychology is typically compared in those authors with that of children, primitives, and neurotics. *Eros e Priapo*'s frenzied female collectivity derives instead from Gadda's own misogynism as a fear of the low joined to the fascist rhetoric against women.

It was Mussolini who claimed to have read Le Bon's work innumerable times and who declared to the German journalist Emil Ludwig: "The crowd loves a strong man. The crowd is a woman!" (Mussolini 1957, xxii, 156; Ludwig 1932, 68). With typical anachronism, Gadda refers to Machiavelli, Caesar, Columbus, and Danton for this view. A constant refrain in *Eros e Priapo* is that the female embodies the conservative, static element in human nature, while the male embodies the dynamic element. The female "does not create the future: she brings the past to perfection"; she is "a companion in the home and useful for traveling over the known road, not for forging forward into the darkness" (EP 256). The male is "form," the woman "material," a declaration Gadda supports with reference to Bergson; the male is the "heuristic" element; the female is the "scarring element after the 'wound of exploration'" (EP 256–57). The assertions that derive from this metaphysics of sexual difference, that women have no place in politics and no aptitude for critical or philosophical thought, reflect those of fascist policy. With its rhetorical sources in the misogynistic sloganism of the futurists, in Gentilian idealism, and in Mussolini's own declared admiration of books such as Weininger's *Sex and Character,* the regime sought to justify and confer intellectual legitimacy to its antifeminist policies. Women were called "incorrigibly frivolous, uncreative and unintellectual" (Mack Smith 1983, 159). Giovanni Gentile, Mussolini's first public minister of education, restricted the rights of women to teach philosophy, and the dictator applauded the reduction of higher education for women "to those subjects where the 'feminine brain' could adequately operate—for example, household management" (Mack Smith 1983, 209). Woman is analytic, not synthetic, Mussolini declared to Ludwig, and he noted that her intellect made her extraneous to architecture, the synthesis of the creative arts. She was to have no importance in the fascist state: "Nel nostro Stato essa non deve contare" (cited in Ludwig 1932, 168).

As political critique *Eros e Priapo* is seriously flawed and incoherent. The attempt to analyze and criticize the fascist phenomenon through the trappings of Freudian theory is shallow and unconvincing. The pamphlet's greatest merit as critique lies beyond its twentieth-century anachronism in a more distant archaism. There is a macaronic interference operating in the pages of *Eros e Priapo* that functions as a corrective to its facile reductionism. The pamphlet invites its reader to participate in the madcap and drunken *danse macabre* of tarantellas, sarabands, and jigs that is man's universal folly (EP 243). We are reminded repeatedly that the satire of the misanthropic De Madrigal is directed not only at Mussolini, or the fascists, or the hysterical Sophonisbas, but at all of the 44 million

Italians, at himself, and at all of us. This carnivalesque all-inclusiveness
is embodied in another traditional satiric motif, the grotesque procession
of the diseased and disfigured:

> Quanti? Quanti? . . . quanti i tubercolotici, meschini!, co'i'ccazzo
> ritto: quanti gli uricemici e gottosi: quanti i colitici: quanti gli epatici:
> quanti i diabetici: quanti i nefritici: quanti i cancerosi, li acromegalici,
> basedowoidi, i luetici: quanti li oppilati sive pilettici: quanti, poi, quelli
> che fanno ciriegie e peperoncini: quanti con privazione d'una gamba:
> quanti i nevrotici, gli psicotici, i maniaci, li ossessi, li ebefrenici, i pazzi:
> e quelli che per dire Caribaldi e' dicano bah bah, poarini! Quanti i gobbi?
> Quante, e tòccati, le quattromila maladette gobbe de la città di Scarica 'l
> ciuccio: che d'una svolti e t'imbuchi e dell'altra svicoli e scappi? E non
> fai a tempo a toccarti le stelle? (EP 234)

> [How many? How many? . . . how many tuberculosis cases, poor
> wretches!, with their pricks straight up: how many with lithemia and
> gout: how many with colitis: how many with liver disorder: how many
> diabetics: how many nephritics: how many with cancer, the acromeg-
> aliacs, those with Basedow's disease, the syphilitics: how many the oc-
> cluded or epileptics: and how many, moreover, those who make cher-
> ries and little peppers: how many missing a leg: how many neurotics,
> psychotics, maniacs, lunatics, hebephrenics, crazy people: and those who
> instead of saying Garibaldi say bah bah, poor fools! How many hunch-
> backed men? How many, and cross yourself, the four thousand cursed
> hunchbacked women in the city of Let's Play Piggback: that you turn
> and hide from one and you slip away and flee from another? And you
> don't even have time to touch your balls for protection.]

Mad dance, grotesque procession, passage on the ship of fools. The macaronic satire in *Eros e Priapo* belongs to a different time, it is dispersive
and silly, and it is an appeal to universality.

The centrifugal impetus is embodied in the pamphlet's macaronic language. *Eros e Priapo* incorporates the most impressive array of languages
in all of Gadda's production. There are the Latinate hypotactical syntax
penetrated by the *diminutio* of dialect (Biasin 1975, 141–42), the neologisms, the foreign borrowings, and the onomatopoeia common to Gadda's
mature works. But in *Eros e Priapo* everything is at its most exaggerated
and extreme. Its dialectal pastiche is a summa of Gadda's linguistic eclecticism. Excursuses in Roman and Lombard are grafted onto a Florentinism
ripe with the archaisms and the morphological peculiarities of the no-

blest Italian literary tradition. Gadda had lived among the Florentines for several years both before and after beginning *Eros e Priapo,* and he was particularly taken with what he called the unmatched "vileness of their daily blasphemies" (EP 1056). Tuscan is the ultimate expressive vehicle for cursing the Duce and his followers and for ridiculing the fascist enterprise by circumscribing it to the highly caricatured and parochial context of the Florentine *borgo.* One has the impression that the Italian scene during the regime has been reduced to a medieval town chronicle or a series of epigrammatic novellas related by a vulgar and sardonic Villani redivivus:

> De Madrigal conobbe e conosce una distintissima e dimolto agiata donna e signora, sua presso che cugina seconda o terza, la quale, venuta alle cittadine botteghe alquanto tardi a ghiribizzare d'attorno Duomo e Batisteo, fu soprappresa dalla notte con una sua dama d'attorno. Chiusi in quell'ora tutti i ricettacoli di sotterra, i Diurni e simili, né si possendo altramente levar di vescica quell'importunissimo litro e mezzo de' suoi rognoni maturato goccia a goccia le precedenti ore senza lei avvedersene, ché tutto dì l'andò stornellando co' la su' dama, e seguitò cicalando e cinguettando a' negozi in su gli sporti di più d'uno di quelli e sorbito anche a un bottegone di molto tè col zuccaro ch'è diuretico forte, lei . . . be' lei poche ciarle: ché è donna deliberata ad ogni suo fatto dopoché loquace ad ogni sua compera o non compera: messa la dama semicieca poco più là come da guardia incontro a le notturne fantasime della vigilanza pubblica, che in quella oscurità non vigilava un fico secco, la sé insinuò in uno cantone fra gli antemurali del duomo e celata ancora dal campanile di messer Giotto. Non sendo plenilunio sereno, Trivia, in quel punto, la non rideva fra le ninfe eterne: talché da niuno lume celata ad occhio, la bellissima donna accosciatasi la mandò fuora in una gran birra quel tepente fiume la l'aveva in fontana. Ché ne schiumò di molto sopra a le selci di piazza. Che da poi te tu stupivi al passare che uno animale n'abbia potuto far cotanta: e ti penseresti alla prima che fussi uno cavallo grandissimo, non fussi che la la viene da uno angulo del cantone, dove caval non ci può. (EP 287)

[De Madrigal knew and knows a most distinguished and very well-to-do lady and gentlewoman, almost a second or third cousin, who, having come somewhat late to muse about the town shops nearby the Cathedral and Baptistery, was taken by surprise, together with one of her ladies-in-waiting, by the night. All of the underground receptacles being closed at that hour, the diurnal conveniences and their like, nor being able to release from her bladder in any other manner that most importunate liter and a half which her kidneys had ripened drop by drop without her notice, since all the day she had gone singing along with her lady, and she had continued chattering and chirruping at more than one or another of the shops and their stalls and having also sipped at one grand establishment quantities of tea with sugar which is a potent diuretic, she . . . Well, she is not one to waste time with talk, for she is a resolute woman in her every action after being loquacious in her every purchase or nonpurchase. Having put her half-blind dame a few paces in front as a guard against the nocturnal phantoms of the public watch, who in that darkness could watch naught, she insinuated herself into a corner between the barbicans of the Cathedral and was hidden still more by Master Giotto's bell tower. There not being a clear full moon, Trivia, in that instance, was not smiling amongst her eternal nymphs. And so, hidden to the eye by the lack of light, the most beautiful gentlewoman crouched and let flow in a mighty beer that warm flood she had in her fountain. And much indeed frothed over the paving stones of the square, so that later, crossing by, you were astonished that an animal could have produced such a quantity, and you might think at first that it was a greatly large horse, except that it's flowing from the deepest angle of the corner, where a horse can't do it.]

One understands the accusations of triviality and "bozzettismo"; they are well-taken. Nonetheless, scenes like the above are an integral part of *Eros e Priapo*'s universal satire. The satirist, in a reaction similar to that of the astonished passerby, is amazed by the gigantesque and wondrous inanity of the world around him. Most importantly, this stupor is not only that of the solitary nightwalker in a 1943 Florence under a wartime blackout but that of a medieval Calandrino as well. It is an example of what Guido Baldi called *Eros e Priapo*'s "purest, but also, practiced in the middle of the twentieth century, most anachronistic 'macaronic' and burlesque Italian tradition" (Baldi 1972, 163). Yet it is precisely this macaronic anachronism that is responsible for the satire's expansive centrifugality.

With respect to Gadda's other macaronic works, *Eros e Priapo* constitutes a significant movement toward the original Renaissance parameters of the macaronic. Gadda's satirical pamphlet not only exploits the macaronic interference between high and low codes, it recuperates what Cesare Segre has called the "diachronic perspective" of macaronic discourse: "What characterizes the macaronic writers is not just that they place side by side two or more linguistic strata (language, dialect, etc.), but their utilization of the internal historical and tonal contrasts of the strata. . . . The revolution of the tonal hierarchies is for this reason realized concomitantly on the language-dialect polarity and on the ancient language–modern language polarity" (Segre 1979, 179). The historical breadth of *Eros e Priapo*'s macaronic pastiche is enhanced by Florence's ancient legacy of fierce municipalism and its strong tradition of satiric ribaldry, but it is truly manifest in the unique situation of the Florentine tongue itself, a language that is both a highly connotated local vernacular and the archaic nucleus of the national language and its grand literary tradition.

Eros e Priapo continually exploits the peculiar diachronic status of Florentine as the essence of a language that is unmistakably different from that language, or, with its perennial opening on the past, that is not yet that language. The pamphlet flows in a linguistic form which is a constant reminder of the primordial difference of language, of its always amorphous and ambiguously inscribed coming into being. In its parodic ebb and flux from language to not-quite-language, *Eros e Priapo*'s Florentine pastiche destabilizes all notions of linguistic wholeness and the sense of indisputable "truth" that such a wholeness conveys. This enables its diachronic interference to go beyond language to the deautomatization of official ideology and its tyranny of received ideas.

All of this is important for the mockery of fascist discourse. *Eros e Priapo*'s satire employs numerous strategies to discredit the regime's manipulation of false rhetoric. From Le Bon, Mussolini had learned to work the crowd with images, words, and slogans to produce a magnetic fascination and dependence on his charismatic presence (Koon 1985, 4–5). The Duce's exaggerated posturing, gesticulation, calibration of voice, repetition, and synergy with the crowd below are all exploded by the pamphlet into a bestial parody. Even more significantly, Mussolini operated a tremendous centripetal narrowing of political discourse, especially when compared with the linguistic eclecticism of D'Annunzio or experimentalism of Marinetti, two of fascism's more famous literary cotravelers. Technical precision and breadth of critical discourse were anathema to the Duce, whose political idiolect has been described as consisting of only a few hundred words manipulated in a rhetorical refrain of work, country, and a vacuous idealism of spirit over matter (Simonini 1978, 10–13). Add to this the regime's attempted Romanization of place names and its political crusades against dialect, foreign expressions, and customs, or even the late and ridiculous campaign against the use of the formal singular form of address ("Lei"), and one is confronted with a linguistic policy diametrically contrary to Gadda's own. Gadda's linguistic expressionism, macaronism, and dialectism, his forays into the language of psychoanalysis, are a de facto rebellion against the linguistic and cultural constrictions of the regime. Nowhere is this more apparent than in the plurilingual satire of *Eros e Priapo*. The Duce's centripetal rhetoric of repeated slogans is countered by continual rebuttal that language, history, and life are a variegated movement from chaos to cosmos, a continual process of differentiation and becoming.

In true macaronic fashion, the pamphlet's linguistic and diachronic destabilization affects every form of official linguistic reductionism or monolanguage. Not only is fascist dysfunctionalism subjected to psychoanalytic critique, psychoanalytic discourse itself is dislocated and de-automatized by the pamphlet's ancient macaronic tongue. Freudian crowd theory is infiltrated by Machiavellian discourse. Narcissism is explained in the anachronistic scholasticism of Dante's "anima semplicetta" while the Tuscan poet's own life becomes a comic example of the analytical concept of sublimation. In Gadda's postwar essays on psychoanalysis and in *Eros e Priapo*, Freudian discourse pales as a late and less creative version of the psychoanalytic insights of the great Latin writers and historians, Virgil and Ovid, Suetonius and Tacitus.

Municipal chronicler, medieval theologian, licentious *novelliere*, Machiavellian historian, and Renaissance satirist, the cantankerous De Madrigal subjects all received ideas and all reality to the anachronistic and subversive perspective of the past and its languages. Through this diachronic sieve the inanity of the present is sucked into history while that of the past is superimposed on our own. The anachronistic discrepancies highlight an even more ludicrous similarity. The satire is always pertinent because its object, the stupidity of man, never changes.

FERTILITY, MYTH, AND MAGIC

> Un mito è pur necessario a travolgere gli umani verso il futuro ("Mito e consapevolezza," MS 901).

> [A myth is absolutely necessary to sweep human beings toward the future.]

Macaronic dislocation plunges *Eros e Priapo*'s satire into history's continuum. But the essay strives for even more distant and archaic lands. It invokes the primordial magic of satire. Satire is the most archaic of the Western literary forms. Turn-of-the-century anthropological Hellenists and their successors have corroborated Aristotle's assertion on the genesis of the satirical Old Comedy from the Phallic Songs of the Dionysian cults (see Cornford 1914, Elliott 1960). The songs had their origins in magical fertility rituals that consisted of both a positive invocation of the god and a negative element of invective and curse against evil forces or individuals. The phallus was the sacred emblem of fertility, but it too was of a dual nature: a positive agent of fertilization but also a negative magical charm against evil spirits. Ritual magic is highly efficacious for its believers. It can kill at a distance; it can expel evil; it can give man the power to impose order on a hostile world; it is highly pragmatic and practical.

Eros e Priapo recuperates the genesis of satire in ritual magic, especially its origins in the abusive and scurrilous invective of the phallic rites. The Nietzchean Dionysus is replaced with his sexually obscene son Priapus. The ritualistic thrust of the satire resides in its exorcism of Mussolini as the degenerate and false Priapus. The dictator is a false fertility; he is denounced and cursed as the opposite of fecundity; he is revealed to be death itself. Contrary to the demagogue's proclamation that he was "the possessor of the central and only barrel of sperm" (EP 236), the pamphlet stresses from its opening paragraph that he and his cohorts were instead "the destruction and the cancellation of life, the total obliteration of the signs of life" (EP 221). With a not infrequent recurrence to classical mythology, the dictator, his henchmen, and the disastrous policy of agricultural autarchy are accused of having provoked the catastrophic reversal of nature's abundance through their own blasphemy of the gods of fertility: "They would tread pompously in their boots alongside the grain harvest and the rice fields [in] their black and cemeterial adornments. For they were death, and they were not anything else. Blustering aside the ditches and rows of stacks, they vituperated the eternal sanctity of Maia, the benign and parched divinity of Pales and Ceres, or later the lavish abundance of the overturned horns of Pomona and Vertumnus. The Rogations they proposed were tempests. With walnuts of hail, and, later, the figs of howling wind" (EP 284). The agrarian image of "ducismo" propagated through photos and newsreels of the bare-chested dictator loading grain into a threshing machine or standing astride a tractor is mocked in Gadda's pamphlet via the image of two hairs surrounding withered nipples of no interest to any hungry babe (EP 267–68).

The appropriation of the invocative power of the ritualistic curse to harm and kill is most evident in the anti-Mussolinian fables in Gadda's *Il primo libro delle favole.* When they were published in 1952, Gadda's enigmatic Florentine fables elicited a largely unappreciative response from the critics much as *Eros e Priapo* would, but for Gadda there was satisfaction enough in having put Mussolini into hell: "This is my paradise," he declared (Cattaneo 1973, 60–61). Several of the fables (111, 129, 134, 137, 138) constitute a demonic wish-fulfillment. Mussolini has been cast into the underworld ("Pocolume" [Littlelight]) where he is subjected to continual verbal abuse: "Testa di Morto," "Grugnone Sanguemarcio," "Mascella d'asino Maltone" [Head of the Dead, Rottedblood Snoutmug, Jackass Jaw Maltone].[6] He is defecated on by darting bats ("they pissed on his doge's nape, they crapped on his bald head . . . he received more shit on his nose") and greeted by the "mighty latrine breath" and "waves of feces" spewing forth from the lewd mouth of his infernal bride (PLF 35–36, 41). The satiric attack in these sketches is vicious and personal (more obscene comments are reserved for Clara Petacci, the dictator's mistress who was executed with him during his flight to the Swiss border and exposed with him to the public's rage in Milan's Piazzale Loreto). The vilification is an inversion of the phallic ritual. The dictator's "genital trunk" is not the emblem of fecundity but is "full of leprosy" (PLF 43). His hellish *contrappasso* locks him into a second Perillian bovine artifice where he mates in eternity with his Pasiphae-Clara while a fiery cauldron bubbles in eternity under his scrotum: "so the Maltone had his balls burnt, with his ass, and he let out in brays: hee haw!, so that Pocolume screeched with that sound all the way to the king's throne. May he remain that way forever. Amen" (PLF 44).

The Mussolinian fables and curses are astonishingly puerile. They are a regression to the author's personal mythos of denial and blasphemous revenge. Throughout his career Gadda had conveyed the myth in specifically sexual terms, in his motif of the denial of love of the repressive father-God, in his jealousy of the sexual dominance of father-brother substitutes, in his sadistic revenge against the female or maternal object of desire. Nowhere is the primitive sexual agon as obsessive as in *Eros e Priapo*.

What elicits the most savage name-calling in Gadda's satire against the dictator as the "fallo paterno padronale" [paternal padronal phallus] was the latter's representational usurpation and hording of sexual power, the decree that he alone was "il solo genitale-eretto disponibile sulla piazza" [the only erect-genital available in the square], "il portatore del sublime" [the bearer of sublimity], "l'organo generatore dominante" [the dominant generating organ] (EP 259). This arrogation of sexual power was made possible by "putting to silence and shame the 'other males'" and especially the intellectuals, poets, and philosophers who were made to appear as "impotent sluggards" (EP 257–58). Responsible for much of the pamphlet's phallic imagery and misogynistic denigration, the motif of the perceived imagery of impotency of the intellectual is obsessive and ubiquitous in *Eros e Priapo:* "Women dislike philosophers, they hate every disquisitional manner of mangy intellects and every form of critical thought, reason for them is sophism, and they call civil restraint impotence. Woe to the Hesitater! . . . He who hesitates or stutters incurs blame: since he presents them with the image of another hesitation and of another stammering that annoys them at all hours and more than any other thing on earth" (EP 255).

The obsession is not new. One is reminded of the unusual argument in *Racconto italiano* that an author often achieves literary success in accordance with his sexual potency. In *Eros e Priapo* sexuality is validated only if it can be sublimated into creative teleology (Dante is the repeated example). In all other cases, De Madrigal's denunciation is vehement: "I certainly shall not be the one to deny that undeniable relationships, that multiple and complex interferences exist between sex and the work of art: it may happen that sex inspires a work of art, that's fine: but for you to tell me because at noon you visited Madame Zenaide and her *demoiselles en chemises* . . . that you have begun a great poem, and that you expect from me that laurel I don't even have for myself, go fuck yourselves till the devil take you, you ill-bred louts. Thus concluded Oco De Madrigal in a fit of rage" (EP 255).

Sexuality and creativity are conjoined again and again in *Eros e Priapo;* they are the low and the sublime mechanics of heuristic becoming. It is an old story. The author's exclusion from artistic or heroic greatness— the laurel he does not have for himself—had habitually been depicted as a sexual denial: "nor will a goddess deign him her bed. Nec dignata cubili est" ("Dalle specchiere dei laghi," GA 229).

Gadda's polemic against the dictator's sexual usurpation, false fecundity, and histrionic sublimity is ultimately a primordial struggle for the magical word. The word-mongering Mussolini is denounced as the "Verbo sterile" [sterile Word] (EP 260). In the economy of the sexual-verbal exchange, the phallic signifier ("fava") is also the verbal signifier ("favola"), and the vituperous deflation of the one is that of the other (PLF 71). The poet's weapon in this agon is the curse. The single most striking and archaic element of *Eros e Priapo* is its unrestrained profusion of invective. The inexhaustible heaping of insult upon insult as if to bury the opponent under the weight of verbal abuse is immanently ritualistic. The whole imposing edifice of the Gaddian linguistic castle has its source in the formulaic structure and magical coercion of this primordial invective.

In a distant 1936, during the dictator's highest moment of rhetorical triumph with the conquest of Ethiopia and the creation of the new Italian empire, Gadda had written that even in enlightened societies the word retains the obsessive and re-creating value that it had with magic and necromancy. "It is up to us," he wrote, "to redeem it from the obsession of fraud and to re-create the magic of truth" ("Meditazione breve circa il dire e il fare," VM 453). There is no direct reference to the regime or the dictator in Gadda's 1936 essay, but there is an imagery so similar in the 1944 "I miti del somaro" ("The Myths of the Jackass") that one is led to believe that Gadda's credo of the polyphonic and imminently ethical use of language was determined in part by his disgust for Mussolini's fraudulent manipulation of the "sacred" and "magical" words of incantation: "A paranoiac half-wit enchanted millions of Italians and Italian women in the guise of a 'genius,' a 'prophet,' a 'man sent by Providence.' . . . He discovered in his immeasurable vulgarity the pentacle of facile magic, the filthy formula and the inane enchantment. He showed himself off and made during two double lustrums a single puffed-up turkey's pirouette, with a fine psychagogic pretext: that to sway the crowd he had to excite it sexually with a myth, which was that funerary carnival of knives, black headbands and giant cardboard heads, empty and funereal" (MS 922).

In 1944 Gadda wrote "I miti del somaro" and two other brief essays on the fascist phenomenon, "Mito e consapevolezza" ("Myth and Awareness") and "La consapevole scienza" ("The Aware Science"). The essays, later found among the papers of critic and editor Giacomo Debenedetti, were never published in Gadda's lifetime. They constitute the initial nucleus of many of the arguments and imagery in *Eros e Priapo* (Pinotti 1993).[7] Gadda's references to the magical power of words and myth on the crowd are indicative of the presence of Freud's *Group Psychology,* and through it, of Le Bon's *Psychologie des foules.* But the essays have not yet appropriated the Freudian language on unsublimated narcissism. The argumentation is based instead on the necessity of myths in the heuristic becoming of the collectivity. A religion is necessary, Gadda states, perhaps with echoes of Machiavelli, but it cannot be a false religion. The battle lines are drawn. Against the purveyors of the false myths, of the Mussolinian "theatrical myth" and "any myth whatsoever so long as it is a myth" (MS 909), are arrayed the positive forces of the useful, pragmatic myth. This useful myth is the "psychodynamic myth"; it is grounded in "the authenticity of a consciousness"; it "transforms into pragma or at least into pragmatic tension the most profound instances of our being" (MS 904).

Every author conscious of what his craft is truly about knows he is a spinner of myths. Gadda knew this. His myth, his dream, had always been to forge the heroic poetics of rational synthesis. The scenario is a familiar one. The poetics of rational synthesis is denied, by fate, by nature, by the gods, by the repressive superego-father. The agon degenerates into the tragedy of the vulgar and buffoonish railer. Positive ritualism becomes negative ritual.

Freud liked to study myths. He was as much a writer as a psychologist, and he forged his own myths. Perhaps the most sweeping of these was the myth of the birth of the individual consciousness from the psychology of the group. The primal horde of brothers kills the repressive primal father. They ingest him and thereby complete their identification with him and appropriate to themselves his strength, his potency. From this murder is born the universal remorse and sense of guilt of the son. This is Freud's myth, which he presents as a truth. It is the artist, he argues, who is responsible for the lying myth. A man breaks with the group in his exigency to take over the father's part. He invents the heroic myth: a sole hero slew the totemic monster-father. The lie culminates in the deification of the hero. This liar and hero is the first epic poet. Freud's myth is elaborated specifically in the pages of *Totem and Taboo* and *Group Psychology and the Analysis of the Ego*. Gadda had read both works and was well aware of the totemic inheritance in himself. He declared that the towering Monte Rosa had been his Freudian "totem-papà" (EP 1046).

The lie of the hero myth becomes the fragmentation of the hero myth in Gadda. The broken myth reappears throughout his work. It is what pushes his prose from epic to satire. The satirist is the primitive antihero par excellence. He, as Walter Benjamin noted, is the true anthropophagite. No one ingests the father more than he, but he cannot sublimate the meal into sublime poetry. It weighs on his stomach like a bilious toad and comes out in a vomit of curses and blasphemies. This is how the satirist kills; this is how he forges his own topsy-turvy hero myth. He is always punished and mocked for his efforts. The ugly and vulgar Thersites is thrashed in public and brought to tears by the true pragmatic hero, Ulysses. Eventually Thersites is killed by the true tragic hero, Achilles, precisely for his vituperation and vilification of the warrior woman-queen.

Eros e Priapo was a regression for Gadda, a return to the primitive antiword that lies at the core of his poetics and frustrated sublimity and blasphemous revenge. But personal regression in Gadda is always redeemed by its translation into literary regression, the ability of his works to plumb the historical geneses of literary genres and forms. The works reach beyond their immediate autobiographical and synchronic boundaries to penetrate to the core of literary evolution. They recuperate literature's tragic metaphoricity, the grotesque, macaronic, and satirical origins of novelistic discourse, satire's origins in ritual invective. In this sense, it is misleading to approach Gadda as a forerunner of the Italian neo-avant-garde (Seroni 1969), to see him as an author who matured in synchrony with the experimentation of the *nouveau roman* (Dombroski 1975) or narrowly to tag him as a final, exasperated exemplar of nineteenth-century "bozzettismo" (Baldi 1972). He is far more puerile and primitive. He romps with buffoonish giants. He curses with Archilochus.

Notes

Introduction: The Modern Macaronic

1. Butor's and Enzenberger's essays appeared with others by Juan Petit, Drago Ivanisevic, and Pier Paolo Pasolini under the title "Gadda Europeo" in *L'Europa letteraria* 4, nos. 20–21 (1963): 52–67.

La cognizione del dolore and *Quer pasticciaccio brutto de via Merulana* are the only works by Gadda to have been translated into English. Both translations are by William Weaver.

2. Contini's first contact with Gadda's writing was with the "Polemiche e Pace nel direttismo" (1933) (CU 245–81), a satirical fiction on the "contenutisti-calligrafi" controversy that Contini remembers having irritated him more than anything (LGC 7).

As Gian Carlo Roscioni points out, Contini speaks of Gadda's "spontaneous" association with the macaronic tradition and in so doing indicates more a typology than a true and proper genealogy (Roscioni 1994, 147). This is also my own understanding of Gadda's macaronic heritage, although this typology is characterized by a strong sense of historical reminiscence.

3. On the language debate in Italy across the centuries see Maurizio Vitale's definitive *La questione della lingua* (Palermo: Palumbo, 1960). On the historical evolution of Italian see Tullio De Mauro's *Storia linguistica dell'Italia unita* (Bari: Laterza, 1979).

4. Among the Italian macaronics, other than Folengo, can be included Tifi Odasi, Fossa da Cremona, Bassano da Mantova, Giovan Giorgio Alione, Partenio Zanclaio, Bartolomeo Bolla, Cesare Orsini, and Bernardino Stefonio. Among the French, Remy Belleau, Étienne Tabourot, and Antonius de Arena. Among the English, William Drummond, George Ruggle, and Alexander Geddes. There were also macaronic schools in Holland, Germany, Portugal, and Spain. See *Lessico universale italiano* (Roma: Istituto della Enciclopedia Italiana, 1973), xii, 463.

5. Otherwise it would make sense to recur to a less historical term than *macaronic* to describe literary manifestations so distant in time. This is what Ivano Paccagnella argues, suggesting the alternative labels of *plurilingualism* or *pastiche* (Paccagnella 1983, 250).

6. Published in English as "New Linguistic Questions" in *Heretical Empiricism* (Bloomington: Indiana University Press, 1988), 3–22. Citations come from this translation.

For an overview of the entire debate see Oronzo Parlangèli's *La nuova questione della lingua* (Brescia: Paideia, 1971).

7. Renato Barilli is the literary critic who has most eloquently argued against any prescriptive validity for the Gaddian literary line. For Barilli, writing in the mid-1960s and early 1970s, Gadda's linguistic torment was already "outdated," the last throes of the crisis of mimetic realism which had not gotten beyond the "barrier of naturalism." He argues instead that the Svevo-Pirandello line is the only valid tradition for the future of Italian letters, a line which he dates to a Renaissance tradition of a poetics of linguistic transparency in the name of a literature of "ethos" over "mythos" (Barilli 1964, 105–28; 1972, 5–15). I agree with Barilli's thesis that Gadda is involved in an exacerbation of the crisis of mimetic realism, but I feel he misses the historical complexity of Gadda's literature by speaking of him as not going beyond the barrier of naturalism as opposed to returning to the genre origins of Western realism. In essence, Gadda's literary practice, like that of other modern macaronic authors, is a backward-looking art. For that matter, the choice by Pirandello and Svevo of a transparent prose style is conditioned in part by their hostile response to the immediate historical pressure of D'Annunzian and Crocean aesthetics. This helps to explain why their works are substantially devoid of the lyrical expressionism that is an important feature of European modernism.

8. The answer to the question of the liberating or reactionary quality of the Renaissance carnivalesque or modern humor ultimately lies not in a metahistorical approach but in the examination of their symbolic function in concrete historical, cultural, and sociopolitical contexts. This is what Peter Stallybrass and Allon White suggest concerning the carnivalesque in their argument that it "makes little sense to fight out the issue of whether or not carnivals are *intrinsically* radical or conservative, for to do so automatically involves the false essentializing of carnivalesque transgression" (Stallybrass and White 1986, 14; see also White 1982, 62).

9. The macaronic distortion of Charles's name combines French and Latin to foreground his rustic and "bovine" characteristics: French *char* = *cart* or *wagon*; Latin *bovarius* whence French *bouvier*, "keeper of oxen" but also "a coarse and awkward person." See *Le grand Robert de la langue française* (Paris: Le Robert, 1986), 2:144.

10. Mercier defines the language of *Finnegans Wake* in Delepierre's terms as "Hybrido-Pedantesque" (27).

11. The comparisons of Céline to Joyce have also been numerous. Patrick McCarthy, for example, writes that Céline's Rabelaisian style "sets him apart from all other modern French writers and in looking for parallels one turns inevitably to Joyce. Both men have faith in language and believe it can express

anything. Both use it in its own right as a triumphant, independent entity. The creation of a new style that Céline carries out in *Mort à crédit* is the task Joyce undertook in *Finnegans Wake*" (McCarthy 1975, 115). In "Rabelais, il a raté son coup," Céline declares that he owed nothing to Joyce, and that like Rabelais he found everything in French itself.

CHAPTER ONE: THE POETICS OF POLARITY

1. The philological approach counts Gianfranco Contini, Dante Isella, and Cesare Segre among its more prominent spokespersons and dates to Contini's 1934 essay "Carlo Emilio Gadda, o del pastiche." The speculative approach evolves later with the publication of Gian Carlo Roscioni's *La disarmonia prestabilita* (1969)—which remains, in my opinion, the best overall study on Gadda—and Roscioni's publication in 1974 of Gadda's 1928 philosophical treatise *Meditazione milanese.* In his later years Gadda was often distrustful of literary critics but he was amiable to Roscioni, calling him "Doctor R.," "a philosopher and an Anglicist" who has "helped me much and with great effort has helped with Einaudi's publication or republication of some of my works" (LPGC 124, 126; LAM 84).

2. The two quasi-biographies of Gadda to date are *Le confessioni di Carlo Emilio Gadda* (1974), in which Piero Gadda Conti provides a running exegesis to cousin Carlo Emilio's letters, and Giulio Cattaneo's anecdotal *Il gran lombardo* (1973). The best biography is to be found in the numerous volumes of Gadda's correspondence published since his death, constituting what Roscioni laments "risks being the last great epistolary collection of Italian literature" (Roscioni 1988).

3. It was the embracing Europeanism of *Solaria's* otherwise rarefied literary pages that drew the greatest censure from fascist intellectuals and authorities: "I became a contributor to a small Florentine journal," remarked Elio Vittorini. "I was a Solarian—and Solarian was a word that in the literary circles of the times meant antifascist, Europeanist, universalist, antitraditionalist.... Giovanni Papini insulted us from one side, and Farinacci from another. They even called us dirty Jews because of the hospitality given to authors of the Hebrew religion and for the good things we said about Kafka and Joyce" (Vittorini 1976, 192–93).

4. In a 1968 interview with Dacia Maraini, Gadda reiterated that he considered Leibniz the philosopher closest to his own ideas and "certainly not those long-haired hippies of modern philosophy" (IDM 15). Roscioni, citing a reference to Bergson in Gadda's 1927 "I viaggi la morte" (VM 581), makes an argument for a strong Bergsonian influence on Gadda's thought (see Lucchini [1988, 53] for a rebuttal), but he also notes elsewhere that much of Gadda's knowledge of nineteenth-century and twentieth-century authors was secondhand (Roscioni 1969b, 28–30; 1974, xvii).

5. Gadda would seem to have in mind Leibniz's affirmation in paragraph 61 of the *Monadology* that "every body responds to all that happens in the universe" ("tout corps se ressent de tout ce qui se fait dans l'univers") (Leibniz 1973, 265;

Roscioni 1969b, 29), or that of Dostoyevsky's Father Zosima that "all is like an ocean, all is flowing and blending; a touch in one place sets up movement at the other end of the earth" (Dostoyevsky 1950, 383–84).

The image of the distant effects of the dragonfly's flight bears an iconographic similarity to what has become known in chaos science as "the butterfly effect," coined by meteorologist Edward Lorenz in a 1979 paper on sensitive dependence on initial conditions in weather forecasting, "Predictability: Does the Flap of a Butterfly's Wings in Brazil Set Off a Tornado in Texas." Other affinities with chaosology can be found in Gadda's obsession with the nonlinear or "baroque" forms of nature (camel humps, thighbones, livers, beans, squash, oblong watermelons, churchbells shaped like Kaiser pears [C 760, 765]), or in his reference to the lapse of periodic movement into chaos at increased velocities, as in the episode the "catastrophic *itinéraire*" of a lightning bolt caught between two rooftop rods in *La cognizione del dolore* (C 587–88; AWG 24–25). Given Gadda's technical and scientific background, one could argue that his attraction-repulsion complex toward disorder assumes at times the contours of a Kuhnian paradigm crisis.

6. I have chosen the Greek neologism *heuresis* to translate Gadda's *euresi*, a term which he uses to indicate reality's evolutionary process of creation, invention, becoming. His use of the adjective *euristico* [heuristic] typically conveys a similar meaning. Both usages are idiosyncratic, so much so that Salvatore Battaglia's exhaustive *Grande dizionario della lingua italiana* classifies them as erudite and rare and illustrates them with citations from Gadda's works alone (see vol. 5, E–FIN, 512).

7. Gadda never submitted the unfinished *Racconto* for consideration, and the jurors (among whom were Giuseppe Antonio Borgese, Benedetto Croce, and Luigi Pirandello) were not satisfied with the 245 submissions they did receive. In a clear indication of the crisis of the novel in Italy during this period, not one entrant was found worthy of the prize, and the competition was put off until 1927 when Francesco Chiesa won with *Villadorna* and Francesco Perri with *Emigranti* (Isella 1974, vii–ix).

8. Gadda's "theory of types," as he writes in his copy of Augusto Guzzo's *Pensieri di B. Spinoza*, is linked to Spinoza's differentiation of men according to their knowledge of God: "From this deduce the 'theory of types': that is to say, the nucleating relationships possess a different degree of reality" (cited in Roscioni 1974, 348). There is also perhaps a Balzacian echo in the classification of characters as types. Gadda cites Eugénie Grandet as a model for the type A character (RI 397). For that matter, references to numerous canonical nineteenth-century models recur throughout Gadda's notes: Stendhal's *Le rouge et le noir* for its "hypervolitive" protagonist, turns of phrase and dramatic ending (RI 398, 400, 573); Dickens's *Pickwick Circle* for its caricatural humorism (RI 484); Zola's *Le rêve* for the imagery of its affianced heroine (RI 408); D'Annunzio's *Trionfo della morte* and Fogazzaro's *Malombra* for their dramatic endings (RI 400); Dostoyevsky for images of the jilted woman (RI 537, 548). A special narrative

and ideological debt exists in regard to Alessandro Manzoni's *I promessi sposi* that will be discussed later in this chapter.

9. Despite Gadda's emphasis on the instinct of combination, *Racconto italiano* in no way abandons "determinism-heredity." The latter is present in its motif of "the ethnic, historic and economic insufficiency of the Italian environment" (RI 396), in its construction of character types who behave in accordance with their hereditary constitution (RI 398), in Gadda's emphasis on racial and climatic factors for describing "Italianism" (RI 408). Roscioni argues that Gadda most often effects a fusion of Darwinian evolutionism with Leibniz's combinatory mechanics (Roscioni 1969b, 44).

10. The publication history of Gadda's war diary is convoluted. Three notebooks had been published by Sansoni in 1955 at the request of Alessandro Bonsanti without any revision on Gadda's part. When one of Gadda's Milanese friends, Ambrogio Gobbi, jokingly scolded Gadda in regard to a less than polite reference to himself in the diary, Gadda, in typically excessive fashion, apologized profusely and went to great pains to make various name changes and several minor deletions to protect the innocent when the *Giornale* was republished in 1965 with the inclusion of a fourth notebook. The complete diary has recently been published in volume 4 of the Garzanti edition of the *Opere di Carlo Emilio Gadda* (1992), including the original names, restored deletions, and a previously unpublished fifth notebook. A sixth notebook was lost when Gadda was taken prisoner at Caporetto (Isella 1992, 1103–9).

11. The Fascist Party and Nationalist Association merged in March 1923.

12. Just *how* "private" Gadda intended his war diary and war correspondence with friends to be is uncertain, since in both there are repeated references, most of them tongue-in-cheek, to posterity and possible future readers (see Sassi 1983, xviii).

13. "My sister . . . has a temperament similar to my own" (IDM 10). Upon his return to Milan after the war, Gadda is worried enough about Clara's poor spiritual and physical state to have her undergo a cure (GGP 856). Like Gadda's, many of Clara's problems have familial origins, including what Gadda perceived to be their mother's "coldness" and "distrust" toward her and the veto of her marriage to a family friend (GGP 856). The relationship between brother and sister will deteriorate over the years. Gadda's letters to "Lalla" from Sardinia and Argentina in the early twenties express a mixture of concern for her nervous disorders and failing health, apologetic rebukes of her repeated intentions to visit him, and patronizing suggestions concerning her life goals and career prospects (LAS). In his later years Gadda's correspondence to Clara would decline precipitously and he would show ever less tolerance for her "hysterical crises" (LAM 57). Profoundly saddened by the loss of Clara's infant daughter in 1931 (AF 87), Gadda displayed little sympathy for her subsequent obsession to have children. The sister figure was excluded from the Oedipal economy of the autobiographical *La cognizione del dolore*, but Clara was convinced that the childless and savagely

murdered Liliana Balducci of *Pasticciaccio* was her and that her brother nurtured a homicidal urge in her regard (LAS 14–15).

14. Letters to friends indicate that Gadda had begun ruminating on *La cognizione del dolore* as early as 1934 (L. Orlando 1991, 1236–37). By the time Gadda had begun actively working on the novel he probably had read several important Freudian texts in French translation: *Psychopathology of Everyday Life, Introduction to Psychoanalysis,* and a selection of Freud's writings in the Gallimard edition of *Essais de psychanalyse appliquée* (Manzotti 1988, 854). In a 1963 interview with Alberto Arbasino, Gadda recalled that he had initially approached psychoanalysis between the years 1926–40 and had been guided by Casimiro Doniselli, a professor of psychology at the University of Milan, toward the possibility of the "translation in psychological terms of many positions of theoretical philosophy" (Arbasino 1971, 196).

15. For examples from the fascist press, see Del Buono (1971, 346–54). Gadda's defense of Freudianism is not so much an attack against fascist anti-Semitism as an assault on "Latin" simplemindedness. Minimal strains of anti-Semitism appear throughout Gadda's own writings. In the *Giornale di guerra e di prigionia,* after having met "the very unlikable, pretentious and presumptuous Captain Niccolosi, a Jew," Gadda adds that he always recognizes Jews at first sight, even though he has no "special" aversion toward them. Later he stereotypes a German second lieutenant as "skinny, with glasses and curved shoulders, like a Jewish shopkeeper" (GG 499, 738). In *Racconto italiano* there is a long compositional note on "the children of Israel" that questions how fervently patriotic an Italian Jew can truly be (RI 551–53).

16. The Virgilian motif is referred to specifically in a manuscript sketch for *Cognizione* that bears the title from verse 62 of the fourth eclogue "cui non risere parentes" [to whom his parents did not smile] (C$_2$ 525–35). The reading now commonly preferred is "qui non risere parentes" [who did not smile at his parents] (Manzotti 1987, 339).

17. James Joyce, like Gadda and Vico, was also attracted to the image of the premonitory thunderbolt, and he "wondered where Vico got his fear of thunderstorms" (Ellmann 1983, 554). In Joyce the thunderbolt appears especially in moments of sexual transgression (incest and adultery); in *La cognizione del dolore* Gonzalo's blasphemy against God and his surrogates, the Nistitúo de vigilancia para la noche and the father, is embedded in a tale of repressed incestuous desire that will be punished with the mother's death from a blow to the head. There are other interesting textual similarities between Stephen Dedalus's matricidal angst at the beginning of *Ulysses* and Gonzalo's in *Cognizione* (see Roscioni 1969a, 93–94).

18. On the inane anachronism of villa life in Brianza, Gadda wrote shortly after his mother's death to Contini on May 26, 1936: "Among other things my country house (another big headache!) causes me more problems than a hysterical mother-in-law. It is the domestic, Briantean and rustic whims of a world

that has set forever leaving us only tedious taxes to pay. I will have my re-venge!" Contini identifies this threat of revenge as "the first seed of *Cognizione*" (LGC 19).

19. The mother-brother death link reappears in *Quer pasticciaccio brutto de via Merulana*. The sight of the massacred Liliana Balducci, a surrogate mother figure, triggers detective Ingravallo's memory of the dead soldier-brother in the mountain battlegrounds of World War I and of his mother's grief: "a frightful stream of black blood from Faiti or from Cengio (Don Ciccio remembered sud-denly, with a distant lament in his soul, poor Mamma!)" (P 59; TAM 69). For a moment the Molisan Don Ciccio becomes Gadda-Gonzalo.

CHAPTER TWO: IN SEARCH OF A NECESSARY STYLE

1. A complete bibliography of Gadda's works and their migrations from jour-nals to published volumes is available in *Opere* 5/2:13–67. In a 1953 letter to Contini, Gadda described his fragments as "involuntary expunctions from larger narratives . . . similar to those pieces of a fresco which contain some faces or some surviving figures and objects from a denser and more developed assemblage, which has become submerged in time" (LGC 88–89).

2. Adelaide Gadda's insistence that her son become an engineer because other members of the family had become engineers and because it was financially lucrative was another source of rancor between son and mother (LPGC 14; IDM 14).

3. Gadda announced one of many temporary withdrawals from the trade in a letter to Ugo Betti of November 4, 1927: "My inner crisis, an eternal stomach indigestion, has been resolved recently in a crazy act: I have resigned my posi-tion at the company where I work (and where I am well off in all ways), to see if I can embark on the wretched road of the more or less *"belles" lettres* and the more or less consolatory philosophy. . . . There is this to fear though, that, along the way, hunger and fear do not once again drive the inadequate philosopher toward the city of evil deeds, where circulate the necessary silver coins and the necessary strumpets" (IF 118).

4. From her "casa rossa" in Arenzano, Liguria, Lucia Morpurgo Rodocanachi carried on a flourishing trade in ghost translations for numerous important authors, including Eugenio Montale, Elio Vittorini, and Camillo Sbarbaro (see Marcenaro in LGS 27–44).

5. More than translations, Gadda operates a veritable rewriting of these *Siglo de Oro* authors in which their baroque expressionism is taken to new intensities, as in the following example from Gadda's translation of Quevedo's "El mundo por de dentro." Quevedo: "[M]as las bravatas que en los túmulos sobrescriben podriciòn y gusanos, se podrían excusar. Empero también los muertos tienen su vanidad, y los difuntos y difuntas su soberbia. Allí no va sino tierra de menos fruto y más espantosa de la que pisas, por sí non merecedora de alguna honra ni aun de ser cultivada con arado y azadón" (VS 50). Gadda: "Però, dico io, le

bischeraggini che vanno scrivendo in sul marmo, sì, sì, tutte codeste bravazzate degli epitafî che le gallano al di sopra de' vermini e della putrèdine, quelle almeno, diobono, quelle potrebbono davvero tralasciarle di mettere, o cervelloni! Gli è che fino ai morti, dà retta, fino ai morti e alle morte, anche loro ci hanno pure loro la loro vanità: e appena possano, che ti montano volentieri in superbia, una superbietta minchioncella da andare a paro coi vivi. Laggiù al composanto, senti, la è terra che frutto non dà, nòe? e l'è ancora più spaventosa di quest'altra, che te tu vai pestando co' tuoi piedi per tutto il tempo di vita: e in se stessa . . . di certo che non la merita onore: e nemmeno aratro, o vanga, o zappa che fosse" (TR 275). In 1957 Gadda added a third *siglo de oro* translation, that of Juan Ruiz de Alarcón's "La verdad sospechosa." On Gadda as a translator see Benuzzi Billeter (1977), Contini (1989, 55–60), and Dombroski (1972, 219–21).

6. The desire for "adirectional chaos" in the symbolists represents, Gadda states, a regression to the "primigenial potentiality of the beginning, still devoid of ethical determinations: a relapse into the infancy of being" (VM 581). Similarly, Liliana's "tendency toward chaos" is a "longing to begin all over again from the beginning . . . [s]ince only the Indistinct, the Abyss, the Outer Darkness, can open a new spiritual ascent for the chain of determining causes: a renewed form, renewed fortune" (P 105–6; TAM 138–39). An analogous dilemma was experienced by Italo Calvino in his tension between "possibility" and "form" (see, for example, "The Spiral," in Calvino, *Cosmicomics*).

7. This sublimity of dissolution is not to be confused with Gadda's negative sublimity of heroic annihilation in the cause of the extirpation of evil. The later informs Gadda's Hamlet motif, which he also discusses in "I viaggi la morte" (VM 583–84).

8. Dombroski argues that Martinetti played an important role in Gadda's interpretation of the Kantian concept of noumena. In his reading of Kant, Martinetti argues that empirical reality may constitute a point of departure in a gradual approach to the Kantian "noumenon" (Dombroski 1972, 178, 211). Gadda perhaps took this interpretation to heart in striving to fuse his phenomenology and metaphysics. Just how much of Kant Gadda read firsthand is put in question by Guido Lucchini's discovery that in some of the most important Kantian texts in Gadd's library only a few pages had been opened with a paper cutter (Lucchini 1994, 230).

9. It should be remembered that even for an "outsider" such as the traveling engineer Gadda, the Italian literary establishment of the 1920s, 1930s, and 1940s (headquartered in Florence) was a close-knit community of mutual acquaintances and resonances. Gadda would later dedicate *L'Adalgisa* to De Robertis.

10. Gadda's rebuttal in *Cognizione* is unfair since he ascribes the negative critical appraisals to his (sacred) war reminiscences while it is precisely his pieces on the First World War that these critics tended to praise the most. Gargiulo himself wrote that in the final pages of "Manovre di artiglieria da campagna"

Gadda gives the highest proof of his narrative "possibilities" (Gargiulo 1958, 551).

11. Gadda's critique rapidly matures into a defiant knowledge of diversity in a letter a few years later (1931) to Silvio Guarnieri: "I am incomprehensible, absurd, baroque, ungrammatical, banal, inexperienced in life; but I am also a grammarian, a pedant, one who seeks a pompous and out-of-place display of culture; moreover, I have no sense of rhythm and my prose is antimusical to the point of cachexy, while there is so much good prose out there, smooth, melodious" (LSG 155).

12. On narrative voice see Benveniste (1971), Genette (1983), and Cohn (1978).

13. Various episodes and fragments of the novel appeared over the years with name changes and an increasing use of Milanese and Veneto dialects. The 1970 Garzanti edition of *La meccanica* is an eclectic patchwork of these fragments. The edition contained in volume 2 of Gadda's *Opere* (Garzanti, 1989) is based instead on the integral 1928–29 manuscript and includes for the first time three final less-developed chapters on the war and the novel's dramatic conclusion (Isella 1989b, 1203–4). I refer to this latter edition.

14. In this regard, see Carlo Dionisotti's groundbreaking *Geografia e storia della letteratura italiana*.

15. On the Lombard line see Isella (1984), and in particular his opening essay "La cultura letteraria lombarda" (3–24).

16. "The Predappio" refers to Mussolini. Predappio was the dictator's hometown.

17. Gadda's order out of chaos paradigm is a further link to our own era's "science of chaos," especially in its formulation by Prigogine and Stengers (1984). Years later Gadda confessed he had suffered terrible shocks when some jobs failed and some plants exploded (IDM 17).

18. The article was later renamed "Il Carbone dell'Arsa" and included in *Le meraviglie d'Italia* (MI 181–85). The reference to "the Mussolinian spirit" was replaced by one to fascist autarchy as "the law of autonomy which governs Italy today" (MI 182).

CHAPTER THREE: GROTESQUE TRAGEDY

1. The notion of the pathos of madness is Shoshana Felman's, who argues, in reference to Foucault's *Madness and Civilization*, that the pathos of madness in history begins with the obliteration of the pathos of madness by history (Felman 1978, 53). The conceit is not without relevance for Gadda.

2. Guido Baldi remarks that *Cognizione* is Gadda's most valid work because it combats mystification with critical estrangement, but that its gravitation toward the grotesque and baroque inevitably leads it away from critical responsibility toward the trivial "bozzettismo" of his other works (Baldi 1972, 89–129). Piero Pucci observes that in his delirium of the grotesque, Gonzalo is both pathetic and

paradoxical since his metaphysical rage is not matched by a critical questioning of why things are the way they are (Pucci 1967, 53).

3. *Banzavóis*, an imaginary South American corn, is another instance of macaronic word formation, in this case, in a loose analogy with Hispanic-Italian *mais*, a distortion of Milanese *"panz vöj"* [empty paunches] (see Manzotti 1987, 6).

4. The passage is replete with personal anecdotes. Babylon is Rome, which Gadda had to leave in February 1928 due to "a rather bothersome stomach illness, with which God has unexpectedly but justly punished me for my gluttony, my greed and my rapacity similar to that of Vitellius" (LS 67). Fuerte del Rey is likely Forte dei Marmi on the Tuscan Riviera where Gadda often vacationed. Gadda's taste for lobster is attested to in his correspondence to family and friends (LAS 24; AAF 26). Upon crossing the equator on his voyage to Argentina in 1922, Gadda wrote to Clara that he was baptized with the honorific "Pesce Spada" [Swordfish] (LAS 47). The references to Rome as Babylon, the scarlet coloring of the sea scorpion, and the erotic disembowelment of the sea creature would appear to constitute a parodic allusion to the inebriated harlot of fornication in chapter 17 of the biblical Book of Revelation.

5. The dream shares several similarities with Stephen Dedalus's dream of his dead mother at the beginning of *Ulysses:* "In a dream, silently, she had come to him, her wasted body within its loose graveclothes." Buck Mulligen will goad Stephen, reproaching him for his mother's murder and for not having comforted her in her agony (Joyce 1961, 5–6; see Roscioni 1969a, 93; Manzotti 1987, 180).

6. Gadda's sense of guilt and remorse concerning his dead mother and his ongoing effort to sell the villa and the eventual unsatisfactory sale toward the middle of 1937 are documented in various letters to friends: "Forgive me for responding to you with some delay due . . . to a crisis of ill-being, a crisis due above all to the pain and desperation over the death of my mother to whom I was at times so inhumane. . . . the image of her old and without help returns to me and more than anything else an undescribable remorse overtakes me because of my outbursts, so useless and so vile" (December 27, 1936; LPGC 42); "My spirit is still very downcast from the anguish over the death of my Mother and from the feelings of remorse I have concerning my behavior toward her in her final years—feelings of remorse which sometimes seem unbearable" (January 16, 1938; AAF 127); "We are trying in every way to sell the country house, but it is not easy" (July 3, 1936; AAF 126); "I don't know if I have already told you that I sold, disastrously, my house in Brianza, last spring. I salvaged only my books and papers and a few portraits of aunts and uncles, piled up in a warehouse, as well as possible" (June 27, 1938; LGS 76).

7. See also C 576, 578; AWG 10, 19.

8. Hamlet alludes to the similarity between sleep, dreaming, and death: "To die—to sleep. To sleep—perchance to dream" (*Hamlet* 3.1.72–73). The "rub" lies in the linkage of dreaming to the restrictions of the super-ego, the dreadful dreams

of death. Dreamful oblivion does not liberate the flows of desire but "must give us pause"; "thus conscience does make cowards of us all" (*Hamlet* 3.1.76, 91). Gonzalo, whose dream is a dreadful one, argues nonetheless that to dream is to forget the sclerotic figurations of things seen according to force in order to arrive at a deeper source of truth: "But to dream is a deep river, which rushes to a distant spring, bubbling up again in the morning of truth" (C 632; AWG 82; see Dombroski 1984b).

9. An earlier Caesarian allusion to the impending assault on the mother evokes "the dignity of the eyelids, which fall, fall, like Caesar's toga, over the stupor of death," while Gonzalo sees the peasants, animals, and rustic offerings that surround his mother "like a conspiracy that finally has caught its victim" (C 724, 727; AWG 199, 202). After the mother's bludgeoned body is discovered, the coverlet of her bed, like Caesar's toga, seems to conceal the visitation of death, while her outstretched hands recall her similar pose in the grip of Gonzalo's anger: "The two poor hands raised, skeletal, seemed stretched out toward 'the others' as if in defense or in an extreme imploration" (C 752; AWG 234). The same Caesarian gesture was to mark the mother's reaction to her son in the projected true finale to the novel: "Maintain the detail of the two arms raised in defense, that will strike the son: in symmetry with the arms raised to defend herself against him" (C$_2$ 554–55).

10. Gonzalo's utterance gives credence to the rumors that he had threatened his mother's life. In an unincorporated fragment, the mother's companion Battistina overhears a similar threat and flees in terror (C$_2$ 570).

Roscioni (1969a, 90) points out that in the contrast between Gonzalo's "senseless" threats against his mother and the impossibility that he could commit the actual crime, Gadda's character follows in the footsteps of Shakespeare's Hamlet, who decries: "O heart, lose not thy nature; let not ever / the soul of Nero enter this firm bosom. / Let me be cruel, not unnatural; / I will speak daggers to her, but use none" (*Hamlet* 3.2.400–403). Henry Alden Bunker, to whom Roscioni refers, uses Hamlet's admissions to cast guilt on the character: "Hamlet's dissimilarity to Orestes is much more apparent than real, and he should be placed alongside the Greek hero in being guilty of mother-murder, even though in fantasy rather than in fact" (Bunker 1944, 199). This is also Gadda's position. In his notes to *Cognizione*, he states that "the contemplated thing or act is more real than the thing which has occurred or the act which has been executed" (C 570).

CHAPTER FOUR: MACARONIC PASTICHE

1. The novel was received with critical accolades, as Gadda himself admitted (LAM 59). Although it did not win the coveted Marzotto literary prize (which went instead to recently deceased Umberto Saba), the literary and critical community led by Emilio Cecchi quickly organized a special "Editors' Prize" for Gadda. Gadda's comments over not having won the Marzotto prize are not without embitterment and disdain for what he called the fascist "ex-squadristi" who hypo-

critically honored the Jewish Saba they had persecuted during the regime while rejecting Gadda's novel because of its attacks on Mussolini (LPGC 93–94).

2. The screenplay appears to have been written sometime between 1946 and 1948 for Michelangelo Antonioni who never utilized it (see Pinotti 1989, 1403–4; Andreini 1988, 138–52).

3. For a documented archaeology of *Pasticciaccio*'s publishing history see Pinotti 1989, 1137–69; Andreini 1988, 79–94. The project did not end with the novel's publication in 1957. In September of that same year, Gadda detailed his program for continuing work on the novel including either additional insertions with notes, a concluding sequel, and a short glossary in an enlarged edition, or, if that should prove economically unfeasible, a separate second volume for the sequel. The project was gradually abandoned during the course of the following two years.

4. In his 1957 essay on the novel, "Il Pasticciaccio," Gadda declared that the digressive attacks on the regime in the 1946 *Letteratura* version were the result of "an unrestrainable and explosive urgency of my 1945–46 state of mind" after so many years of forced silence (VM 507–8). Even Filippo Angeloni's epicurean gluttony had its genesis, Gadda added, in his own desperate situation as a war refugee in Florence in the aftermath of the fascist debacle: "In my anger, in my desperation, I dreamed of little truffles, I dreamed of chicken in aspic" (VM 509).

5. *Er Maccheronaro* appears several times in the novel and is another figurative inscription of *Pasticciaccio*'s macaronic poetics. His famous, multilayered roast-beef sandwiches will evoke the same astonishment in onlookers as does Liliana's mutilated corpse: "The customers present, envious, were stunned. A full-scale torpedo boat, something exceptional. To see it from the outside . . . quite decorous: but ponderously stuffed, within (P 162; TAM 221–22).

6. Ingravallo's opinions on the necessary reform of the notion of cause into that of a multiplicity of causes echoes Gadda's own repeated comments in *Meditazione milanese:* "'Every effect has its cause' is an assertion which I absolutely do not understand. I say 'every effect (lump of relationships) has its causes'"; "A single cause? No: that has no sense"; "Here I want to conclude that causes and effects are a pulsation of an ensnarled multiplicity and are never thinkable in the singular" (MM 647–48, 649, 650).

7. In a 1934 letter to Giuseppe De Robertis, Gadda wrote that he had wished that at least "La festa dell'uva a Marino" should have incurred the critic's favor, since "in it the 'baroque' has a sense of adhesion to the real baroque of our environment, our customs, our festivals" (TLI 28).

8. Textual analyses of Gadda's manipulation of the Bellian source are available in Gelli (1969), Gibellini (1975), and Papponetti (1985).

9. There is a humorous nod to Rossini's *Barber of Seville* (1.1) in Gadda's substitution of "de oro" in the 1946 *Pasticciaccio* with "de quer metallo" in the 1957 version (see Andreini 1988, 130).

10. Alba Andreini argues that Gadda's distaste for "trade-union" situations

probably spurred him to eliminate the word *padrone*, with its class-struggle connotations, from the 1957 revision of *Pasticciaccio* (Andreini 1988, 86).

11. Gadda, however, had no tolerance for the postwar leftist wave of prosouthern nationalism and accusations against the northern bourgeois and capitalist class as exploiters of the south: "These shithead Southern barons and false populists," as he put it in a letter to cousin Piero (LPGC 82). See also Gadda's 1945 essay "Nord-Sud, ancora" (SD 914–19).

12. Gadda was firm in protesting the classification of *Pasticciaccio* as a "romanzo dialettale": "The landslide of novels in dialect (read Testori in Lombard dialect and Pasolini in Romanoid slang from the slums) is not imputable to me. My work is embroidered on an Italian foundation, very Italian in fact" (LPGC 106). "As far as Roman dialect goes, I did not intend to dish up actual dialect, that vigorous way of speaking of those who come from dialect-speaking families. . . . In essence mine is a 'contamination' between conventional Italian and Roman dialect" (cited in Pinotti 1989, 1164).

13. Pasolini (1960, 319) puts forward this tripartite division, but the class associations are not as rigid as he argues. Dialect is not only the expressive vehicle of "the culture of the working classes which are Southern and thus of the subproletariat"; it is the affective language of the middle-class and upper-class characters as well.

14. A *sympathetic* ironic adherence between authorial and character perspective via macaronic free indirect discourse is present instead in the narration of Ines Cionini's inner thoughts: "Quando il Signore l'aveva richiamata, col suo sguardo di raggi d'oro nella sera, dal finestrone rotondo di Crocedomini, lei, ar Zignore, che aveva avuto er core d'arisponneje? 'Io vado cor mi' amore,' j'aveva arisposto a quelo sguardo, a quela voce. Sicché 'r Zignore, adesso, bisognava lassallo stà" ("When the Lord had called her back, with his gaze of golden rays in the evening, from the round window of *Croce domini*, she, to the Lord—who had the heart to answer Him? 'I'm going with my love,' she had answered that gaze, that voice. So as for the Lord, now, He had to be left out of it") (P 169; TAM 233).

15. See Gadda's ironic comments in the 1949 essay "Psicanalisi e letteratura": "An affirmation repeated many times (or even only appearing superficially in our speech) tends to push the methods of research and results of psychoanalysis beyond the borders of the so-called Latin world and thought. According to this affirmation, to insist with a turbid and reprehensible curiosity on the most innermost motives of organic activity, of the psychological (or even biological) mechanism, or to acknowledge the supposed links between the life of the instincts (of the 'lowest' instincts) and the luminous discipline of the academic garden is a motive that is extrinsic and esoteric to Latin culture, smoke and scribbles from beyond the Alps or even Europe, a monstrous practice, repugnant to the clarity, the purity, the elegance and the decorum of the Latin mind and soul" (VM 455).

CHAPTER FIVE: SATURA TOTA NOSTRA EST

1. The pamphlet is mentioned in a footnote on fascist persecution of the innocent in the 1946 *Pasticciaccio* with a revealing slippage from the novel's Roman
pastiche to *Eros e Priapo*'s Florentine pastiche: "Te t'hai a vedere per questo i bei
ragionari ti farò nel mio volume novo dell'Eros e del Logos" [You will have to
consult on this matter the fine arguments I will present in my new volume on
Eros and Logos] (PL 364).

2. One finds a similar albeit more vulgar mixture of misogynism and racism
in Céline's *Bagatelles pour un massacre:* "Vous pouvez partir tranquilles . . .
vous serez remplacés dans vos boulots promptement, dan vos maisons et dans
vos lits . . . la femme, surtout la Française, raffole de crépus, des Abyssins, ils vous
ont des bites surprenantes!" ("You can go off without worry . . . you'll be promptly
replaced in your jobs, your homes and in your beds. . . . Women, especially
Frenchwomen, admire men with fuzzy hair, Abyssinians, my dear, they have
surprising cocks!") (Céline 1938, 89; cited and translated in Thomas 1979, 149–
50).

3. A similar episode appears in the 1949 "Come lavoro" (VM 429). Mussolini
served for a year and a half during World War I and spent six months in the
trenches. He was wounded early in 1917 by a grenade thrower in a training exercise and was released from active service for the remainder of the conflict. His
military valor was later trumped up in the official fascist hagiography to the
point of the absurd declaration that the war began going badly for Italy from the
moment Mussolini was forced to leave the front (Mack Smith 1983, 28).

4. Early on in his office Mussolini was fond of assuming the air of aristocratic
dignity by dressing in spats and derby. *Kuce* is a distortion of *Duce* meant to
highlight the inanity of the senseless repetition.

5. *Hè-jà, hè-jà* [hey-ya, hey-ya] is a distortion of the Fascist yell *eia, eia, eia,
alalà!* appropriated from D'Annunzio's Arditi during their occupation of Fiume.

6. Maltoni was Mussolini's mother's maiden name.

7. They are now gathered together under a single title, *I miti del somaro*, in
Gadda's *Opere* 5/1:899–923.

Selected Bibliography

Adorno, Theodor. 1984. *Aesthetic Theory.* Translated by C. Lenhardt. Edited by Gretel Adorno and Rolf Tiedemann. London: Routledge and Kegan Paul.

Amoruso, Vito. 1960. "Stratificazione linguistica e mondo storico di Gadda." *Nuova corrente* 20 (October–December): 33–52.

Anderson, Laurie Jane. 1977. *Challenging the Norm: The Dialect Question in the Works of Carlo Emilio Gadda.* Stanford Honor Essays in the Humanities, no. 20. Stanford: Stanford University.

Andreini, Alba. 1988. *Studi e testi gaddiani.* Palermo: Sellerio.

Angelini, Franca. 1978. *Il teatro del Novecento da Pirandello a Fo.* Bari: Laterza.

Arbasino, Alberto. 1971. "Carlo Emilio Gadda." In *Sessanta posizioni,* 185–210. Milan: Feltrinelli.

Auerbach, Erich. 1953. *Mimesis: The Representation of Reality in Western Literature.* Translated by Willard R. Trask. Princeton: Princeton University Press.

Avellini, Luisa, ed. 1978. *La critica e Dossi.* Bologna: Cappelli.

Bakhtin, Mikhail. 1981. *The Dialogic Imagination.* Translated by Caryl Emerson and Michael Holquist. Edited by Michael Holquist. Austin: University of Texas Press.

———. 1984a. *Problems of Dostoevsky's Poetics.* Translated and edited by Caryl Emerson. Minneapolis: University of Minnesota Press.

———. 1984b. *Rabelais and His World.* Translated by Hélène Iswolsky. Bloomington: Indiana University Press.

Baldi, Guido. 1972. *Carlo Emilio Gadda.* Milan: Mursia.

Bàrberi Squarotti, Giorgio. 1978. *Le sorti del tragico. Il Novecento italiano: romanzo e teatro.* Ravenna: Longo.

Barilli, Renato. 1964. "Gadda e la fine del naturalismo." In *La barriera del naturalismo. Studi sulla narrativa italiana contemporanea,* 105–28. Milan: Mursia.

———. 1968. "Carlo Emilio Gadda. Eros e Priapo." *Il verri* 26:113–16.

———. 1972. "Introduzione." In *La linea Svevo-Pirandello,* 5–15. Milan: Mursia.

Barthes, Roland. 1975. *S/Z.* Translated by Richard Miller. London: Jonathan Cape.

Belli, Giuseppe Gioachino. 1961. *Lettere.* 2 vols. Edited by G. Spagnoletti. Milan: Mondadori.

Benedetti, Carla. 1983. "Un espressionismo contro l'io: Gadda e *La cognizione del dolore.*" *Il centauro* 7:124–39.

Benjamin, Walter. 1986. *Reflections: Essays, Aphorisms, Autobiographical Writings.* Translated by Edmund Jephcott. Edited by Peter Demetz. New York: Schocken Books.

Benuzzi Billeter, Manuela. 1977. "Introduzione." In *La verità sospetta. Tre traduzioni di Carlo Emilio Gadda,* by Carlo Emilio Gadda, edited by Manuela Benuzzi Billeter, 5–30. Milan: Bompiani.

Benveniste, Emile. 1971. *Problems in General Linguistics.* Translated by Mary Elizabeth Meek. Coral Gables: University of Miami Press.

Bernstein, J. M. 1984. *The Philosophy of the Novel: Lukács, Marxism, and the Dialectics of Form.* Minneapolis: University of Minnesota Press.

Bertone, Manuela. 1990. "L'incompiutezza 'necessaria': Carlo Emilio Gadda tra finitezza e non finito." *Romance Languages Annual* 2:182–88.

———. 1993. *Il romanzo come sistema. Molteplicità e differenza in Carlo Emilio Gadda.* Rome: Editori Riuniti.

Bettini Filippo, et al. 1975. *L'alternativa letteraria del '900: Gadda.* Quaderni di critica. Rome: Savelli.

Bevilacqua, Mirko. 1985. "*Eros e Priapo:* trattato, romanzo o divagazione parodistica?" *Rassegna della letteratura italiana,* 89, series 7 (January–April): 142–47.

Biasin, Gian-Paolo. 1975. "The Pen, the Mother." In *Literary Diseases: Theme and Metaphor in the Italian Novel,* 127–55. Austin: University of Texas Press.

———. 1993. "The Cornucopia of the World: Carlo Emilio Gadda, *La cognizione del dolore* and *Quer pasticciaccio brutto de via Merulana.*" In *The Flavors of Modernity: Food and the Novel.* Princeton: Princeton University Press.

Birtolon, Andreia. 1973. "Proposta per una nuova classificazione del linguaggio del *Pasticciaccio.*" In *Storia linguistica dell'Italia del Novecento,* edited by Maurizio Gnerre et al., 41–46. Rome: Bulzoni.

Bo, Carlo. 1946. "Nota su C. E. Gadda." In *Nuovi studi,* 197–205. Florence: Vallecchi.

Bodei, Remo. 1973. "Conoscenza e dolore. Per una morfologia del tragico." *Il centauro* 7 (January–April): 3–27.

Bory, Jean-Louis. 1960. "Bardamu à nouveau seul contre tous." In *Les Critiques de notre temps et Céline,* edited by Jean-Pierre Dauphin. Paris: Editions Garnier Frères, 1976.

Brilli, Attilio, ed. 1985. *Dalla satira alla caricatura. Storia, tecniche e e ideologie della rappresentazione.* Bari: Dedalo.

Buckley, William K., ed. 1989. *Critical Essays on Louis-Ferdinand Céline.* Boston: G. K. Hall.

Bucolo, Placido, ed. 1980. *The Other Pareto.* Translated by Placido and Gillian Bucolo. London: Scolar Press.

Budgen, Frank. 1934. *James Joyce and the Making of Ulysses*. New York: Harrison Smith and Robert Haas.

Bunker, Henry Alden. 1944. "Mother-Murder in Myth and Legend: A Psychoanalytic Note." *Psychoanalytic Quarterly* 13:198–203.

Butor, Michel, Juan Petit, Hans Magnus Enzensberger, Drago Ivanisivic, and Pier Paolo Pasolini. 1963. "Gadda Europeo." *L'Europa letteraria* 4, nos. 20–21:52–67.

Calvino, Italo. 1980. *Una pietra sopra. Discorsi di letteratura e società*. Turin: Einaudi.

Cane, Eleanora. 1969. *Il discorso indiretto libero nella narrativa italiana del '900*. Rome: Silva.

Cannon, JoAnn. 1989. "*La cognizione del dolore* and the Autobiographical Project." *Symposium* 43 (Summer): 94–106.

Carlino, Marcello, et al., eds. 1987. *Gadda progettualità e scrittura*. Rome: Editori Riuniti.

Cattaneo, Giulio. 1973. *Il gran lombardo*. Milano: Garzanti.

———. 1987. "L'affermazione di Gadda." In *Gadda progettualità e scrittura*, edited by Marcello Carlino et al., 245–50.

Cavallini, Giorgio. 1977. *Lingua e dialetto in Gadda*. Messina: D'Anna.

Ceccaroni, Arnaldo, ed. 1978. *Leggere Gadda. Antologia della critica gaddiana*. Bologna: Zanichelli.

Celati, Gianni. 1975. *Finzioni occidentali. Fabulazione, comicità e scrittura*. Turin: Einaudi.

Céline, Louis-Ferdinand (Louis-Ferdinand Destouches). 1937. *Bagatelles pour un massacre*. Paris: Denoël.

———. 1965. "Rabelais, il a raté son coup." *Cahiers de l'Herne*, 5:44–45.

———. 1983. *Journey to the End of the Night*. Translated by Ralph Manheim. New York: New Directions.

Citati, Pietro. 1963. "Il male invisibile." *Il menabò* 6:12–41.

Clément, Catherine, and Hélène Cixous. 1986. *The Newly Born Woman*. Translated by Betsy Wing. Minneapolis: University of Minnesota Press.

Cohen, J. M. 1955. "Translator's Introduction." In *The Histories of Gargantua and Pantaguel*, by François Rabelais, translated by J. M. Cohen, 17–31. London: Penguin.

Cohn, Dorrit. 1978. *Transparent Minds. Narrating Modes for Presenting Consciousness in Fiction*. Princeton: Princeton University Press.

Contini, Gianfranco. 1989. *Quarant'anni d'amicizia: Scritti su Carlo Emilio Gadda (1934–1988)*. Turin: Einaudi.

Cordié, Carlo. 1977. "Nota introduttiva a Teofilo Folengo." In *Opere di Teofilo Folengo*, edited by Carlo Cordié, xi–lii. Milan: Ricciardi.

Cornford, Francis MacDonald. 1914. *The Origin of Attic Comedy*. Reprinted and edited by Theodore H. Gaster. Garden City, N.Y.: Anchor, 1961.

David, Michel. 1965. *La psicanalisi nella cultura italiana.* Turin: Boringhieri.

De Grand, Alexander. 1982. *Italian Fascism: Its Origins and Development.* Lincoln: University of Nebraska Press.

De Mauro, Tullio. 1979. *Storia linguistica dell'Italia unita.* 2 vols. Bari: Laterza.

De Robertis, Giuseppe. 1946. "C. E. Gadda: *La Madonna dei Filosofi, Il Castello di Udine.*" In *Scrittori del Novecento* (3rd ed.), 325–34. Florence: Le Monnier.

De Sanctis, Francesco. 1973. *Storia della letteratura italiana.* Milan: Bietti.

Dionisotti, Carlo. 1967. *Geografia e storia della letteratura italiana.* Turin: Einaudi.

Dombroski, Robert. 1970. "The Meaning of Gadda's War Diary." *Italica* 47 (Winter): 373–86.

———. 1971. "Some Observations on the Revision of *Quer pasticciaccio.*" *Modern Language Notes* 86, no. 1:61–72.

———. 1972. "Moral Commitment and Invention in Gadda's Poetics." *Rivista di letterature moderne e comparate* 25 (September): 210–21.

———. 1975. *Introduzione allo studio di Carlo Emilio Gadda.* Florence: Vallecchi.

———. 1984a. "Gadda: Fascismo e psicanalisi." In *L'esistenza ubbidiente. Letterati italiani sotto il fascismo.* Naples: Guida.

———. 1984b. "Overcoming Oedipus: Self and Society in *La cognizione del dolore.*" *Modern Language Notes* 99 (January): 125–43.

Domenichelli, M. 1985. "La satira è de-costruttiva (de-compositiva)." In *Dalla satira alla caricatura,* edited by Attilio Brilli, 179–82. Bari: Dedalo.

Dossi, Carlo. 1981. *La desinenza in A.* Milan: Garzanti.

Dostoyevsky, Fyodor. 1950. *The Brothers Karamazov.* New York: Modern Library.

Eagleton, Terry. 1981. *Walter Benjamin: Towards a Revolutionary Criticism.* London: Verso.

Eco, Umberto. 1979. "The Semantics of Metaphor." In *The Role of the Reader.* Bloomington: Indiana University Press.

———. 1980. "The Comic and the Rule." In *Travels in Hyperreality,* translated by William Weaver, 269–78. San Diego: Harcourt Brace Jovanovich, 1986.

Eliot, Thomas Sterns. 1934. "Hamlet and His Problems." In *The Sacred Wood. Essays on Poetry and Criticism,* 95–103. London: Methuen.

Elliott, Robert C. 1960. *The Power of Satire. Magic, Ritual, Art.* Princeton: Princeton University Press.

Ellmann, Richard. 1959. *James Joyce.* New York: Oxford University Press.

Felman, Shoshana. 1978. "Cogito et folie ou raison de la littérature." In *La folie et la chose littéraire,* 37–55. Paris: Seuil.

Ferrero, Ernesto. 1972. *Invito alla lettura di Carlo Emilio Gadda.* Milan: Mursia.

Ferretti, Gian Carlo. 1987. *Ritratto di Gadda.* Bari: Laterza.

Fiorillo, Francesca. "Verso il dolore universale: la riscrittura del *Pasticciaccio.*" *Italica* 60 (Spring): 24–37.

Flaubert, Gustave. 1965. *Madame Bovary.* New York: Norton.

———. 1979. *The Letters of Gustave Flaubert. 1830–1857.* Selected, edited, and translated by Francis Steegmuller. Cambridge, Mass.: Belknap Press/Harvard University Press.

Flores, Enrico. 1973. *Accensioni gaddiane. Strutture, lingua e società in C. E. Gadda.* Naples: Loffredo.

Folengo, Teofilo. 1977. *Opere di Teofilo Folengo.* La letteratura italiana. Storia e testi, vol. 26, Folengo * Aretino * Doni, no. 1. Edited by Carlo Cordié. Milan: Riccardo Ricciardi.

Foucault, Michel. 1988. *Madness and Civilization. A History of Insanity in the Age of Reason.* New York: Vintage.

Fratnik, Marina. 1990. *L'écriture détournée. Essai sur le texte narratif de C. E. Gadda.* Turin: Albert Meynier.

Freud, Sigmund. 1938. *The Basic Writings of Sigmund Freud.* Translated and edited by Dr. A. A. Brill. New York: Modern Library.

———. 1959. *Group Psychology and the Analysis of the Ego.* Translated and edited by James Strachey. New York: W. W. Norton.

———. 1963. *Three Case Histories.* Edited by Philip Rieff. New York: Collier Books.

Frullini, Andrea. 1973. "La tessitura del dolore." *Letteratura* 29:21–34.

Furst, Lilian. 1984. *Fictions of Romantic Irony.* Cambridge, Mass.: Harvard University Press.

Gabici, Franco. 1982. "Gadda: il dolore della cognizione." *Otto/Novecento* 4, nos. 3–4:305–19.

Gadda, Carlo Emilio. 1969. *Acquainted with Grief.* Translated by William Weaver. New York: George Braziller.

———. 1973. "Carlo Emilio Gadda con le sue parole." *Studi cattolici* 148 (June): 365–69.

———. 1975. "Lettere inedite di C.E. Gadda e di C. Sbarbaro ad A. Camerino." Edited by Maria Corti. *Strumenti critici* 9, no. 2:209–18.

———. 1977. "Due lettere 'foscoliane.'" Edited by Piero Bigongiari. *Paradigma* 1:395–98.

———. 1977. *La verità sospetta. Tre traduzioni di Carlo Emilio Gadda.* Edited by Manuela Benuzzi Billeter. Milan: Bompiani.

———. 1978. "Tre lettere inedite di C.E.G. alla cugina Luisa." Edited by Giuditta Podestà. *Lettere italiane* 30, no. 2:207–12.

———. 1979. "Lettere a Valentino Bompiani." *L'unità* (November 29): 8.

———. 1982. *Carteggio dell'ing. Carlo Emilio Gadda con l'"Ammonia Casale S.A."* Edited by Dante Isella. Verona: Ammonia Casale.

———. 1983. *Lettere agli amici milanesi.* Edited by Emma Sassi. Milan: Il Saggiatore.

———. 1983. *Lettere a una gentile signora.* Edited by Giuseppe Marcenaro. Milan: Adelphi.

———. 1983. "Tre lettere di C.E. Gadda a Silvio Guarnieri." Edited by Marcello Carlino and Francesco Muzzioli. *L'Ombra d'Argo* 1, nos. 1–2:155–59.

————. 1983. "Tre lettere inedite a Giuseppe De Robertis." *Rinascita* 40 (October 21): 28.

————. 1984. *A un amico fraterno. Lettere a Bonaventura Tecchi.* Edited by Marcello Carlino. Milan: Garzanti.

————. 1984. *L'ingegnere fantasia. Lettere a Ugo Betti.* Edited by Giulio Ungarelli. Milan: Rizzoli.

————. 1984. "Lettere a Enrico Vallecchi." *Nuovecarte* (January–February).

————. 1984. *That Awful Mess on Via Merulana.* Translated by William Weaver. New York: George Braziller.

————. 1987. *La cognizione del dolore.* Edited by Emilio Manzotti. Turin: Einaudi.

————. 1987. *Lettere alla sorella. 1920–1924.* Edited by Gianfranco Colombo. Milan: Rosellina Archinto.

————. 1988. *Lettere a Gianfranco Contini a cura del destinatario.* Edited by Gianfranco Contini. Milan: Garzanti.

————. 1988. *Opere di Carlo Emilio Gadda.* Vol I. Romanzi e racconti, I: La Madonna dei Filosofi/Il castello di Udine/L'Adalgisa (disegni milanesi)/La cognizione del dolore. Directed by Dante Isella. Edited by Raffaella Rodondi, Guido Lucchini, and Emilio Manzotti. Milan: Garzanti.

————. 1989. *Opere di Carlo Emilio Gadda.* Vol II. Romanzi e racconti, II: Quer pasticciaccio brutto de Via Merulana/Quer pasticciaccio brutto de via Merulana (redazione di *Letteratura*, 1946–47)/La meccanica/Accoppiamenti giudiziosi/ Racconti dispersi/Racconti incompiuti. Directed by Dante Isella. Edited by Giorgio Pinotti, Dante Isella, and Raffaella Rodondi. Milan: Garzanti.

————. 1991. *Opere di Carlo Emilio Gadda.* Vol. III. Saggi, giornali, favole e altri scritti, I: Le meraviglie d'Italia/Gli anni/Verso la Certosa/I viaggi la morte/ Scritti dispersi. Directed by Dante Isella. Edited by Liliana Orlando, Clelia Martignoni, and Dante Isella. Milan: Garzanti.

————. 1992. *Opere di Carlo Emilio Gadda.* Vol. IV. Saggi, giornali, favole e altri scritti, II: Il primo libro delle Favole/I Luigi di Francia/Eros e Priapo/Il guerriero, l'amazzone, lo spirito della poesia nel verso immortale del Foscolo/Giornale di guerra e di prigionia/Schede autobiografiche. Directed by Dante Isella. Edited by Claudia Vela, Gianmarco Gaspari, Giorgio Pinotti, Franco Gavazzeni, Dante Isella, and Maria Antonietta Terzoli. Milan: Garzanti.

————. 1993. *Opere di Carlo Emilio Gadda.* Vol. V, part I. Scritti vari e postumi: Pagine di divulgazione tecnica/Traduzioni/Racconto italiano di ignoto del novecento/Meditazione milanese/I miti del somaro/Il palazzo degli ori/ Gonnella buffone/Háry János/Il Tevere/Ultimi inediti/Altri scritti. Directed by Dante Isella. Edited by Andrea Silvestri, Claudio Vela, Dante Isella, Paola Italia, and Giorgio Pinotti. Milan: Garzanti.

————. 1993. *Opere di Carlo Emilio Gadda.* Vol. V, part II. Bibliografia e indici: Bibliografia degli scritti di C.E. Gadda/Indice dei titoli/Indice dei nomi/Indice generale. Directed by Dante Isella. Edited by Dante Isella, Guido Lucchini, and Liliana Orlando. Milan: Garzanti.

Gadda Conti, Piero. 1974. *Le confessioni di Carlo Emilio Gadda.* Milan: Pan.

Garboli, Cesare. 1967. "Non sono un misantropo." *La fiera letteraria* (August 10): 8–9.

Gargiulo, Alfredo. 1958. "Carlo Emilio Gadda." In *Letteratura italiana del Novecento,* 547–60. Florence: Le Monnier.

Gelli, Piero. 1969. "Sul lessico di Gadda." *Paragone* 230:52–77.

Genette, Gérard. 1980. *Narrative Discourse. An Essay in Method.* Translated by Jane E. Lewin. Cambridge, Mass.: Harvard University Press, 1984.

Gibellini, Pietro. 1975. "Romanesco e ottica narrativa nel *Pasticciaccio* di Carlo Emilio Gadda." *Paragone* 308:75–91.

Gide, André. 1938. "The Jews, Céline and Maritain." In *Critical Essays on Louis-Ferdinand Céline,* edited by William K. Buckley, 195–97. Boston: G. K. Hall.

Gioanola, Elio. 1987. *L'uomo dei topazi. Saggio psicanalitico su C. E. Gadda.* Second edition. Milan: Librex.

Godard, Henri. 1985. *Poétique de Céline.* Paris: Gallimard.

Gorni, Guglielmo. 1972. "Onomastica e altre fonti della *Cognizione.*" *Paragone* 274:87–95.

Greco, Lorenzo. 1983. "L'autocensura di Gadda: gli scritti tecnico-autarchici." In *Censura e scrittura. Vittorini, lo pseudo-Malaparte, Gadda,* 51–98. Milan: Il Saggiatore.

Guglielmi, Angelo. 1963. "Carlo Emilio Gadda." In *Letteratura italiana. I contemporanei,* 1051–67. Milan: Marzorati.

———, ed. 1965. *Vent'anni di impazienza. Antologia della narrativa italiana dal '46 ad oggi.* Milan: Feltrinelli.

———. 1968. "L'officina di Gadda," "Il realismo di Gadda," "Gadda progressista." In *Vero e falso,* 50–65. Milan: Feltrinelli.

Guglielmi, Guido. 1967. "Lingua e metalinguaggio in Gadda." In *La letteratura come sistema e come funzione,* 128–37. Turin: Einaudi.

Harpham, Geoffrey. 1992. *On the Grotesque. Strategies of Contradiction in Art and Literature.* Princeton: Princeton University Press.

Hart, Clive, and David Hayman, eds. 1974. *James Joyce's Ulysses: Critical Essays.* Berkeley: University of California Press.

Isella, Dante. 1958. *La lingua e lo stile di Carlo Dossi.* Milan: Riccardo Ricciardi.

———. 1983. "Prefazione." In *Racconto italiano di ignoto del Novecento,* by Carlo Emilio Gadda, edited by Dante Isella, v–xxvii. Turin: Einaudi.

———. 1984. *I lombardi in rivolta. Da Carlo Maria Maggi a Carlo Emilio Gadda.* Turin: Einaudi.

———. 1989a. "Note alla *Meccanica.*" In *Opere di Carlo Emilio Gadda,* vol. II, 1171–1205. Milan: Garzanti.

———. 1989b. "Note ai 'Racconti dispersi.'" In *Opere di Carlo Emilio Gadda,* vol. II, 1293–99. Milan: Garzanti.

———. 1989c. "Note ai 'Racconti incompiuti.'" In *Opere di Carlo Emilio Gadda,* vol. II, 1301–38. Milan: Garzanti.

————. 1992. "Note al *Giornale di guerra e di prigionia.*" In *Opere di Carlo Emilio Gadda*, vol. IV, 1101–22. Milan: Garzanti.

Isnenghi, Mario. 1970. *Il mito della grande guerra. Da Marinetti a Malaparte.* Bari: Laterza.

Joyce, James. 1961. *Ulysses.* New York: Vintage.

————. 1966. *A Portrait of the Artist as a Young Man.* New York: Viking Press.

Kayser, Wolfgang. 1981. *The Grotesque in Art and Literature.* Translated by Ulriche Weisstein. New York: Columbia University Press.

Kernan, Alvin. 1965. *The Plot of Satire.* New Haven: Yale University Press.

Koon, Tracy H. 1985. *Believe, Obey, Fight. Political Socialization of Youth in Fascist Italy.* Chapel Hill: University of North Carolina Press.

Kristeva, Julia. 1982. *Powers of Horror. An Essay on Abjection.* Translated by Leon S. Roudiez. New York: Columbia University Press.

Lacan, Jacques. 1966. *Ecrits.* Paris: Seuil.

La Capra, Dominick. 1982. *"Madame Bovary" On Trial.* Ithaca: Cornell University Press.

Leibniz, G. W. 1973. *Discourse on Metaphysics/Correspondence with Arnauld/ Monadology.* Translated by Dr. George R. Montgomery. La Salle, Ill.: Open Court Publishing Company.

————. 1981. *New Essays on Human Understanding.* Translated and edited by Peter Remnant and Jonathan Bennett. Cambridge: Cambridge University Press.

Linati, Carlo. 1982. *Il bel Guido e altri ritratti,* edited by Gianfranca Lavezzi and Anna Modena. Milan: Vanni Scheiwiller.

Lopez, Guido, and Silvestro Severgnini. 1978. *Milano in mano.* Milan: Mursia.

Lopreato, Joseph. 1980. "Introduction." In *Compendium of General Sociology,* by Vilfredo Pareto. Minneapolis: University of Minnesota Press.

Lotman, Juri. 1977. *The Structure of the Artistic Text.* Translated by Ronald Vroon. Ann Arbor: University of Michigan Press.

Lucchini, Guido. 1988. *L'istinto della combinazione. L'origine del romanzo in C. E. Gadda.* Florence: La Nuova Italia.

————. 1994. "Gli studi filosofici di Carlo Emilio Gadda (1924–1929)." *Strumenti critici* 9/2 (May): 223–45.

Lucente, Gregory. 1986. "System, Time, Writing, and Reading in Gadda's *La cognizione del dolore:* The Impossibility of Saying 'I.'" In *Beautiful Fables. Self-consciousness in Italian Narrative from Manzoni to Calvino.* Baltimore: Johns Hopkins University Press.

Ludwig, Emil. 1932. *Colloqui con Mussolini.* Verona: Mondadori.

Lukács, Georg. 1971. *The Theory of the Novel. A Historico-Philosophical Essay on the Forms of Great Epic Literature.* Translated by Anna Bostock. Cambridge, Mass.: MIT Press.

Luperini, Romano. 1981. "Nevrosi e crisi dell'identità sociale nella *Cognizione del dolore.*" *Problemi* 60:66–73.

————. 1987. "Il fascismo e la 'repubblica delle lettere': storia e simboli nelle

Occasioni e nella *Cognizione del dolore.*" *Rivista di studi italiani,* 5–6 (December 1987–June 1988): 41–50.

Lyttelton, Adrian, ed. 1973. *Italian Fascisms. From Pareto to Gentile.* Translated by Douglas Parmée. London: Jonathan Cape.

Mack Smith, Denis. 1959. *Italy. A Modern History.* Ann Arbor: University of Michigan Press.

———. 1983. *Mussolini.* New York: Vintage.

Manacorda, Giuliano, ed. 1979. *Lettere a Solaria.* Rome: Editori Riuniti.

Manzoni, Alessandro. 1966. *I promessi sposi.* Edited by Lanfranco Caretti. Milan: Mursia.

Manzotti, Emilio. 1987. "Introduzione" (vii–li) and notes. In *La cognizione del dolore,* by Carlo Emilio Gadda. Einaudi: Turin.

———. 1988. "Note alla *Cognizione del dolore.*" In *Opere di Carlo Emilio Gadda,* vol. I, 851–80. Milan: Garzanti.

Maraini, Dacia. 1973. "Carlo Emilio Gadda." In *E tu chi eri? Interviste sull'infanzia,* 9–21. Milan: Bompiani.

Marcenaro, Giuseppe. 1983. "La casa rossa." In *Lettere a una gentile signora,* by Carlo Emilio Gadda, edited by Giuseppe Marcenaro, 27–44. Milan: Adelphi.

Marinetto, Paola. 1973. "Mito e parodia in Gadda." In *Profili linguistici di prosatori contemporanei,* 113–76. Quaderni del circolo filologico-linguistico padovano, 4. Padua: Liviana.

McCarthy, Patrick. 1975. *Céline.* New York: Viking Press.

McConnell, Joan. 1973. *A Vocabulary Analysis of Gadda's Pasticciaccio.* University, Miss.: Romance Monographs, Inc.

Mercier, Vivian. 1966. "James Joyce and the Macaronic Tradition." In *Twelve and a Tilly. Essays on the Occasion of the 25th Anniversary of Finnegans Wake,* edited by Jack P. Dalton and Clive Hart, 26–35. London: Faber and Faber.

Merry, Bruce. 1989. "The Sound of Revenge in Gadda's Prose." *Romance Quarterly* 36, no. 4:471–84.

Moretti, Franco. 1987. *The Way of the World. The Bildungsroman in European Culture.* Translated by Albert Sbragia. London: Verso.

Muecke, David. 1969. *The Compass of Irony.* London: Methuen.

Murphy, Ann. 1992. "Two Perspectives on Rabelais: Céline and Bakhtin." *Romance Quarterly* 39 (August): 259–70.

Mussolini, Benito. 1957. *Opera Omnia.* Vol. 22. Edited by Edoardo and Duilio Susmel. Florence: La Fenice.

Orlando, Francesco. 1978. *Toward a Freudian Theory of Literature.* Translated by Charmaine Lee. Baltimore: Johns Hopkins University Press.

Orlando, Liliana. 1991. "Note alle *Meraviglie d'Italia.*" In *Opere di Carlo Emilio Gadda,* vol. III, 1229–50.

Paccagnella, Ivano. 1973. "Mescidanza e macaronismo: dall'ibridismo delle prediche all'interferenza delle macaronee." *Giornale storico della letteratura italiana* 150, nos. 470–71:363–81.

———. 1983. "Plurilinguismo letterario: lingue, dialetti, linguaggi." In *Letteratura italiana. II. Produzione e consumo*, edited by Roberto Antonelli et al., 103–67. Turin: Einaudi.

Papini, Giovanni. 1914. "Amiamo la guerra." *Lacerba* 2 (October 1).

Papponetti, Giuseppe. 1985. "*Quer pasticciaccio* di Belli." *Studi romani* 33 (January–June): 56–69.

Pareto, Vilfredo. 1980. *Compendium of General Sociology*. Abridged by Giulio Farina. English text edited by Elisabeth Abbott. Minneapolis: University of Minnesota Press.

Parlangèli, Oronzo, ed. 1971. *La nuova questione linguistica*. Brescia: Paideia.

Pasolini, Pier Paolo. 1963. "Un passo di Gadda." *L'Europa letteraria* 4, nos. 20–21:61–67.

———. 1985. "Gadda." In *Passione e ideologia*, 274–83. Turin: Einaudi.

———. 1988. *Heretical Empiricism*. Translated by Ben Lawton and Louise K. Barnett. Edited by Louise K. Barnett. Bloomington: Indiana University Press.

Patrizi, Giorgio, ed. 1975. *La critica e Gadda*. Bologna: Cappelli.

Paulhan, Jean, and Giuseppe Ungaretti. 1989. *Correspondance Jean Paulhan— Giuseppe Ungaretti, 1921–1968*. Paris: Gallimard.

Paulson, Ronald. 1967a. *The Fictions of Satire*. Baltimore: Johns Hopkins University Press.

———. 1967b. *Satire and the Novel in Eighteenth-Century England*. New Haven: Yale University Press.

———, ed. 1971. *Satire. Modern Essays in Criticism*. Englewood Cliffs, N.J.: Prentice-Hall.

Pedriali, Federica. 1990. "Uno studio in nero: 'La passeggiata autunnale' di Carlo Emilio Gadda." *Paragone* 466:27–40.

Pedullà, Walter. 1968. "Carlo Emilio Gadda." In *La letteratura del benessere*, 367–72. Naples: Libreria Scientifica.

Pinotti, Giorgio. 1989. "Note a *Quer pasticciaccio brutto de via Merulana*." In *Opere di Carlo Emilio Gadda*, vol. II, 1135–69. Milan: Garzanti.

———. 1992. "Note a *Eros e Priapo (Da furore a cenere)*." In *Opere di Carlo Emilio Gadda*, vol. IV, 991–1023. Milan: Garzanti.

———. 1993. "Note a 'I miti del somaro.'" In *Opere di Carlo Emilio Gadda*, vol. V, part I, 1367–80. Milan: Garzanti.

Pirandello, Luigi. 1986. *L'umorismo*. Milan: Mondadori.

Pucci, Pietro. 1967. "The Obscure Sickness." Translated by Ann Hallock. *Italian Quarterly* 11 (Fall): 43–62.

Raimondi, Ezio. 1984. "Language and the Hermeneutic Adventure in Literature." Translated by Albert Sbragia. *Forum Italicum* 18 (Spring): 3–25.

Rank, Otto. 1992. *The Incest Theme in Literature and Legend. Fundamentals of a Psychology of Literary Creation*. Baltimore: John Hopkins University Press.

Richter, Jean Paul. 1973. *Horn of Oberon. Jean Paul Richter's "School for Aesthetics."* Translated by Margaret R. Hale. Detroit: Wayne State University Press.

Ricoeur, Paul. 1977. *The Rule of Metaphor. Multi-disciplinary Studies of the Creation of Meaning in Language.* Translated by Robert Czerny et al. Toronto: University of Toronto Press.

Riffaterre, Michael. 1981. "Flaubert's Presuppositions." *Diacritics* 11:2–11.

Rinaldi, Rinaldo. 1977. *La paralisi e lo spostamento: Lettura della "Cognizione del dolore."* Livorno: Bastogi.

———. 1985. *Romanzo come deformazione. Autonomia ed eredità gaddiana in Mastronardi, Bianciardi, Testori, Arbasino.* Milan: Mursia.

Risset, Jacqueline. 1972. "Carlo Emilio Gadda o la filosofia alla rovescia." In *Il modello e l'invenzione,* 156–64. Rome: Bulzoni.

———. 1975. "Progetto di descrizione del rapporto letteratura-filosofia in Gadda." In *L'alternativa letteraria del Novecento: Gadda,* edited by Filippo Bettini et al., 7–9. Roma: Savelli.

Rodondi, Raffaella. 1988a. "Note al *Castello di Udine.*" In *Opere di Carlo Emilio Gadda,* vol. I, 803–27. Milan: Garzanti.

———. 1988b. "Note alla *Madonna dei Filosofi.*" In *Opere di Carlo Emilio Gadda,* vol. I, 781–801. Milan: Garzanti.

Roscioni, Gian Carlo. 1969a. "La conclusione della *Cognizione del dolore.*" *Paragone* 238:86–99.

———. 1969b. *La disarmonia prestabilita. Studio su Gadda.* Turin: Einaudi.

———. 1974. "Introduzione" and "Note." In *Meditazione milanese,* by Carlo Emilio Gadda, edited by Gian Carlo Roscioni, v–liv, 309–423. Turin: Einaudi.

———. 1975. *La disarmonia prestabilita.* Revised edition. Turin: Einaudi.

———. 1988. "L'arduo Gianfranco." *La Repubblica* (September 22).

———. 1994. "Gadda umorista." *Strumenti critici* 9, no. 2:147–62.

Sassi, Emma. "Introduzione." In *Lettere agli amici milanesi,* by Carlo Emilio Gadda, edited by Emma Sassi, ix–xxvii. Milan: il Saggiatore.

Sbragia, Albert. 1990. "From the Novel of Self-Ridicule to the Modern Macaronic." *Italiana,* Rosary College Italian Studies, 4:169–80.

Segre, Cesare. 1979. "La tradizione macaronica da Folengo a Gadda (e oltre)." In *Semiotica filologica,* 169–83. Milan: Feltrinelli.

———. 1985. "Punto di vista, polifonia ed espressività nel romanzo italiano (1940–1970)." In *Atti dei Convegni Lincei,* vol. 71, 181–94. Rome: Accademia Nazionale di Lincei.

Sereni, Alberta. 1972. "Dinamica e struttura nella *Cognizione del dolore.*" *Studi novecenteschi* 1, no. 3:367–79.

Sergiacomo, Lucilla. 1988. *Le donne dell'ingegnere. Serve, signorine, madri e antimadri nella narrativa di Carlo Emilio Gadda.* Pescara: Medium.

Seroni, Adriano. 1969. *Gadda.* Florence: La Nuova Italia.

Shakespeare, William. 1957. *Hamlet.* New York: Washington Square Press.

——. 1970. *King Lear.* Baltimore: Penguin.

Siciliano, Enzo. 1970. "Il sipario di Carlo Dossi." In *Autobiografia letteraria,* 283–87. Milan: Garzanti.

Simonini, Augusto. 1978. *Il linguaggio di Mussolini.* Milan: Bompiani.

Sontag, Susan. 1962. "The Artist as Exemplary Sufferer." In *Against Interpretation and Other Essays,* 39–48. New York: Noonday Press.

Spackman, Barbara. 1990. "The Fascist Rhetoric of Virility." *Stanford Italian Review* 8, nos. 1–2:81–101.

Speroni, G. B. 1967. "Carlo Emilio Gadda. *Eros e Priapo.*" *Strumenti critici* 1, no. 4:464–67.

Spinoza, Benedict de. 1974. *Ethics.* Edited by James Gutmann. New York: Hafner Press.

Stallybrass, Peter, and Allon White. 1986. *The Politics and Poetics of Transgression.* Ithaca: Cornell University Press.

Steegmuller, Francis. 1968. *Flaubert and Madame Bovary.* London: Macmillan.

Steiner, George. 1961. *The Death of Tragedy.* New York: Oxford University Press.

Tench, Darby. 1985. "*Quel Nome Storia:* Naming and History in Gadda's *Pasticciaccio.*" *Stanford Italian Review* 5, no. 2:205–17.

Tetel, Marcel. 1963. "Rabelais and Folengo." *Comparative Literature* 15 (Fall): 357–64.

Thomas, Merlin. 1979. *Louis-Ferdinand Céline.* London: Faber and Faber.

Ungarelli, Giulio. 1991. "Grandezza e servitù militare per Carlo Emilio Gadda (con documenti inediti)." *Lingua e letteratura* 8, no. 16:5–47.

Vattimo, Gianni. 1988. "The Structure of Artistic Revolutions." In *The End of Modernity,* translated by Jon Synder, 90–109. Baltimore: Johns Hopkins University Press.

Vigorelli, Giancarlo. 1955. "Carlo Emilio Gadda fuori della sigla 'C.E.G.'" *La fiera letteraria* (October 30): 1–2.

Vitale, Maurizio. 1960. *La questione della lingua.* Palermo: Palumbo.

Vittorini, Elio. 1976. *Diario in Pubblico.* Milan: Bompiani.

White, Allon. 1982. "Pigs and Pierrots: The Politics of Transgression in Modern Fiction." *Raritan* 2 (Fall): 51–70.

Worcester, David. 1960. *The Art of Satire.* New York: Russel and Russel.

Index

L'Adalgisa ("Adalgisa"), 73–74, 88, 92–97, 190
Adorno, Theodor, 71
Alarcón, Juan Ruiz de, 190
Alighieri, Dante, 5, 11–12, 39, 99, 176, 179
L'Ambrosiano (newspaper), 30
Amyot, Jacques, 26
Analogy, 97–105, 159
Andreini, Alba, 195
Anti-Semitism, 26, 58, 160, 162, 164–65, 169–70, 185, 188, 194
Antonioni, Michelangelo, 7, 194
Apuleius, 22
Arbasino, Alberto, 3–4, 7–8, 93
Archilocus, 182
Ariosto, Ludovico, 10
Aristotle, 114–15, 134, 162, 176
Ascoli, Graziadio Isaia, 5
Auerbach, Erich, 18
Avanti (socialist newspaper), 84–85

Bakhtin, Mikhail, 13, 15, 18–19, 23, 116, 144
Baldi, Guido, 77, 83, 174, 191
Barilli, Renato, 163, 184
Balzac, Honoré de, 186
Baroque, 27, 43, 87, 92, 100, 131, 146, 186, 189, 194

Barthes, Roland, 21
Bassani, Giorgio, 7
Baudelaire, Charles, 75
Belli, Giuseppe Gioachino, 5, 137–39, 141
Benjamin, Walter, 181
Bergson, Henri, 31, 171, 185
Bernstein, J. M., 21
Berto, Giuseppe, 126
Bertolucci, Bernardo, 165
Betti, Ugo, 29
Biasin, Gian-Paolo, 105, 136, 163
Billanovich, Giuseppe, 11
Blasphemy, 63–65, 68–69, 159, 173, 182, 188
Boccaccio, Giovanni, 12
Bodei, Remo, 57
Boito, Arrigo, 88, 90
Boito, Camillo, 89, 90
Bonaparte, Napoleon, 159
Bonsanti, Alessandro, 129, 187
Bonvesin de la Riva, 88
Borgese, Giuseppe Antonio, 39, 186
Borgia, Francisco, 123
Borgia, Rodrigo, 123
Bory, Jean-Louis, 26
Breton, André, 15
Bruno, Giordano, 25
Budgen, Frank, 25
Bunker, Henry Alden, 193

Butor, Michel, 2
Buonarroti, Michelangelo, 156

Calvino, Italo, 7–8, 190
Caesar, Julius, 52, 80, 123, 128, 170–71, 193
Il caffè (literary journal), 20
Capgras, Joseph, 107
Caravaggio, Michelangelo Merisi da, 38
Carnivalesque, 15–16, 112–19, 130, 135, 184; and food, 113–19, 136; and gigantism, 113–17; inversion, 112
Carocci, Alberto, 91
Il castello di Udine ("The Castle of Udine"), 44, 77, 87, 169
Catholic Partito Popolare, 39–40
Cattaneo, Carlo, 20, 88, 90
Cattaneo, Giulio, 89, 185
Cavani, Liliana, 165
Cecchi, Emilio, 193
Céline, Louis-Ferdinand, 1, 5, 12, 18, 24–27, 160, 163–65, 184–85, 196
Cervantes, Miguel de, 19. See also Don Quixote theme
Christian Democrats, 139
Clément, Catharine, 163
Columbus, Christopher, 171
Commedia dell'arte, 5, 14, 20
La cognizione del dolore (Acquainted with Grief), 2–3, 12, 16, 23, 42–43, 50, 56, 58–59, 61–63, 65–71, 73–74, 76–77, 87–88, 92, 94, 103, 106–28, 130, 135–38, 149, 151, 154–55, 157, 170, 188–89, 191, 193; Formentor Prize for, 2; Gonzalo Pirobutirro as autobiographical figure, 12, 15–17, 50, 55, 57, 61–65, 67–71, 78, 106, 111–13, 116, 121–22, 126, 154, 160, 163; as novel of ridicule, 23–24, 116, 119, 138; published in Letteratura, 59
Il conciliatore (literary journal), 20
Contini, Gianfranco, 2–3, 5, 10, 27, 48, 89–90, 92, 129, 131, 162, 183, 185, 189
Il corriere della sera (newspaper), 141
Croce, Benedetto, 14, 186
Crusca, Accademia della, 6

D'Alcamo, Cielo, 5
D'Annunzio, Gabriele, 40, 44–45, 47, 86, 112, 137, 159, 175, 186, 196
Danton, Georges Jacques, 171
Darwin, Charles, 45, 187
Death, 27, 56–57, 121, 177; as dissipation, 76, 111, 130, 132–33 153, 157, 190; and Eros, 155–58
Debenedetti, Giacomo, 180
Dejanira Classis (Novella seconda), 73, 81, 86, 169
Delepierre, Octave, 24, 184
De Robertis, Giuseppe, 77, 190, 194
De Sanctis, Francesco, 5, 10–12
Detective genre, 41, 129–30, 133–34, 141
Dialect, 4–6, 8, 118, 175, 195; Florentine (Tuscan), 4–6, 74, 96, 163, 172–73, 175, 177, 196; Milanese (Lombard), 4–6, 23, 92, 94–96, 119, 137, 172, 191; Molisan, 134; Neapolitan, 6, 134, 137, 142, 148; Roman 5–6, 132–49, 172, 195–96; Venetian, 5–6, 142, 191
Dickens, Charles, 77, 186
Disorder, 27, 34, 49, 52–54, 68, 71, 123, 127, 133, 186; and madness, 109–11; order from, 102, 190–91
Dolore (pain/suffering/grief), 27, 48, 67, 70; and knowledge, 56–57, 76, 111, 120, 124–25
Dombroski, Robert, 58, 70, 103, 111–12, 139, 161, 182, 190
Doniselli, Casimiro, 188
Don Quixote theme, 107–108, 123
Dossi, Carlo, 2, 87–93
Dostoyevski, Feodor, 32, 83, 186
Douglas, Norman, 150

Eagleton, Terry, 15
Eco, Umberto, 9, 15, 100
Eliot, T. S., 124, 126
Ellmann, Richard, 25
Enzenberger, Hans, 2
Epic, 17–18, 22, 138, 181
Eros (erotic), 116, 148–58; and Logos, 165–66
Eros e Priapo ("Eros and Priapus"), 87, 140, 149, 151, 159–82, 196; Alì Oco De

Madrigal as autobiographical character, 163–64

Euripides, 120

Evil, 27, 33, 37, 67, 133, 157; relationship to good, 33, 42–43, 166

Excrement, 27, 58, 68, 116, 155, 160, 178

Expressionism, 7–8, 10, 24, 34, 79, 89, 97, 189

Faldella, Giovanni, 2, 89

Farinacci, Roberto, 185

Fascism: and censureship, 85–87, 169; in *Cognizione*, 67, 112; and Freud, 58; Gadda joins Fascist Party, 29, 45, 67; Gadda's early idealization of, 40; in *Pasticiaccio*, 130, 139–40, 149; satirized in *Eros e Priapo*, 159–71, 175–77; and technology, 102–103

Father figure, 60, 154; God as, 64–67, 178, 181, 188; Mussolini as, 163, 178

Fellini, Federico, 7

Felman, Shoshana, 191

Fenoglio, Beppe, 3;

Fichte, Johann, 94

Flaubert, 1, 21–26; and novel of ridicule, 21–23; and free indirect discourse, 21, 23

Fo, Dario, 14–15

Fogazzaro, Antonio, 186

Folengo, Teofilo, 1, 3–4, 10–12, 17, 113

Fornasini, Emilio (friend), 44

Forster, E. M., 78

Foscolo, Ugo, 74, 159

Foucault, Michel, 110, 191

Free indirect discourse, 6, 8, 21, 23, 82–83, 146–48, 195

Freud, Sigmund, 25, 55, 58, 64, 93, 119, 155, 164, 170, 180–81, 188

Freudianism 3, 58–59; and fascism, 58–59, 164–68, 171, 176, 188 See also Oedipus complex, Orestes complex, Sublimation

Futurism, 36, 40, 45, 83, 93, 101, 171

Gadda, Carlo Emilio (*see also* individual works):

—biography and biographical traits, 28–30, 47–74, 192: abjection 27, 47; in Argentina, 30, 67, 102, 112, 170, 187, 192; blasphemies, 28, 64; career as electrotechnical engineer, 1, 29–30, 73, 102, 139, 189; childhood, 49, 51, 58, 61–63, 112; conservatism (see also Fascism, Mussolini), 8, 29, 169; denied greatness, 38–39, 43, 47, 108, 179, 181; family (*see also* Clara, Enrico, and Francesco Gadda, and Adelaide Lehr), 49, 51, 59–62; family villa in Brianza, 59, 62, 112, 121, 188–89, 192; gastrointestinal problems, 81, 116, 192; sense of guilt, 51, 63–64, 67–68, 70–71, 121–22, 181, 192; hypersensitivity, 27, 48–52, 61, 64, 68; internment in Germany, 44–45, 47, interventionism, 18, 29, 44–45; late fame, 2, 7, 10, 129; melancholy, 48–49, 159; militarism, 39, 46, 52, 58; misogyny, 48, nationalism, 45, 84–85; neuroses, 48–55; paranoia, 48, 55, 159; racial ideas, 45, 102, 161, 187; Romantic characteristics, 12, 50, 55, 57, 74–75; tragic vision of life, 12, 56; and World War I, 18, 29, 43–49, 52, 60–61, 84–85, 187, 190; and World War II, 59, 72, 161–62

—comparisons to: Céline, 1, 5, 12, 24, 26–27, 163–64, 196; Joyce, 1–2, 5, 24, 26, 37, 188, 192; Pirandello, 10, 15, 37, 50–51, 184; Rabelais, 1, 3, 16–17; Svevo, 2, 10, 37, 51–52, 59, 184

—view of Italy and Italians: criticism of Italian war effort, 29, 46–47, 165; disorderliness, 53, 69; egoism and narcissism, 43, 46, 165; fascism as Italian reaction, 40; insufficiency of Italian environment, 38, 43, 75, 108; "Italian work" motif, 38, 40, 102; in *La meccanica*, 81; lower classes 39, 117, 119, 139–41, 169–70; in *Racconto italiano*, 37–40; shame and anger with fellow Italians, 45–46; Southern Italians, 69, 195

—philosophical thought and formation,

Gadda, Carlo Emilio—*Continued*
30–35, 40–43, 97–101; cause and
effect, 32, 41, 133–34; 194; cognition
and understanding (*see also Dolore
and knowledge*); 34, 42, 76, 104–105;
combination, 27, 41–43, 111, 157, 187;
ethics, 33–35, 43, 45–46, 94, 124;
heuristic becoming, 27, 34–36, 42–43,
165–66, 186; method, 36, 54, 134;
polarity, 32–34; pragmaticism, 40, 45–
46, 57, 94, 101–103, 181; reality, 32–
33, 36, 40, 71, 132; system, 31–32, 54;
and literary form, 97–101, 133–34
—poetics, 35–37; *bozzettismo*, 77, 174,
182, 191; critical epitome, 36, 71;
characters as types and chorus, 38, 40,
78–80, 83, 95–96, 120, 146–48, 186–
87; fragmentation of writings, 1, 18,
30, 37, 73, 191; lyricism, 12, 37–38,
79–83; modernism, 1–2, 10, 24, 37, 51,
184; plot, 40, 43, 120; narrative voice,
79–87, 146–48, 163–64; "necessary"
style, 72–74, 87, 90–91; stylization, 79,
81–82, 111, 120, 146
—short stories and essays: "L'Adalgisa"
("Adalgisa"), 96; "*Amleto* al Teatro
Valle," ("Hamlet at the Valle Theater"), 57, 124–25; "Anastomòsi"
("Anastomosis"), 104–105; "Arte del
Belli" ("The Art of Belli") 72, 137,
139; "Le belle lettere e i contributi
espressivi delle techniche" (Belles
Lettres and the Expressive Contributions of Technology"), 9, 35, 101, 103;
"Un cantiere nelle solitudini" ("A
Construction Site in the Outback"),
102; "Carabattole a Porta Ludovica";
"Cinema," 88, 91–92; "Combustibile
italiano" ("Italian Combustibles") 103,
191; "Come lavoro" ("How I Work"),
28, 33–34, 50, 97, 196; "Un `concerto'
di centoventi professori" ("A Concert
of One Hundred and Twenty Profes-
sors") 93, 95–97; "Crociera
mediterranea" ("Mediterranean
Cruise"), 93; "Dalle specchiere dei
laghi" ("From the Mirrors of the

Lakes"), 62–63; "L'egoista" ("The
Egoist"), 32, 164; "Fatto personale . . .
o quasi" ("A Personal Affair . . . or
Almost"), 11–12, 131, 133, 135, 149; "I
grandi uomini," ("Great Men"), 50;
"Impossibilità di un diario di guerra"
("Impossibility of a War Diary"), 44;
"Intervista al microfono" ("Micro-
phone Interview"), 63; "Lingua
letteraria e lingua dell'uso" ("Literary
Language and Everyday Language"),
7; "La Madonna dei Filosofi" ("The
Madonna of the Philosophers"), 78,
93; "Manovre di artiglieria da
campagna" ("Field Artillery Maneuvers"), 73, 190; "Una mattinata ai
macelli" ("A Morning at the Slaughterhouse"), 104; "Meditazione breve
circa il dire e il fare" ("A Meditation
on Thinking and Doing"), 12, 180;
"Milano" ("Milan"), 88; "I miti del
somaro" ("The Myths of the Jackass"),
180; "Un'opinione sul neorealismo"
("An Opinion on Neorealism"), 7, 12,
55; "La passeggiata autunnale"
("Autumn Walk"), 74–75, 78, 140,
148; "Il Pasticciaccio," ("That Awful
Mess"), 130, 159, 194; "Polemiche e
Pace sul direttissimo" ("Polemics and
Peace on the Direct Train"), 183;
"Preghiera" ("Prayer"), 64, 75;
"Psicanalisi e letteratura"
("Psychoanalysis and Literature"), 59,
164, 195; "Un romanzo giallo nella
geologia" (A Detective Novel in
Geology"), 103–4; "San Giorgio in
Casa Brocchi" ("Saint George in the
Brocchi Home"), 88; "La scapigliatura
milanese," ("The Milanese
Scapigliatura"), 90; "Teatro" ("The-
ater"), 91–92, 97; "Tecnica e poesia"
("Technology and Poetry"), 101; "Il
terrore del dáttilo" ("Terror of the
Dactyl") 94–95; "Una tigre nel parco"
("A Tiger in the Park"), 58; "L'umanità
degli umili" ("The Humanity of the
Humble"), 141; "I viaggi la morte"

("Journeys and Death"), 76, 124, 185, 190
—translations, 73–74, 189–90
Gadda, Clara (sister), 49, 62, 162, 169, 187–88, 192
Gadda, Emilia (half sister), 59
Gadda, Enrico (brother), 29, 44, 48–49, 56, 60–61, 69–70, 75
Gadda, Francesco Ippolito (father), 39, 51, 59–60, 112. See also Father figure
Gadda Conti, Piero, 85, 168–69, 185
Galilei, Galileo, 12
Garibaldi, Giuseppe, 112, 172
Gargiulo, Alfredo, 77, 89, 190
Garzanti, Livio, 129, 160
La Gazzetta del Popolo (newspaper), 103
Gentile, Giovanni, 58, 171
Gide, André, 164
Gioanola, Elio, 61, 68, 152–55
Giolitti, Giovanni, 44–45
Giornale di guerra e di prigionia ("War and Prison Diary"), 30, 44–56, 58–62, 64, 75, 137, 187–88
Giotto, 173–74
Gobbi, Ambrogio (friend), 93, 137, 187
Goldoni, Carlo, 5, 14, 20
Gozzi, Carlo, 87
Grotesque, 12–13, 18, 26–27, 35, 42, 53, 111–19, 127–28, 131, 172;
groviglio (knot/tangle), 28, 32–33, 133–34
Gruppo '63, 8
Il guerriero, l'amazzone, lo spirito della poesia nel verso immortale del Foscolo ("The Warrior, the Amazon, and the Spirit of Poetry in the Immortal Verse of Foscolo"), 159
Guglielmi, Angelo, 8

Hamlet theme, 42, 57, 123–27, 190, 192–93
Homer, 80, 163
Humor (humorism): v. carnivalesque comic, 15, 184; Gadda and Dossi, 89, 92; Pirandellian, 13–15; Romantic, 13

"Interpretative delirium," 27, 106–109

Irony, 13, 21; Ironic dissonance, 80, 82, 146, 195;
Isella, Dante, 89, 185

Joyce, James, 1–2, 5, 24–26, 37, 184–85, 188, 192
Jung, Carl, 25

Kafka, Franz, 55, 185
Kant, Immanuel, 31, 37, 75–76, 134, 190
Kitchener, Horatio Herbert, 52
Kristeva, Julia, 26–27

Lacan, Jacques, 109–10
Larbaud, Valery, 24
Lawrence, D. H., 150
Le Bon, Gustave, 170, 175, 180
Lehr, Adelaide (Adele, mother), 48–49, 51, 59, 62, 73, 189, 192 See also Mother figure
Leibniz, Gottfried, 30–32, 41, 100, 185, 187; Gadda's thesis on, 30; mal physique, 107; monadism, 30–32, 100, 125; preestablished harmony, 32, 100
Leopardi, Giacomo, 98
Le Temps (newspaper), 107
Letteratura (literary journal), 2, 59, 129, 194
Levi, Primo, 101
Linati, Carlo, 77, 89–90
Logre, Joseph, 107–109
Lombard line of Italian writers, 88
Lombroso, Cesare, 41
Longanesi, Leo, 85
Lorenz, Edward, 186
Lucchini, Guido, 77, 161, 190
Lucini, Gian Pietro, 89
Ludwig, Emil, 170–71
Lukács, György, 17–18, 21

Macaronic: in Gadda, 2, 10, 12, 23, 26–27, 53, 74, 129–48, 162, 171–76, 182–83, 194; modern, 1, 11, 17, 24–27; and names, 112, 141–44; and the novel, 19, 22–23, 144; original Renaissance, 3–4, 10–11, 183

Machiavelli, Niccolò, 10, 171, 180

Madness, 51–52, 106–11, 117; in Celine, 26; in Pirandello and Fo, 14–15

La Madonna dei Filosofi ("The Madonna of the Philosophers"), 30, 73, 76–77, 89, 91

Maggi, Carlo Maria, 88

male invisibile (oscuro) (invisible/ obscure illness), 12, 27, 63, 110–11, 117, 126–27, 157

Mann, Thomas, 79

Manzoni, Alessando, 7, 12, 20, 85, 88–89, 123, 137, 187; ethical lesson for Gadda, 39, 87

Manzotti, Emilio, 125

Maraini, Dacia, 59

Marchetti, Domenico (friend), 2

Marinetti, Filippo Tommaso, 101, 175

Martinetti, Piero, 30, 33, 76, 190

Mastronardi, Lucio, 3

Matricide, 27, 67–68, 70–71, 121, 123–24, 128, 130, 149, 154, 166, 188, 193

Matteotti, Giacomo, 168, 170

Mazzini, Giuseppe, 46, 85

McCarthy, Patrick, 26

La meccanica ("Mechanics"), 30, 73, 80–86, 88, 95, 159, 169, 191; Luigi Pessina as autobiographical character, 86

Meditazione milanese ("Milanese Meditation"), 12, 30–37, 40, 42, 44, 54–56, 58, 68, 77, 81, 98–101, 108, 127, 157, 170, 185, 194

Melancholy, 13, 16–17, 24, 27; in Gadda, 104, 116–17, 149, 152–53, 162

Le meraviglie d'Italia ("The Marvels of Italy"), 103, 191

Mercier, Vivian, 24, 184

Misogyny, 81, 151, 164, 179; and critique of fascism, 149–50, 161–63, 170–71; Gadda shares with Céline, 196; Gadda shares with Dossi, 92–93; and satire, 162

Molière, Jean Baptiste, 15, 110, 123

Momigliano, Attilio, 11

Mondadori (publishing house), 30, 37–38, 129, 160

Montale, Eugenio, 2, 96, 189

Moravia, Alberto, 160, 169

Mother figure, 56, 61, 67–68, 70–71, 104, 106, 119–23, 126–28, 151, 153–54, 157, 178, 189, 192–93

Mussolini, Benito, 40–41, 44, 72, 87, 112, 130, 139, 146, 149, 159–68, 170–71, 175–80, 194, 196; and phallus, 150–51 162–63, 167–68, 177–80; as Predappio (his birthplace), 90, 191; Gadda's early admiration of, 67, 103, 191

Narcissism, 57–58, 110, 176, 180; and fascism, 160–61, 164–69; and Resistance partisans, 169

Naturalism, 41, 184

Neorealism, 7, 140

Novel, 17–25; *Bildungsroman*, 20–21; as genre of modernity, 17–21; and irony, 21; and macaronic, 19, 23–25, 144, 182; and satire, 19, 21–24; of self-mutilation, 14, 17, 22–24, 55, 66, 71, 157

Odasi, Tifi 3

Oedipus complex, 27, 57–59, 62, 111, 120, 123, 126, 130, 154, 164

Officina (literary journal), 160

Olmi, Ermanno, 3

Orestes complex, 27, 120, 123–24, 193

Ovid, 176

Paccagnella, Ivano, 183

Il palazzo degli ori ("The Apartment Building of Riches"), 129, 140

Palinuras complex, 75–76

Panzini, Alfredo, 77

Papini, Giovanni, 45

Paranoia, 83, 108; and philosophy, 55; shared with Celine, 26–27

Pareto, Vilfredo, 41, 86

Parini, Giuseppe, 116

Parody: in Flaubert, 21–23; 26; in Gadda, 16, 23, 79–86, 89, 115, 163, 166, 175; and the novel, 13, 18–19, 26

Pascoli, Giovanni, 145

Pasolini, Pier Paolo, 3–4, 7–9, 16–17, 92, 195

Pasticcio (mixture, mess, pastiche), 29, 70, 104, 132–33

Pastiche, 2, 16, 24, 129–148, 183
Pavese, Cesare, 56
Petaci, Clara, 178
Petronius, 22
Pettine, Renzo, 86, 169
Pirandello, Luigi, 10, 13–15, 51, 184, 186
Pius XI (Achille Ratti), 139
Plurilingualism 1, 4, 8, 10, 26, 183
Plutarch, 26
Politics, 14–15, 20; and Gadda, 38–40, 45, 85–87, 102, 139, 169, 171, 175. *See also* Fascism, Socialism
Pomponazzi, Pietro, 11
Il popolo d'Italia (Mussolinian newspaper), 44
Porta, Carlo, 5, 88, 96, 137
Positivism, 41, 93
Postmodernism, 9, 101
Praga, Emilio, 88
Prati, Giovanni, 145
Pratolini, Vasco, 169
Il primo libro delle favole ("The First Book of Fables"), 177–79
Pucci, Piero, 87, 109–10, 191

Quevedo, Francisco, 74, 189
Quer Pasticciaccio Brutto de Via Merulana (*That Awful Mess on Via Merulana*), 1–2, 7–8, 32, 42, 70, 76, 129–60, 188–89, 194–196; Filippo Angeloni as autobiographical character, 130, 194; Remo Balducci as autobiographical character, 160; Francesco Ingravallo as autobiographical character, 130, 133, 152, 154, 189, 194; published in *Letteratura*, 129, 194
Quintilian, 160
Questione della lingua (Italian language question), 3–10

Rabelais, François, 1, 3–4, 16–17, 19, 22, 24, 117, 131
Racconto italiano di ignoto del Novecento ("An Italian Tale by an Unknown Author of the Twentieth Century"), 18, 30, 37–45, 56–58, 67, 73, 77, 79–80, 84, 94, 97, 108, 123, 157, 162, 168, 179, 186–88; *ab interiore* v. *ab exteriore* narrative style, 79–80, 84, 98; Grifonetto Lampugnani as autobiographical character, 39–40; and Mondadori Prize, 30, 37, 186
RAI (Italian radio-television network), 90, 129
Rationality (reason), 43, 46, 57, 71, 76, 109–10, 181; disrupted by disorder, 54, 69; as Logos, 165–66; and method, 53, 69; and the novel, 20; and order, 52–53, 69, 165
Realism, 1, 18–19; crisis of, 21, 24–26, 184
Relativity, 14, 36–37
Retribution (revenge, punishment), 55–57, 63–71, 116, 153–55, 166, 181–82; and fascism, 67, 86, 178; and Hamlet, 57, 123–27
Richter, Jean Paul, 12–13, 87
Ridiculous (ridicule): Flaubertian novel of, 21–23; in Gadda, 23–24, 27, 116; Richter's view of, 13
Rimbaud, Arthur, 75
Rinascita (literary journal), 8
Robespierre, Maximilian, 93
Rodocanachi, Lucia, 74, 189
Romance, 19–20
Romanticism, 12–13, 24, 57; in Gadda, 16, 74–75
Roscioni, Gian Carlo, 15, 35, 83, 91, 98, 101, 131, 185, 193
Rosenkranz, Karl, 10
Rossellini, Roberto, 165
Rossini, Gioacchino, 194
Ruzante (Angelo Beolco), 14

Saba, Umberto, 193–94
Sade, Marquis de, 1
Sadism, 68–69, 153–57
Salandra, Antonio, 46, 84
Salas Barbadillo, Alonso Jerónimo de, 74
Satire: in Gadda, 11–12, 23–24, 159–82; and the macaronic, 11, 172–76; and the novel, 19, 21–24; and political censorship, 86–87; ritual origins of, 167, 176–182; figure of satiric railer, 140, 160, 163, 181
Sbarbaro, Camillo, 189

Scapigliatura (literary movement),
2–4, 87–93; Gadda's dissociation
from, 89–90
Segre, Cesare, 4, 10–11, 174, 185
Semenza, Luigi (friend), 44
Sereni, Vittorio, 160
Sérieux, Paul, 107–108
Sex and sexuality: author's sexual
potency, 80, 179; dysfunc-
tionalism, 152–58, 164;
homophobic homosexuality, 48,
165, 169; incest, 70–71, 149,
154, 188. See also Eros
Shakespeare, William: 57, 122–24,
126, 193; Coriolanus, 120–21,
123; Hamlet, 57, 123–27, 193;
King Lear, 122–23, 128;
Macbeth, 104; The Tempest, 123
Socialism, 39–40, 81, 83–86, 102,
140, 170
Società Umanitaria, 85–86
Solaria (literary journal), 2, 28–30,
73, 76–77, 81, 84, 91–92, 101,
185
Spinoza, Baruch, 31, 33, 55, 57,
186
Stallybrass, Peter, 20, 119, 184
Stendhal, 186
Sterne, Laurence, 15
Subjectivity: and authenticity, 96–
97; desecration of, 106, 112,
123–25, 148, 163; dismantlement of ego, 34; ego ideal, 66;
empirical v. transcendental self,
13, 17, 148; and humorism, 12–
18; Lacanian interpretation of,
109–10; linguistic, 79, 96, 142,
148; and mimesis, 21–24;
negativity of 21; and transgression, 70–71
Sublimation, 166–67, 169, 176,
180–81; of female, 152–53
Sublime: and authorial bovarism,
81–83; disorder disrupts, 53–54,
68, 71, 119; and disperion
(death), 76, 96, 157; in Flaubert,

23; Gadda's exclusion from, 64–65, 75;
humor disrupts, 78–79
and mountains, 52, 74–75, 81–82;
associated with order, 52, 68, 71; as
wholeness, 70–71; and women, 152–53
Suetonius, 128, 176
Svevo, Italo, 2, 10, 51–52, 59, 184

Tacitus, 87, 176
Tarchetti, Iginio Ugo, 88
Tasso, Torquato, 111
Tecchi, Bonaventura, 28, 49, 55, 73, 77
Technology: and literature, 97, 101–105
Testori, Giovanni, 8, 195
Theater: Gadda's satire of, 91–92; and
Gonzalo Pirobutirro, 119–20, 124–25;
and humorous discourse, 14–15, 20
Thunderbolt, 65–69, 155, 186, 188
Tolstoy, Leo, 91,
Tragedy (tragic): agon, 62, 178, 181;
exclusion, 63, 75; in Cognizione, 119–
28; and knowledge, 56–57, 70, 76;
metaphoricity, 120–22

Umberto I, 170
Ungaretti, Giuseppe, 1

Vattimo, Gianni, 101
I viaggi la morte ("Journeys and Death"),
11
Vico, Giovanni Battista, 25, 65, 188
Victor Emmanuel II, 5, 47
Vigorelli, Giancarlo, 91
Villani, Giovanni, 173
Villon, François, 25
Virgil, 62, 75, 99, 176, 188, 189
Vittorini, Elio, 169, 185
Voyeurism, 27, 149–50, 156

Weaver, William, 10, 145, 183
Weininger, Otto, 162, 171
Wertmüller, Lina, 165
White, Allon, 20, 119, 184

Zola, Emile, 186